Suicide as Psychache

Suicide as Psychache:
A Clinical Approach to
Self-Destructive Behavior

Edwin Shneidman, Ph.D.

JASON ARONSON INC.
Northvale, New Jersey
London

This book is set in 11 pt. Palacio by Lind Graphics of Upper Saddle River, New Jersey, and printed by Haddon Craftsmen in Scranton, Pennsylvania.

Library of Congress Cataloging-in-Publication Data

Shneidman, Edwin S.
    Suicide as psychache : a clinical approach to self-destructive behavior /
by Edwin Shneidman.
        p.   cm.
    Collection of previously published articles.
    Includes bibliographical references and index.
    ISBN 0-87668-151-8
    1. Suicide.   I. Title.
    [DNLM: 1. Suicide—collected works.   HV 6545 S558s]
RC569.S47   1993
616.85′8445—dc20
DNLM/DLC
for Library of Congress   92-49478

Manufactured in the United States of America. Jason Aronson Inc. offers books and cassettes. For information and catalog write to Jason Aronson Inc., 230 Livingston Street, Northvale, New Jersey 07647.

To

Avery D. Weisman, M.D.

Exemplar in every way,

from Alpha to Omega

Contents

III. RESPONSE

IV. FOLLOW-UP

Preface

My purpose in preparing this volume is both simple and straight-forward: to bring together my work—in this case, a dozen chapters and papers written between 1971 and 1993—for the broad range of mental health clinicians who are seeing and treating suicidal patients. The pieces include an empirical study, some single-case analyses, some theoretical think pieces, some suggestions for psychotherapy, and an extended psychological autopsy. Like many other scientific writers, I seem to write by "accretion," modifying my ideas and adding conceptual bits and pieces as I try to refine and focus, through successive publications, my own understanding about human self-destruction.

Writing by accretion necessarily results in a certain amount of repetition of my favorite ideas among successively written chapters. I am not especially troubled by this—as I hope the reader will also not be—not only because I believe in the effectiveness of repetition as a learning principle, but, more importantly, I believe that these ideas have merit and thus deserve to be emphasized in this way.

I have always felt that there ought to be a productive tension between theory and practice, and that they ought to fructify each other. I make no apologies—after a lifetime of clinical practice—for an emphasis in my writings on the theoretical side of things, believing as I do that there may not be anything as practical as a good theory. (The decisions about the merits of my theorizing remain in the empirical marketplace.)

My neologisms are meant to clarify; to make sharper distinctions. (I see nothing frivolous in them.) *Suicidology* simply defines the field of knowledge of suicide and the practice of suicide prevention; *psychache* throws emphasis on the central role of psychological pain in suicide (and suicide's irreducible psychological character); *psychological autopsy* clarifies the mode of death in those cases where the mode is equivocal because of the ambiguity of the decedent's intentions; *subintentioned death* throws the action into the decedent's court by admitting, in some deaths, the key role of unconscious motivations; *post-self* refers to the reputation that living people hope they will have created to survive their deaths; and *postvention* relates to activities that can be performed after the dire death of a loved one, and that look to the mental health of the survivors.

I hope to have the opportunity to revise this volume—dropping some chapters, adding some new ones—several years from now. I do not believe that the principal enigmas of suicidal phenomena will be solved by then—but I am reasonably optimistic that we shall be thinking more clearly about them.

E.S.S.
UCLA
April 1993

PART ONE

FOUNDATIONS

1

Definition of Suicide

My principal assertion about suicide has two branches. The first is that suicide is a multifaceted event and that biological, cultural, sociological, interpersonal, intrapsychic, logical, conscious and unconscious, and philosophical elements are present, in various degrees, in each suicidal event.

The second branch of my assertion is that, in the distillation of each suicidal event, its essential element is a *psychological* one; that is to say, each suicidal drama occurs in the *mind* of a unique individual. Suicide is purposive. Its purpose is to respond to or redress certain psychological needs. There are many pointless deaths but there are no needless suicides. Suicide is a concatenated, complicated, multidimensional, conscious and unconscious "choice" of the best possible practical solution to a perceived problem, dilemma, impasse, crisis, or desperation.

To use an arborial image: the psychological component in suicide is the "trunk" of it. An individual's biochemical states, for instance, are the roots. An individual's method of suicide, the contents of the suicidal note, the calculated effects on the survivors, and so on, are the branching limbs, the flawed fruit, and the camouflaging leaves. But the psychological component, the problem-solving choice—the best solution to the perceived problem—is the main trunk.

We may now proceed to my proposed definition of suicide.

Currently in the Western world, suicide is a conscious act of self-induced annihilation, best understood as a multidimensional malaise in a needful individual who defines an issue for which the suicide is perceived as the best solution.

Now I shall attempt an exegesis of this definition by clarifying the meaning of each word.

CURRENTLY

What is meant to be implied in this study of suicide is a contextual endeavor, embedded in the historical epic or era in which it occurs and in which it is either historically or concurrently studied. For example, if it were possible, it would not be enough simply to contrast suicide rates in pre-Christian Rome with suicide rates in Rome today. The whole meaning of the suicidal act for the person who did it and the contemporary witnesses is vastly different from that time to now. I believe that the definition of suicide offered in this book would become out of date in time and would not be applicable without appropriate modification even to suicidal occurrences as recent as the nineteenth century.

WESTERN WORLD

There are publications of studies of suicides in Africa (Bohannan 1960), in Hong Kong (Yap 1958), and other places around the world. I believe that this proposed definition is applicable only to the Western world (which may very well, in certain circumstances, include Japan and other countries). But this cautionary needs to be cited so that cross-cultural comparisons do not make the error of assuming that a suicide is a suicide.

SUICIDE

Two comments about this word. First is that after much thought I have concluded we are well advised to use this word rather than to venture on a substitute for it or to create a neologism. The use of the word admittedly has some disadvantages, but it has such wide usage that it is tactically best to employ it.

The second point is that an examination of a number of previous definitions of suicide reveals that the word is often (perhaps typically) used with not one, but two meanings. These two meanings are: the definition of the *act* of self-destruction, and some delineation of the *person* who commits that act. I have followed this practice in my proposed definition.

CONSCIOUS

What is implied here is that first of all suicide—at least the kind of suicide we are talking about—is limited to *human* acts. We shall not be concerned at all with migrating lemmings or mourning dogs inasmuch as suicide devolves in part on reportable intention, as we shall see.

A second important issue reflected in this word is the entire domain of the unconscious mind. The use of the word *conscious* in this definition is not meant to gainsay or to deny the notion that there may be important (even vital or anti-vital) unconscious elements in a total suicidal scenario. Rather it is meant to indicate that, by definition, suicide can occur only when an individual has some conscious meditation or, better, some conscious intention to stop his or her own life. There is always an element of some awareness and conscious intentionality in suicide.

This is not to say there are not many deaths—I would venture to assert even a majority of all deaths—that do not have a *subintentioned* quality to them. A subintentioned death is any death other than a suicidal death (accidental, natural, or homicidal) in which the decedent has played some significant covert, latent, or unconscious role in hastening his or her demise. No suicide is a subintentioned death. Rather, every suicide is an intentioned death with a conscious advertent element in it.

ACT

This word is meant to carry some special meanings. One direct implication is, I believe, that we should totally eschew the words *attempt* or *threat* when they are preceded by the adjective *suicidal*. (I am now obviously discussing other than lethal suicidal acts.) I make this suggestion because the words "attempt" and "threat" are often used in a judgmental, pejorative way, impuning even the worthlessness of the person or the seriousness of the personal crisis which in part impelled the act, as in the phrase "We sewed her up and sent her home. It was *only* a suicide attempt." My suggestion is that we reject the words "attempt" and "threat" and try to describe every suicidal act. Instead, we should use words like suicidal act, event, occurrence, deed, maneuver, phenomenon, and indicate our *lethality rating*. The lethality rating that might run, say, from 1 to 9, is the common-sense ascription of the probability of that act or deed or event having a lethal outcome. In this sense *any* act, deed, or event in the world can be rated on a lethality dimension. The main merit of the use of the word "act" is that it clarifies and appropriately simplifies what suicide is: namely, a behavior that leads to death.

Two ratings should be made for each suicidal act or event or deed: lethality, as indicated above, and *perturbation*, as discussed below. The rating of perturbation—also from 1 to 9—is an indication of how upset, agitated, depressed, psychotic, or perturbed the individual was deemed to be at the time of the act. It is very important in assessing a suicidal act or treating a suicidal person to distinguish between how perturbed the individual is and how lethal that individual is.

No one has ever died from elevated perturbation alone. It is elevated lethality that is dangerous to life. The two concepts need to be separated in order to have a clear understanding of the total event and the chief protagonist in it.

SELF-INFLICTED

The fulcrum word in the definition of suicide is the word *self-inflicted*. If suicide is anything, it is a *mort ius dese*, a death by oneself. This would seem to be clear enough, although there are problems with the biblical incident in which Saul asked another soldier to kill him, and in cases of what are now called assisted suicides. But in these instances the suicidal person changes only the voice of the grammar of the event and instead of killing himself directly has himself killed at one remove only by the asked-for action of another agent.

In the same sense, the suicide is also self-inflicted even in the instance when Seneca was ordered by the mad Roman emperor Nero to kill himself. We can reasonably assume that until the moment of that imperial order, Seneca had no intention of killing himself, but after the order he then consciously intended to kill himself when he did because the alternative—disgrace, enforced death, or punishment to his family—was worse.

ANNIHILATION

This word is meant to imply that the life of an individual is the life as that individual experiences it. It is the life of the mind. (The activities of the mind are the products of a living brain. No brain, no mind; no mind, no life.) One's life is the history—the introspective history—of one's mind. Suicide is the stopping or cessation of consciousness. It is redundant to say "forever." Cessation is thus distinguished from interrupted states (i.e., sleep, coma, anesthetic unconsciousness) and altered continuation states (i.e., intoxication, fugue states, psychotic states). Termination is what others see to have happened to your body. You can never experience cessation—being dead. A committed suicide results in cessation but we know that often the person who does it wants only to stop the flow of unbearable anguish or intolerable emotion or a change of locale from this world to a hoped-for other existence. But operationally speaking, suicide is a conscious act of self-inflicted cessation. Synonyms are cessation, nothingness, oblivionation, and naughtment.

These seven terms above, especially terms three to seven, define the *act* of suicide. The remaining ten terms define the *actor*, the person who does the act.

We have already defined what suicide is. It is the consciously intended act of self-inflicted cessation. Every definition is a tautology and it turns upon itself in a more or less obvious way. A definition is like an equation in which the word and its meaning have equal weight on the two sides of the copula (usually the word "is"). Now having defined the act, we shall go on and explicate some of the omnipresent characteristics of the actor (limited, of course, to currently in the Western world).

MULTIDIMENSIONAL

No single learned discipline is sufficient to explain any individual suicidal event. I believe it is most accurate to define, in addition to the definition above, suicide as a biological/biochemical/sociocultural / sociological / interpersonal / intrapsychic / philosophic /exi- stential event. It is certainly possible to write about suicidal phenomena from, say, a sociological point of view (as Durkheim

[1897] has done with great success) or from a psychodynamic point of view (as Menninger [1938] has done, also with great success). But those are simply elaborations of one point of view and cannot be thought to tell the whole story. The main point is that suicide is a multidimensional event and requires, for its understanding, a multidisciplinary approach.

MALAISE

The history of suicide is a record that involves words like sin, crime, and disease. Battin (1982), reminds us that even today the narrower definition used in the Catholic tradition (which emphasizes the moral signification under which the act is done synonymous with morally repugnant self-killing) seems closest to much ordinary usage. The notion of suicide as sin is very much present in current talk of it. A contemporary scientist, on the other hand, eschewing religion, has attempted to express suicide in medical terms, insisting that suicide is best understood not as a sin, not as a crime, and certainly not as a disease. From everything we know about a human event as complicated as suicide, we can be certain that such human disorders as malaria, syphilis, and tuberculosis are not accurate paradigms of suicide. In this sense suicide is more akin to delinquency or prostitution or craziness. I believe it is best conceptualized as a malaise, not a disease (for which we might hope to find a virus, coccus). It is a state of being, a human malaise.

PERTURBED

In the assessment of any living, potentially suicidal person, evaluations along two continuum should be made: how oriented toward death the individual is (lethality), and how upset or disturbed the individual is (perturbation). By its very definition, no one commits suicide who is not highly lethal. We know, of course, it is possible to be highly perturbed and not highly lethal at the same time—the living presence of many disturbed individuals attests to this. But our clinical observations affirm to us that no one commits suicide who is unperturbed. If a totally unperturbed individual were to commit suicide "for no reason at all," that in itself would be an aberrant act. There are several implications and corollaries of the above statements. It is not implied that all, or even most, individuals who commit suicide are insane or psychotic. It is implied that some elevated state of perturbation is necessarily present. This could be relatively innocuous, like the truncated scope of choices induced by severe psychical pain, sudden threat of torture, loss of health, or loss of status. The point is that an individual in his or her normal or modal state of being-in-the-world (by which is meant being in his or her accustomed world) does not ever commit suicide. Some elevated perturbation is the trigger, the *sine qua non*, the omnipresent component of the suicidal act.

One obvious and important implication (supported by the totality of my clinical experience) is that the most effective way to treat a potentially suicidal, highly lethal person is for the helping person to address not the lethality directly, but the perturbation. The most effective way to treat a suicidal person is to do whatever is humanly possible to decrease the lethality to a point below its critically explosive level. This means that one is not limited to addressing the suicidal individual's psyche. Instead, one attempts to make whatever changes are required in that individual's interpersonal relationships (especially with his or her significant others) and with other aspects of that person's environment, job, jail, cancer, and so on.

NEEDFUL

It is difficult to conceptualize an individual's committing suicide apart from that individual's seeking to satisfy certain innerfelt needs. Of course, these needs always operate within the context of a surrounding psychological situation—and there is something to be said for the subsidiary role of the environmental determinants of action. Murray's classification of human needs (1938) provides us with a set of usable terms. That approach is not the be-all and end-all but it certainly is a good beginning and perhaps the very best set of usable terms now available. I dare to repeat my own dictum in this matter: there are many pointless deaths but there can never be a needless suicide.

It might be argued that the word *needful* is unnecessary, almost redundant, in this definition in that every living individual is needful. The point of including this word in the definition of suicide is to focus on the fact that aside from whatever else suicide represents, it focally involves the attempt to fulfill some urgently felt psychological needs. Operationally, these heightened unmet needs make up, in large part, what the suicidal person feels and reports as his or her perturbation.

INDIVIDUAL

Fedden (1938) distinguishes between two kinds of suicide: personal and institutional (or sacrificial) suicide. In this he is simply wrestling, as Deshaies (1947) and others have done, with the tag end of sacrificial suicide, not knowing where to put it and needing to create a separate category for it. Just as we do not believe in the mob mind or in the collective unconscious, so we do not believe in institutional suicide. All suicides are individual acts. Granted that they reflect degrees of social or societal or group pressure. At the furthest remove, all suicide might be considered institutional or social to some degree in the sense that the individual has learned about it. There is no history of a feral person (that is, a person raised by animals) ever committing (i.e., inventing) suicide.

The task of the suicidologist who wishes to understand or to assess a suicidal act, whether that of a samurai warrior, a traditional Hindu widow who has practiced suttee, or a child at Jonestown, is no different from assessing a suicide of a middle-class Westchester teenager who kills herself by taking an excessive amount of barbiturates and permits herself to drown in her swimming pool.

In each case what is to be rated is the intention of the decedent vis-à-vis death. We can now answer the question that was discussed by European intellectuals during World War II. That question was: if you kill yourself when the Gestapo knocks on your door, have you—without any moral judgment in it (except, perhaps, about the Gestapo)—committed suicide? What else would you call it? Accident? Natural death? Homicide? In a terrible sense all suicides—*every* suicide—is committed because the real or figurative or imagined or hallucinated "Gestapo" is knocking at the psychic door.

If one could arrange it—and one cannot—it would be "appropriate" to die at one of the apogees of one's life, but it would be pointless if it were done. To commit suicide at the high point (when one is healthy, successful, happy, etc.) would be pointless and aberrant. The examples in Durkheim (1897) of individuals who kill themselves on the occasion of attaining sudden wealth are always referred to as being overwhelmed by their good fortune. One man's apogee is another man's perigee.

It seems sensible to say that no person left entirely to his or her own devices would commit suicide. A feral adult would not have the conceptualization of suicide and, more importantly, that concept without which suicide has absolutely no meaning, death. In that sense and in the further sense that many, perhaps most, suicidal events are intensely dyadic (involving some significant other), suicide may be said to be an interpersonal and certainly an intracultural event. But in its essence suicide is always an individual occurrence. It is separate people who kill themselves (albeit on occasion in a group setting) and always, as I have indicated, within a cultural nexus. All this may sound fairly obvious but those readers whose orientations are tenaciously sociological may well take umbrage at the seemingly rather innocuous words. To do so would be to misunderstand what I wish to say: suicide is always an individual event, *but* (or *and*) it always occurs in an individual who, willy-nilly, holds one or more citizenships in one or more cultures and who can never emigrate to *no where* (there is *no where* in suicide). In addition, there can be no suicide without some independent conceptualization of death, nullity, naughtment, cessation, and surcease and their opposites survival, continuance, and immortality. The emphasis on the individual does not at all preclude interest and concern with social (including economic) and especially cultural forces as they reside or swirl within the individual psyche.

DEFINES

Psychic life is perception and imagining and thinking and feeling. Perception involves, by its very nature, distortion by the living brain, which performs the act of perceiving. We are defining our world all the time, misperceiving it in our own idiosyncratic way—albeit with such commonplace agreements that no one but a sophist would quibble over a vast percentage of our perceptions. All this is to say that the word *defines* and the subsequent key word *issue* need to be discussed together since an issue is always defined by someone, that is, the very act which makes some matter in the world an image in the first place.

Inasmuch as the various words in this definition are organically related to one another, an additional point can be made about the word *defines*. We have already indicated that the individual who commits suicide is perturbed. More specifically that perturbation is manifested by a constriction and narrowing of the perceptional "diaphragm" in the camera of the mind. There is a narrowing and a tunneling and a closing down—much more light is needed for an ordinary common-sense picture of what is going on. This means that the very act of defining is done with some constriction and is not done in the relatively more open way of which that individual is capable. Operationally it means that fewer options than would ordinarily occur to that individual are

present for the perturbed mind's consideration. A suicidal individual who is defining any issue is not at his etymological best.
He is rather like Dr. Samuel Johnson might have been if he had
worked on his famous *Dictionary* with a mind truncated by drugs,
fatigue, or extraordinary emotional stress.

ISSUE

There is a notion in the watered-down popular misconception of
psychoanalytic theory that the individual (usually in the course of
psychotherapy) need only discover that one traumatic incident or
moment in the earlier life, at which point the complexes were
fixed. We can call this the magic moment theory of the neuroses.
It is a point of view that looks for *the* cause of relatively complex
nexuses of human behaviors. In the same sense there is some
danger of focusing on the issue in a suicidal drama. At the outset
we are aware that the causes of suicide are multiple and layered.
We can speak of primary causes, sustaining causes, resonating
causes, exacerbating causes, and precipitating causes. (Most
discussions of the causes of suicide—for instance, ill health,
financial failure, emotional rejection—deal only with precipitating
situations.) Nonetheless it makes sense in the linguistic analysis
of the typical suicidal scenario to speak of *the* issue which is
paramount in the consciousness of the suicidal person. The
implication of this view is that the unconscious factors, the
psychodynamics, which admittedly do play an important role in
the entire suicidal drama, play their role indirectly by making
what could be an issue in an individual's life *the issue* around
which that individual then conducts a life-or-death debate.

PERCEIVED

No brain, no life. Everything we experience is processed through
our living brain. In that sense all perception has some idiosyn-

cratic components. The words *perceive* and *misperceive* are synonymous. There is some distortion, by definition, in all perception. In the cases of suicidal individuals, the issue is the extent of this distortion. Our definition of suicide could have as easily read "for which the suicide is misperceived as the best solution." The pathology in suicidal perception is linked most directly with the *constriction* of the individual's then-present perceptual processes. This tunneling or focusing of the mind's set seems stimulated by the increase in perturbation. It is a commonplace observation that when one is upset, one does not, or is unable to, think clearly. Operationally, "clearly" implies capacity internally to scan and to choose among several viable options. Confusion is not so much a jumbling of possible options as it is a falling away of viable options and an arbitrarily operational focusing on only one seemingly possible solution (i.e., suicide) where more than one solution is realistically possible.

BEST

Suicide is an act done by a perturbed individual who, with a somewhat truncated perception of the options possible in the world, decides that cessation is the *best* possible solution that he can choose. Pascal, in his *Pensées* (1658) talked about the Bet Situation in which he asserted each individual must bet his soul on whether or not God exists. In a comparable way we can say that the suicidal person places himself in a Bet Situation where, under duress, he jumps to what he considers to be the best choice among the possible options—all of which may be noxious or offensive in some degree: an *aristos*, the best one can do under the circumstances. One implication of this view is that the treatment of the suicidal person almost always involves an effort to broaden the scope or range of his perceptions—"to widen his blinders" and to increase the number of more or less onerous options available in his consciousness.

SOLUTION

We have described suicide as an act or a deed. We have said that it is an event done in the service of certain unfilled psychological needs. It is all purposeful; its purpose is to solve a problem. In the mind of the chief protagonist suicide is a solution—*the* solution—to a perceived problem, dilemma, challenge, difficulty, seemingly inescapable or intolerable situation. "It was the only thing I could do. What else could I do? It was the best way out of that terrible situation."

In this definition, "suicide" has an adaptive and a self-serving function. Suicide is always done in the individual's "best interests"; that is, in the service of the individual's most pressing yearnings—to be free of intolerable emotion. In this sense, suicide can be said to be a selfish act. The individual's first fealty is not to his own preservation, but to himself. In this paradoxical sense, we are reminded of Richard Dawkins' brilliantly reasoned but not totally convincing presentation, *The Selfish Gene* (1976), whose major thesis is "that a predominant quality to be expected in a successful gene is ruthless selfishness" (p. 2). Neither for Dawkins in his book, nor for me in this context is it a moral judgment to say that both successful evolution and "successful" suicide are ruthlessly committed self processes—the "best" that can be done under the circumstances.

REFERENCES

Battin, M. P. (1982). *Ethical Issues in Suicide*. Englewood Cliffs, NJ: Prentice-Hall.

Bohannan, P. (1960). *African Homicide and Suicide*. Princeton, NJ: Princeton University Press.

Dawkins, R. (1976). *The Selfish Gene*. New York: Oxford University Press.

Deshaies, G. (1947). *Psychologie du Suicide*. Paris: Presses Universitaires de France.

Durkheim, E. (1897). *Le Suicide (Suicide)*. Trans. J. A. Spaulding and G. Simpson. Glencoe, IL: The Free Press of Glencoe, 1951.

Fedden, H. R. (1938). *Suicide: A Social and Historical Study*. London: Peter Davies.

Menninger, K. A. (1938). *Man against Himself*. New York: Harcourt, Brace and Company.

Pascal, B. (1658). *Pensées*.

Yap, P. M. (1958). *Suicide in Hong Kong*. London: Oxford University Press.

2

Aphorisms of Suicide

INTRODUCTION

No one can speak with total objectivity about a topic as complicated as suicide. Thinking about death and self-destruction can be
endlessly intriguing—and always has important subjective elements. Even if one were to limit one's discourse to the objective
statistics and demographic facts about suicide, that in itself would
imply a statement of one's view of things. It is probably best for
anyone who seeks to discuss suicide to show his flags and
allegiances explicitly, saying, as it were, "Here are some of my
views on this matter." Such a presentation has the advantage of
the author sharing with the reader where he stands, what his
beliefs are, and who—vis-à-vis suicide—he is (Shneidman 1973).

The driving thought behind this essay is that psychotherapy
is most effective when it flows from understanding, that remediation follows definition. This assertion might seem too obvious
to belabor, but the present difficulties and inefficiencies in treating, as one example, schizophrenia—where we do not definitely

know its cure, its causes, and (most importantly) its nature, if it is an "it" which clearly it is not—should alert us to the importance of clear conceptualization. This essay cannot seek to solve the problem, but it hopes to clarify the issue, specifically to comment on suicide in such a way as to yield direct implications for intervention.

The comments will take the form of aphorisms. An aphorism is a pithy short statement stating a general doctrine or truth. It is a maxim or saying; a principle expressed tersely in a few telling words. Historically—see the article on aphorisms in the *Encyclopaedia Britannica* (1973)—aphorisms are closely tied to the development of medicine.

The name was first used in the *Aphorisms of Hippocrates*, a long series of propositions concerning the symptoms and diagnosis of disease and the art of healing in medicine. . . . The first aphorism, perhaps the best known of all, runs as follows: "Life is short, art is long, opportunity fleeting, experimenting dangerous, reasoning difficult; it is necessary not only to do oneself what is right, but also to be seconded by the patient, by those who attend him, by external circumstances." [p. 109]

In the Western world at large probably the most acclaimed set of aphorisms are those philosophic ruminations of Pascal known as the *Pensées* (1657–1658). In those notes and fragments Pascal posits and then discusses the "Bet Situation," by which he means the bet on whether or not God exists. In a series of aphorisms he gives arguments for betting on the side of His existence.

In our own time the famous English novelist John Fowles— *The Collector, The Magus, The French Lieutenant's Woman, The Ebony Tower,* and so forth—has written a set of contemporary aphorisms entitled *The Aristos* (1964), in which he (like Pascal) creates aphorisms about death, immortality, and the Bet Situation. Not unexpectedly, his truths are quite different from those of Pascal.

It is obvious that one way to define and to discuss a topic is to do so aphoristically. In a set of aphorisms there is usually, if not a thread of logic, then at least a flow of thought from one aphorism to the next, building a general point of view. That is what I hope to do with my aphorisms on suicide.

APHORISMS ABOUT SUICIDE

1. There are two basic, albeit contradictory, truths about suicide: (A) Suicide should never be committed when one is depressed (or disturbed or constricted); and (B) almost every suicide is committed for reasons that make sense to the person who does it.
2. We can empathize with every person who has committed suicide and yet we should seek to thwart every suicidal plan that has not yet been consummated.
3. There is no such act as a rational suicide; but every suicide is a rational act — except possibly one committed by an actively psychotic person.
4. Suicide is both a logical and psychological phenomenon. As a logical thought disorder it is fueled by an individual's emotional turmoil and grounded in his psychological history.
5. The primary thought disorder in suicide is that of a pathological narrowing of the mind's focus, called constriction, which takes the form of seeing only *two* choices: either something painfully unsatisfactory *or* cessation.
6. There is nothing intrinsically wrong (or aberrant) in thinking about suicide; it is abnormal only when one thinks that suicide is the *only* solution.
7. The chief shortcoming of suicide is that it unnecessarily answers a remediable challenge with a permanent negative solution. In contrast, living is a long-term set of resolutions with oftentimes only fleeting results.
8. Wilhelm Stekel and the other early psychoanalysts (1910 and after) overstated the case when they proclaimed that no one commits suicide who has not wished the death of another; that suicide is basically hostility directed toward the image of a loved one incorporated within the psyche. Not only is this explanation often off the mark, but even more, the individual who commits suicide usually does not even wish to kill himself.

9. Suicide should not be misunderstood as hostility directed toward the introjected love object; but rather suicide is better understood as anguish over the plight of the writhing self.

10. When suicide is a hostile act, it is often not the hostility of the perpetrator but rather the hostility of the significant others who have provoked or permitted the act.

11. The central issue in suicide is not death or killing; it is, rather, the stopping of the consciousness of unbearable pain which—unfortunately—by its very nature entails the stopping of life.

12. If tormented individuals could somehow stop consciousness and still live, why would they not opt for that solution? In suicide, "death" is not the key word. The key words are "psychological pain."

13. If the pain were relieved then the individual would be willing to continue to live. Nobody wants to embrace pain; we just want to get out of the way of the hooves that hurt us.

14. As a psychological disorder suicide relates specifically to unmet or frustrated needs, such as the need for acceptance, achievement, dignity, self-regard, clear conscience, safety, and succorance. There are many pointless deaths, but never a needless suicide. Every suicide act is addressed to certain unfulfilled needs.

15. Suicide is not only a reaction to unmet needs, but also the need for important psychological freedoms, such as freedom from pain, freedom from guilt, freedom from shame, freedom from rejection, and aloneness. When these freedoms are traumatically violated, an individual who realistically lacks "a court of appeal" may take matters into his own hands and remove his consciousness from the painful scene.

16. Much of what has been written about suicide is relatively useless for actual prevention. There can be little meaningful practical research on suicide until the obfuscating categories of "attempted suicide" and "threatened sui-

cide" are eschewed and the continua of "perturbation" and "lethality" are understood and employed.

17. Suicide is not a right any more than is the right to belch. If the individual feels forced to do it he will do it. That capacity for untoward action cannot be taken away.

18. A definition of suicide should never be undertaken lightly. Much—especially implications for individual rescue and for global survival—depends upon it. The task of defining suicide is worthy of a separate book.

19. With some few clear exceptions, I am against suicide committed by other people, but I want to reserve that option for myself.

20. Nietzsche said that "The thought of suicide is a great consolation; by means of it one gets successfully through many a bad night." I can say that the topic of suicide has been a great preoccupation that has kept me up more nights than I care to remember.

THEORETICAL IMPLICATIONS

There are certain notions on which the aphorisms rest (that are propaedeutic to them) and certain notions which flow out of them (that are implications of them). For purposes of this discussion they need not be separated. At least five relatively important general notions about suicide can be delineated:

A. That suicide is best understood not so much as a movement toward death as it is a movement away from something and that something is always the same: intolerable emotion, unendurable pain, or unacceptable anguish. Reduce the level of suffering and the individual will choose to live.

B. That suicide is best understood not so much in terms of some sets of nosological boxes—for example, depression or any of the labels in *DSM-III*—but rather in terms of two continua of general personality functioning: perturbation and lethality. Everyone is omnipresently rateable (by himself or by others) on how disturbed he is (perturbation) and how deathfully suicidal he is (lethality). To say that an individual is "disturbed" or "suicidal" simply indicates that there is an elevation in that individual's perturbation and lethality levels, respectively. Moreover, it often happens that an individual is highly perturbed but not suicidal. It infrequently occurs that an individual is highly lethal but not perturbed. Experience has taught us the important fact that it is neither possible nor practical in an individual who is highly lethal and highly perturbed to attempt to deal with the lethality directly, either by moral suasion, confrontational interpretations, exhortation, or whatever. (It does not work any better in suicide than it does with alcoholism.) The most effective way to reduce elevated lethality is by doing so indirectly, that is by reducing the elevated perturbation. Reduce the individual's anguish, tension, and pain, and his level of lethality will concomitantly come down, for it is the elevated perturbation that drives or fuels the elevated lethality.

C. That suicide is best understood not so much as a psychosis, a neurosis, or a character disorder but rather as a more-or-less transient psychological constriction of affect and intellect. Synonyms for constriction are a tunneling or focusing or narrowing of the range of options usually available to *that* individual's consciousness when the mind is not panicked into dichotomous thinking: either some specific (almost magical) total solution *or* cessation. The range of choices has narrowed to two—not very much of a range. The usual life-sustaining images of loved ones are not only disregarded, they are not even within the range of what is in the mind.

One of the most dangerous aspects of a suicidal state (high lethality, high perturbation) is the presence of constriction. Any attempt at rescue or remediation has to deal almost from the first with the pathological constriction.

D. That suicide is best understood not so much as an unreasonable act (or a defect in cognition) but as a reaction to frustrated psychological needs. These needs—taken from the monumental work on personality by Henry A. Murray (1981)— include the needs for affiliation, avoidance (of pain), succorance,[1]—among many others. A suicide is committed because of frustrated or unfulfilled needs. In an even wider sense the systems theorist Ludwig von Bertalanffy (1965)—emphasizing that self-destruction is intimately connected with man's symbolic and psychological world—says:

The man who kills himself because his life or career or business has gone wrong, does not do so because of the fact that his biological existence and survival are threatened, but rather because of his quasi-needs, that is, his needs on the symbolic level are frustrated. [p. 114]

Given that there are no suicides in the absence of thwarted needs, if one will but address the frustrated needs, the suicide will then not have to occur (Shneidman 1980a).

E. That suicide is best understood not so much in relation to the idea of a reified Death as it is in terms of the idea (in the mind of the chief protagonist) of cessation, specifically when cessation—the complete stopping of one's consciousness of unendurable pain—is seen by the suffering individual as a solution, indeed the perfect solution, to life's painful and pressing problems. The moment that the idea of the possibility of stopping consciousness occurs to the mind as the answer or as the way out in the presence of unusual constriction and elevated perturbation and high lethality, then the active suicidal scenario has begun.

With these several theoretical supplements (of the twenty aphorisms) in mind, we can now turn to the main point, namely, the implications for psychotherapy of this general point of view.

IMPLICATIONS FOR PSYCHOTHERAPY

Initially I had developed implications for each of the twenty aphorisms but in the end it seems both tedious and somewhat

---

[1]A partial listing of Murray needs includes the following: the need for abasement, achievement, affiliation, aggression, autonomy, counteraction, defendance, deference, dominance, exhibition, harm-avoidance, pain-avoidance, inviolacy, nurturance, order, play, rejection, sentience, sex, succorance, and understanding.

repetitious to present them in this fashion. Instead, I decided to combine my twenty sets of working notes into one amalgam or synthesis of what seemed to me to be the most important implications for therapy from the view of suicide implicit in the aphorisms. The careful reader can easily match the implications for therapy with one or more aphorisms.

Some of the implications for psychotherapy are:

1. The therapist should ascertain the separate levels of the patient's perturbation and lethality (on a scale of 1 to 9) and make a day-to-day assessment of each of them. A lethality rating of 7, 8, or 9 indicates that the patient may be hazardously suicidal and that special measures need to be taken.

2. With a highly lethal suicidal person the main goal is, of course, to reduce the elevated lethality. The most important rule to follow is that *high lethality is reduced by reducing the patient's sense of perturbation.* One way to do this is by addressing in a practical way those in-the-world things that can be changed, if ever so slightly. In a sensible manner, the therapist should contact (preferably by telephone) the patient's spouse, lover, employer, government agencies, and so forth. In these contacts the therapist acts as ombudsman for the patient, promoting his interests and welfare. The subgoal is to reduce the real-life pressures that are driving up the patient's sense of perturbation.

A psychotherapist decreases the elevated perturbation of a highly suicidal person by doing almost everything possible to cater to the infantile idiosyncrasies, the dependency needs, the sense of pressure and futility, the feelings of hopelessness and helplessness that the individual is experiencing. In order to help a highly lethal person, one should involve others; create activity around the person; do what he or she wants done—and, if that cannot be accomplished, at least move in the direction of the desired goals to some substitute goals that approximate those which have been lost. Remind the patient that life is often the choice among lousy alternatives. The key to well-functioning is often to choose the least lousy alternative that is practicably attainable.

The basic principle is this: To decrease lethality one puts a hook on perturbation and, doing what needs to be done, pulls the level of perturbation down—and with that action brings down the active level of lethality. When the person is no longer highly suicidal, then the usual methods of psychotherapy can be usefully employed.

As to how to help a suicidal individual, it is best to look upon a suicidal act as an effort to stop unbearable anguish or intolerable pain by "doing something." Knowing this usually guides us as to what treatment should be. In the same sense the way to save a person's life is also to do something. Those somethings include putting that information (that the person is in trouble with himself) into the stream of communication, letting others know about it, breaking what could be a fatal secret, talking to the person, talking to others, proffering help, getting loved ones interested and responsive, creating action around the person, showing response, and indicating concern.

3. It is vital to counter the suicidal person's constriction of thought by attempting to widen the angle of the mental blinders and to increase the number of options, certainly beyond the two options of either having some magical resolution or being dead.

4. The mental pain of the suicidal person relates to the frustration or blocking of important psychological needs, that is, needs deemed to be important by that person. It should be the therapist's function to help the patient in relation to those thwarted needs. Even a little bit of improvement can save a life. Often just the possibility of a small amount of gain gives the perturbed individual enough hope and comfort to divert the suicidal course. In general, the goal of psychotherapy is to increase the patient's psychological *comfort*. One way to operationalize this task is to focus on the thwarted needs. Questions such as "What is going on?," "Where do you hurt?," and "What would you like to have happen?" can usefully be asked by a therapist helping a suicidal person.

The psychotherapists can focus on feelings, especially such distressing feelings as guilt, shame, fear, anger, thwarted ambition, unrequited love, hopelessness, helplessness, loneliness. The key is to improve the external and internal situations at the least a noticeable amount. This can be accomplished through a variety of methods: ventilation, interpretation, instruction, and realistic manipulation of the world outside the consultation room. That last means to do things, involve significant others, and invoke agencies. All this implies—when working with a highly lethal person—a heightened level of interaction during the period of elevated lethality. The therapist needs to work diligently, always giving the suicidal person realistic transfusions of hope until the perturbation intensity subsides enough to reduce the lethality to a tolerable, life-permitting level.

A highly suicidal state is characterized by its transient quality, its pervasive ambivalence, and its dyadic nature. Psychotherapists are well advised to minimize, if not totally to disregard, those probably well-intentioned but shrill writings in this field which naively speak of an individual's right to commit suicide—a right which in actuality cannot be denied.

A dozen other special features in the management of a highly lethal patient can be mentioned. Some of these special therapeutic stratagems or orientations reflect the *transient*, *ambivalent*, and *dyadic* aspects of almost all suicide acts.

1. *Monitoring.* A continuous (preferably daily) monitoring of the patient's lethality.

2. *Consultation.* There is almost no instance in a psychotherapist's professional life when consultation with a peer is as important as when one is dealing with a highly suicidal patient.

3. *Hospitalization.* Hospitalization is always a complicating event in the treatment of a suicidal patient but it should not, on those grounds, be eschewed. Obviously, the quality of care—from doctors, nurses, and attendants—is crucial. It helps if the hospital personnel are familiar with the therapist.

4. *Transference.* The successful treatment of a highly suicidal person depends heavily on the transference. The therapist can be active, show his personal concern, increase the frequency of the sessions, invoke the magic of the unique therapist-patient relationship, be less of a *tabula rasa*, give transfusions of (realistic)

hope and nurturance. In a figurative sense I believe that Eros can work wonders against Thanatos.

5. *The involvement of significant others.* Suicide is often a highly charged dyadic crisis. It follows from this that the therapist, unlike his usual practice of dealing almost exclusively with his patient (and even fending off the spouse, lover, parents, grown children), should consider the advisability of working directly with the significant other. If the individual is married, it is important to meet the spouse. The therapist must assess whether, in fact, the spouse is suicidogenic; whether the patient ought to be separated from the spouse; whether there are misunderstandings which the therapist can help resolve; or to what extent the spouse is insightful and concerned. At the minimum the role of the significant other as hinderer or helper in the treatment process needs to be assessed.

6. *Careful modification of the usual canons of confidentiality.* Admittedly this is a touchy and complicated point, but the therapist should not ally himself with death. Statements given during the therapy session relating to the patient's overt suicidal (or homicidal) plans should not be treated as a secret between two collusive partners.

Working with highly suicidal persons borrows from the goals of crisis intervention: not to take on and ameliorate the individual's entire personality structure and to cure all the neuroses, but simply to keep the person alive. That is the sine qua non without which all other psychotherapy could not have an opportunity to function.

REFERENCES

Aphorism. *Encyclopaedia Britannica* (1973). 14th Edition. Vol. 2, p. 109. Chicago: William Benton.
Bertalanffy, L. von (1965). Comments on aggression. In *Psychoanalysis*

and the Study of Behavior, ed. I. G. Sarason, p. 114. Princeton, NJ: Van Nostrand.

Fowles, J. (1964). *The Aristos*. Boston: Little, Brown.

Murray, H. A. (1981). *Explorations in Personality*. New York: Oxford University Press.

Pascal, B. (1657–1658). *Pensées*.

Pasternak, B. (1959). *I Remember: Sketch for an Autobiography*. New York: Pantheon.

Shneidman, E. S. (1973). Suicide. In *Encyclopaedia Britannica*, 14th ed., vol. 21, pp. 383–386. Chicago: William Benton.

———— (1980a). A possible classification of suicidal acts based on Murray's need system. *Suicide and Life-Threatening Behavior* 10:175–181.

———— (1980b). Psychotherapy with suicidal patients. In *Specialized Techniques in Individual Psychotherapy*, ed. T. B. Karasu and L. Bellak, pp. 305–313. New York: Brunner/Mazel.

3

A Conspectus of the Suicidal

Scenario

THE EXPERIENCE OF SUICIDE: ACCOUNTS OF THREE CASES

Let us consider some verbatim excerpts from the case transcripts of three failed suicides—each of whom performed an act that is ordinarily fatal, and fortuitously, against all realistic odds, survived to tell us something about the inside view of the suicidal scenario. What are the common threads of psychological gold and silver in the ore and slag of these heated reports? Both as a preview to all of the following text and as a guide to the proactive reading of the three excerpts, let us keep in mind these half-dozen key words (to be defined and discussed in this chapter): *pain, needs, frustration* (of needs), *constriction, ambivalence,* and *cessation* (of pain).

Immolator: I remember sitting in the car, and it was sort of like a blank in my mind. I felt very calm. I felt a kind of hush over my body. That everything was going to be OK. And I remember then pouring the gasoline first over the front seat, and of course over myself to a great extent. Even then, no thoughts went through my head at all of the pain that it was going to entail, the misery, hurt, any of that. I guess I didn't think that burns would really hurt, but none of that went through my head. It just felt good. It was the first time, in fact, that I had felt at peace, that I wasn't hurting inside. And for once it seemed like I had taken care of my problems and that my pain would just go away. It was not going to exist any more, especially my mental pain. And I remember very slowly striking the match and at that moment the fumes ignited, just a tremendous explosion.

Jumper: I was so desperate, I felt, "My God, I can't face this thing." Everything was like a terrible whirlpool of confusion. And I thought to myself, "There's only one thing to do: I just have to lose consciousness." That's the only way to get away from it. The only way to lose consciousness, I thought, was to jump off something good and high. I just figured I had to get outside. I just slipped out. No one saw me. And I got to the other building by walking across that catwalk thing, sure that someone would see me, you know, out of all those windows. The whole building is made of glass. And I just walked around until I found this open staircase. And as soon as I saw it, I just made a beeline right up to it. And then I got to the fifth floor and everything got very dark all of a sudden, and all I could see was this balcony. Everything around it just blacked out. It was just like a circle. That was all I could see, just the balcony. I climbed over it and I just let go. I was so desperate.

Shooter: There was no peace to be found. I had done all I could and was still sinking. I sat many hours seeking answers and all, but there was a silent wind and no answers. The answer was in my head. It was all clear now: Die. The next day a friend of mine offered to sell me a shotgun. I bought it. My first thought was, What a mess this is going to make. The next day I began to say goodbye to people. Not actually saying it, but expressing it silently. I didn't sleep. The dreams were reality and reality dreams. One by one I turned off my outside channels to the world. My mind became locked on my target. My thoughts were, Soon it will all be over. I can obtain the peace I have sought so long for. The will to survive and succeed had been crushed and defeated. I was like a general alone on a battlefield being encroached upon by my enemy and its hordes: fear, hate, self-depreciation, desolation. I felt I had to have the upper hand, to control my environment, so I sought to die rather than surrender. Destiny and reality began to merge. Those around me were as shadows, apparitions, but I was not actually conscious of them, only aware of myself and my plight. Death swallowed me long before I pulled the trigger. I was locked within myself. The world through my eyes seemed to die with me. It was like I was to push the final button to end this world. I committed myself to the arms of Death. There comes a time when all things cease to shine, when the rays of hope are lost. As I look back on that day it is as if this was another person's life. I was ending. I placed the gun under my chin. Then I remember a tremendous explosion of lights like fireworks consumed within a brilliant radiance. Thus did the pain become glorious, becoming an army rallied to the side of death to help destroy my life which I could feel leaving my body with each rushing surge of blood. I was engulfed in total darkness.

It is possible to conceptualize the commonalities of these (and all other) suicides in terms of the basic and omnipresent elements of the suicidal scenario—a "conspectus" of suicide, as it were. These fundamentals are as follows:

1. A sense of unbearable psychological *pain*, which is directly related to thwarted psychological *needs*.
2. Traumatizing *self-denigration*—a self-image that will not include tolerating intense psychological pain.
3. A marked *constriction* of the mind and an unrealistic narrowing of life's actions.
4. A sense of *isolation*—a feeling of desertion and the loss of support of significant others.
5. An overwhelmingly desperate feeling of *hopelessness*—a sense that nothing effective can be done.
6. A conscious decision that *egression*—leaving, exiting, or stopping life—is the *only* (or at least the best possible) solution to the problem of unbearable pain.

All these elements combine to result in suicide.

THE TEN COMMONALITIES OF SUICIDE

In previous publications (Shneidman 1985, 1986, 1987, 1989, 1990), I have referred to "the ten commonalities of suicide"— specifically, the common psychological features in human self-

TABLE 3-1. The Ten Commonalities of Suicide

   I. The common purpose of suicide is to seek a solution.
  II. The common goal of suicide is cessation of consciousness.
 III. The common stimulus in suicide is intolerable psychological pain.
  IV. The common stressor in suicide is frustrated psychological needs.
   V. The common emotion in suicide is hopelessness-helplessness.
  VI. The common cognitive state in suicide is ambivalence.
 VII. The common perceptual state in suicide is constriction.
VIII. The common action in suicide is egression.
  IX. The common interpersonal act in suicide is communication of intention.
   X. The common consistency in suicide is with lifelong coping patterns.

Note. From *Definition of Suicide* by E. S. Shneidman, 1985, New York: Wiley. Copyright © 1985 by Edwin S. Shneidman.

destruction. They are reproduced in Table 3-1 and are discussed briefly below. But first, a few preliminary remarks.

Suicidal phenomena can be understood in various ways. (I discuss these different approaches at the end of the chapter.) Clearly, one of the principal ways is the psychological approach, and the key to the psychological understanding of suicide is *pain*—psychological pain, the pain that the suicidal individual feels in *that* situation in his or her life. In this sense, suicide is a practical act intended to stop the unbearable flow (in consciousness) of intolerable pain. As Murray (1938) says in his great book, *Explorations in Personality,* suicide is clearly not adaptive, but it is just as clearly uniquely adjustive. Similarly, Baechler (1975), in his intensive book-length essay on suicide, tells us that in order to understand a specific case of suicide we must know what problem it was intended to solve. And Kelly (1961), in a way that is both philosophical and psychological, views suicide by proposing that each individual has his or her own private (unique, idiosyncratic) epistemology—his or her personal construct of the world—and that a suicide is to be understood as that individual's efforts to validate this personal construct.

Let us now consider the ten psychological commonalities of suicide (see Table 3-1), together with some illustrative quotations from the three suicidal vignettes presented above:

I. *The common purpose of suicide is to seek a solution.* First of all, suicide is not a random, pointless, or purposeless act. To the sufferer, it seems to be the only available answer to a real puzzler: "How am I to get out of this? What am I to do?" Its purpose is to seek a solution to a perceived crisis—the problem of over-whelming pain—that is generating intense suffering. To understand what a suicide is about, one must know the psychological problems it was intended to resolve. The general question one must put to the suicidal person is this: "What is going on?"

Excerpts: "And for once it seemed like I had taken care of my problems."

"And I thought to myself, 'There's only one thing to do . . .' "

"The answer was in my head."

II. *The common goal of suicide is cessation of consciousness.* Suicide is both a moving toward and a moving away. The common practical goal of suicide is the stopping of the painful flow of consciousness. Suicide is best understood not so much as a movement toward a reified Death as it is in terms of "cessation"—the complete (and irreversible) stopping of one's consciousness of unendurable pain. Suicide, as R. E. Litman (personal communication, 1990) points out, involves not only pain, but the individual's unwillingness to tolerate that pain, the decision not to endure it, and the active will to stop it. This means that in psychotherapy one needs to focus on the amelioration of the pain, as well as the "character" that has chosen not to tolerate it.

Excerpts: "It [the mental pain] was not going to exist any more."

"I felt, 'My God, I can't face this thing. . . . I just have to lose consciousness.' "

"Die. . . . Soon it will all be over."

III. *The common stimulus in suicide is unendurable psychological pain.* In any close analysis, suicide is best understood as a combined movement toward cessation *and* a movement away from intolerable, unendurable, unacceptable anguish. It is psychological pain of which I am speaking: "metapain," the pain of feeling pain. From a traditional psychodynamic view, hostility, shame, guilt, fear, protest, longing to join a deceased loved one, and the like have singly and in combination been identified as the root factor(s) in suicide. It is none of these; rather, it is the pain involved in any or all of them, together with the unwillingness to endure that idiosyncratically defined pain. Psychological pain is the center of suicide and constitutes the chief hurdle that must be lowered before any kind of therapy can be effectively lifesaving. The basic clinical rule is this: If the level of suffering is reduced (often just a little bit), the individual can choose to live.

Excerpts: "It was the first time . . . that I wasn't hurting inside. And for once it seemed . . . the [mental] pain would just go away."

"I was so desperate."

"I can obtain the peace I have sought so long for."

IV. The common stressor in suicide is frustrated psychological needs. The psychological pain that is central to suicide is driven, created by, and sustained by frustrated, blocked, or thwarted psychological needs. Suicide is best understood not so much as an unreasonable act—every suicide seems logical to the person who commits it (given that person's major premises, styles of syllogizing, and constricted focus)—as it is a reaction to unfulfilled psychological needs.

In order to understand suicide in this kind of context, we need to ask a much broader question, which I believe is the key: What purposes do most human acts (including suicide) intend to accomplish? The best nondetailed answer to that question is that, in general, human acts are intended to satisfy a variety of human needs. There is no compelling *a priori* reason why a typology (or classification or taxonomy) of suicidal acts might not parallel a general classification of human needs. Such a classification of psychological needs can be found in Murray's *Explorations in Personality* (1938). Murray's discussion of human needs is a ready-made, viable taxonomy of the essential underpinnings of suicidal behaviors. Table 3–2 presents a partial listing of Murray's explication of psychological needs.

Most suicides represent combinations of various needs, so that a particular case of suicide may properly be understood in terms of two or more different need categories. There are many pointless deaths, but never a needless suicide. If the frustrated needs are addressed, the pain they cause will be lessened, and the suicide will not occur. The therapist's function is to decrease the patient's acute discomfort and to increase the patient's comfort. One way to operationalize this task is to focus on the thwarted needs. Questions such as "Where do you hurt?" can be useful in clarifying the suicidal picture.

The assessment of needs related to suicide may be a more complicated epistemological task than the identification of the other commonalities of suicide. Psychological needs are more conceptual and abstract, and there is more inference necessary to name them. One requires access to a detailed anamnestic record or case history for the raw data from which inferences can reasonably be made. In the case of the shooter whose words are quoted above, I have concluded that the half-dozen most important needs (see Table 3–2) related to his suicidal state were the needs for dominance, autonomy, counteraction, succorance, affiliation, and order. These constitute a quite different constellation of vital psychological needs from the frustrated needs that ignited the immolator or those that pushed the jumper. I should note also that the use of the language of psychological needs immediately and radically changes the way in which one then conceptualizes that individual's suicidal behavior, and in which one can think of ways to help the suicidal person.

Excerpt: "I was like a general . . . being encroached upon by my enemy and its hordes: fear, hate, self-depreciation, desolation."

TABLE 3-2. A Partial Listing of the Murray Psychological Needs

Abasement. To submit passively to external force. To accept injury, blame, criticism, punishment. To surrender. To become resigned to fate. To admit inferiority, error, wrongdoing, or defeat. To confess and atone. To blame, belittle, or mutilate the self. To seek and enjoy pain, punishment, illness, and misfortune.

Achievement. To accomplish something difficult. To master, manipulate, or organize physical objects, human beings, or ideas. To do this as rapidly and independently as possible. To overcome obstacles and attain a high standard. To excel oneself. To rival and surpass others. To increase self-regard by the successful exercise of talent.

Affiliation. To draw near and enjoyably cooperate or reciprocate with an allied other (who resembles the subject or who likes the subject). To please and win affection of a respected person. To adhere and remain loyal to a friend.

Aggression. To overcome opposition forcefully. To fight. To attack or injure another. To oppose forcefully or punish another.

Autonomy. To get free, shake off restraint, break out of social confinement. To resist coercion and restriction. To avoid or quit activities prescribed by domineering authorities. To be independent and free to act according to desires. To defy convention.

Counteraction. To master or make up for a failure by restriving. To obliterate a humiliation by resumed action. To overcome weakness; to repress fear. To efface a dishonor by action. To seek for obstacles and difficulties to overcome. To maintain self-respect and pride on a high level.

Defendance. To defend the self against assault, criticism, or blame. To conceal or justify a misdeed, failure, or humiliation. To vindicate the ego.

Deference. To admire and support a superior. To praise, honor, or eulogize. To yield eagerly to the influence of an allied other. To emulate an exemplar. To conform to custom.

Dominance. To control one's human environment. To influence or direct the behavior of others by suggestion, seduction, persuasion, or command. To dissuade, restrain, or prohibit.

Exhibition. To make an impression. To be seen and heard. To excite, amaze, fascinate, entertain, shock, intrigue, amuse, or entice others.

Harmavoidance. To avoid pain, physical injury, illness, and death. To escape from a dangerous situation. To take precautionary measures.

Infavoidance. To avoid humiliation. To quit embarrassing situations. To avoid conditions that lead to scorn, derision, or indifference of others. To refrain from action because of fear of failure.

Inviolacy. To protect the self. To remain separate. To resist attempts of others to intrude upon or invade one's own psychological space. To maintain a psychological distance. To be isolated, reticent, concealed, immune from criticism.

(continued)

TABLE 3–2.(*continued*)

Nurturance. To give sympathy and gratify the needs of another person, especially an infant or someone who is weak, disabled, tired, inexperienced, infirm, defeated, humiliated, lonely, rejected, sick, or mentally confused. To feed, help, support, console, protect, comfort, nurse, heal; to nurture.

Order. To put things or ideas in order. To achieve arrangement, organization, balance, tidiness, and precision among things in the outer world or ideas in the inner world.

Play. To act for "fun" without further purpose. To like to laugh and make jokes. To enjoy relaxation of stress. To participate in pleasurable activities for their own sake.

Rejection. To separate oneself from a negatively viewed person. To exclude, abandon, expel, or remain indifferent to an inferior person. To snub or jilt another.

Sentience. To seek and enjoy sensuous experience. To give an important place to creature comforts of taste, touch, and the other senses.

Succorance. To have one's needs gratified by the sympathetic aid of another person. To be nursed, supported, sustained, protected, loved, advised, guided, indulged, forgiven, consoled, taken care of. To remain close to a devoted protector. To have a supporter.

Understanding. To ask and answer questions. To be interested in theory. To speculate, formulate, analyze, and generalize. To want to know the answers to general questions.

Note. Adapted from *Explorations in Personality* (pp. 142–242) by H. A. Murray, 1938, New York: Oxford University Press. Copyright © 1938 by Oxford University Press. Adapted by permission.

V. The common emotion in suicide is helplessness-hopelessness. In the suicidal state, there is a pervasive feeling of helplessness-hopelessness: "There is nothing I can do [except to commit suicide] and there is no one who can help me [with the pain that I am suffering]." Underlying all of the emotions—hostility, guilt, shame—is the emotion of impotent ennui, the feeling of helplessness-hopelessness. The most effective way to reduce the elevated lethality is to reduce the elevated perturbation of which the feelings of helplessness-hopelessness are an integral part.

Excerpt: "There comes a time when all things cease to shine, when the rays of hope are lost."

VI. The common cognitive state in suicide is ambivalence. The (non-Aristotelian) accommodation to the psychological realities of mental life—simultaneous contradictory feelings (such as love and hate toward the same person)—is called "ambivalence." It is the common internal attitude toward suicide: to feel that one has to do it, and at the same time to yearn (even to plan) for rescue and intervention. The therapist uses this ambivalence, and plays for time so that the affect rather than the bullet can be discharged.

Excerpt: "[I was] sure that someone would see me [and rescue me] . . . The whole building is made of glass."

VII. The common perceptual state in suicide is constriction. Suicide is not best understood as a psychosis, a neurosis, or a character disorder (100 percent of suicides are highly perturbed). It is more accurately seen as a more or less transient psychological constriction of affect and intellect. A synonym for "constriction" would be a "tunneling" or "focusing" or "narrowing" of the range of options usually available to that individual's consciousness when the mind is not panicked into dichotomous thinking: either some specific (almost magical) good solution or cessation; *Caesar aut nihil;* all or nothing. The range of life choices has narrowed to two—not very much of a range. The usual life-sustaining images of loved ones are not even within the mind. The fact that suicide is committed by individuals who are in a special constricted condition suggests that no one should ever commit suicide while disturbed. It takes a mind capable of scanning a range of options greater than two to make a decision as important as taking one's life. At the outset, it is vital to counter the suicidal person's constriction of thought by widening the mental blinders and increasing the number of options beyond only two dichotomous options of either achieving a magical resolution or being dead. The dangerous word that the therapist must be alert for is the word "only."

Excerpts: "[It] was sort of like a blank in my mind. . . . I didn't think that burns would really hurt . . ."

" 'There's only one thing to do . . . That's the only way . . .' The only way to lose consciousness, I thought, was to jump off something good and high. . . . [E]verything got dark all of a sudden . . . Everything around it just blacked out. It was just like a circle. That was all I could see . . ."

"My mind became locked on my target. . . . I sought to die rather than surrender."

VIII. The common action in suicide is egression. "Egression" or escape is a person's intended departure from a region of distress. Suicide is the ultimate egression, besides which all others (running away from home, quitting a job, deserting an army, leaving a spouse) pale. The therapist needs to give the person other exits, other ways of doing something. (The therapist and those close to the patient also need to close a possible lethal exit by, for example, removing a gun.) This notion is very much related to expanding the patient's constriction.

Excerpts: "It [I] was not going to exist any more . . ."

"I just have to lose consciousness."

"I committed myself to the arms of Death."

IX. The common interpersonal act in suicide is communication of intention. Perhaps the most interesting finding from large numbers of psychological autopsies of suicidal deaths is that in most cases (80 percent) there were clear verbal or behavioral clues to the impending lethal event. Individuals who are intent on committing suicide (albeit ambivalent about it) consciously or unconsciously emit signals of distress, whimpers of helplessness, or pleas for response; or they provide opportunities for rescue in the usually dyadic interplay that is an integral part of the suicidal drama. The common interpersonal act of suicide is paradoxical communication of intention with the usual verbal and behavioral clues.

Excerpt: "The next day I began to say goodbye to people."

X. *The common consistency in suicide is with lifelong coping patterns.* In suicide, one may be initially thrown off the scent because suicide is an act that, by definition, that individual has never committed before; thus, there seems to be no precedent. And yet there are some deep consistencies with lifelong coping patterns. The therapist must look at previous episodes of deep perturbation, distress, duress, and threat, and at the person's capacity to endure psychological pain, for patterns of egression in that person's life.

Excerpt: "I felt I had to have the upper hand, to control my environment, so I sought to die rather than surrender."

A THEORETICAL MODEL OF SUICIDE

It is now possible to combine these ten items into a more succinct theoretical model. Let us imagine a cube (see Figure 3–1) made up of 125 cubelets, with twenty-five squares on a plane, and five cubelets in each row and each column. I call these three faces of the cube (and the three corresponding components of this theoretical model) "pain," "perturbation," and "press," which are defined as follows:

1. *Pain.* "Pain," represented on the front of the cube, refers to the psychological pain resulting from thwarted psychological needs. The left-most column of cubelets represents little or no pain, the next column some bearable pain, and so on until the rightmost column, which represents intolerable psychological pain.
2. *Perturbation.* "Perturbation," assigned to the side plane of the large cube, is a general term meaning the state of being upset or perturbed. Ranked here on a five-point rating scale, perturbation includes everything in the *Diagnostic and Statistical Manual of*

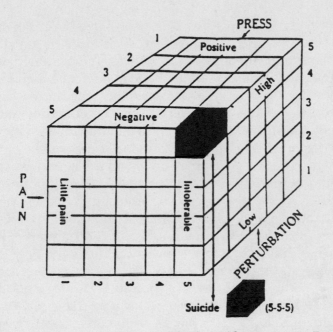

Figure 3-1. A theoretical cubic model of suicide. From "A Psychological Approach to Suicide" by E. S. Shneidman, 1987, in G. R. VandenBos and B. K. Bryant (Eds.), *Cataclysms, Crises and Catastrophes: Psychology in Action.* Washington, DC: American Psychological Association. Copyright © 1987 by the American Psychological Association. Reprinted by permission.

Mental Disorders, third edition, revised (*DSM-III-R* 1987). In relation to suicide, perturbation includes (a) perceptual constriction, and (b) a penchant for precipitous self-harm or inimical action. "Constriction" refers to the reduction of the individual's perceptual and cognitive range. At its worst, the individual reduces the viable options to two, and then to one. On this plane in the cube, the bottom row reflects open-mindedness, wide mentational scope, and relatively clear thinking. The top row reflects constriction of thought, tunnel vision, and a narrowing of focus to few options, with cessation, death, and egression as one (and ultimately the only) solution to the problem of pain and frustrated needs. "Penchant for action" refers to something akin to impulsiveness—a tendency to get things over with; to bring them inappropriately to a quick resolution; to have little patience and low tolerance for open and stressful situations; to jump to conclusions; and to jump at opportunities for more immediate resolution. The row of cubelets at the bottom reflects a high tolerance for ambiguity, a capacity for patience and waiting. As we move upward on this plane, we come closer to this tendency for precipitous and consummatory action, this lethal impulsivity. That is what the topmost row on the side plane represents.

3. *Press.* Murray (1938) may have had the word "pressure" in mind when he decided to use the word "press" ("press" is both the singular and the plural form) to represent those aspects of the inner and outer world or environment that impinge on, move, touch, or affect the individual and make a difference. The term refers to the things done *to* the individual (and the way they are incorporated and interpreted), to which he or she reacts. There is positive press (good genes and happy fortune), and there is negative press (conditions or events that perturb, threaten, stress, or harm the individual). It is the latter that are relevant to suicide. Press includes both actual and imagined events, in the sense that everything is mediated by the mind. In this cubic model, press ranges from positive (in the back row of the top plane) to negative (in the front row of the top plane).

In this theoretical cube of 125 cubelets, there is only one cubelet that is numbered 5-5-5. Not every individual who is in a 5-5-5 cubelet commits suicide—he or she may commit homicide, or go crazy, or become amnesic, or destroy a career—but in this conceptual model no one commits suicide *except* those in the 5-5-5 cubelet (maximum pain, maximum perturbation, maximum negative press). The implications for therapy and lifesaving redress would seem to be obvious: Reduce any of these three dimensions from a 5 to a 4 (or less); preferably, reduce all three. Individuals can lead long, unhappy lives as 4s and 3s, but the specific goal in suicide prevention is to remove the individual from the 5-5-5 cubelet—to save his or her life. All else (demographic variables, family history, previous suicidal history) is peripheral, except as those and other factors bear on the presently felt pain, perturbation, and negative press.

CONCLUSION: FIELDS CONTRIBUTING TO SUICIDOLOGY

Now, finally, to put this presentation of the psychological approach to suicide in a wider perspective, I can speak of a variety of fields of knowledge that have a legitimate interest in suicidology (see Table 3-3). Each of these approaches can contribute to our knowledge of suicidal phenomena. In this same sense, any one of them errs when it claims that *its* sector represents the whole circle of etiology—that it is clearly the only way to achieve a real understanding of suicide. Furthermore, proponents of all the approaches need to be vigilant that they do not confuse concomitance (events [in the brain, in the blood, in society, in interpersonal relations, within the psyche] that happen at the

TABLE 3-3. Various Contemporary Approaches to the Study of Suicidal Phenomena

Sector	Key references	Principal assertion: That suicide is best understood primarily—
Life history	Allport (1937) Murray (1967) Runyon (1982)	As an episode in a long life history; precursors of the suicidal death can be seen in previous patterns of response to comparable life situations.
Personal documents	Allport (1942) Shneidman and Farberow (1957) Leenaars (1988)	Through the analysis of such personal documents as letters, diaries, autobiographies, and especially suicide notes.
Demographic; epidemiological	Graunt (1662) Süssmilch (1741) Dublin (1963) Hollinger and Offer (1986)	In terms of census data (the statistics for sex, age, race, religious affiliation, marital status, socioeconomic status, etc.).
Systems theoretical	Blaker (1972) Miller (1978) Tyler (1984)	As an act within a living system; both the individual and the individual-within-the-society are considered as living systems.

(continued)

TABLE 3–3. *(continued)*

Sector	Key references	Principal assertion: That suicide is best understood primarily—
Philosophical; theological	Pepper (1942) Fowles (1964) Choron (1972) Battin (1982)	In terms of answers to questions such as these: What is the purpose of life? Are there forces beyond ourselves? What is our relation to the universe? Is there life after death?
Sociocultural	Hendin (1964) Lifton, Kato, and Reich (1979) Iga (1986)	In terms of sociocultural data (e.g., knowledge of various countries and cultures such as Sweden, Japan, etc.).
Sociological	Durkheim (1897/1951) Douglas (1967) Maris (1981)	In terms of an individual's relationship to his or her society (estrangement from it, ties to it).
Dyadic and family	Pfeffer (1986) Richman (1986)	In terms of the stressful interaction between two people or within a family nexus.
Psychiatric	Kraepelin (1883/1915) American Psychiatric Association (1987)	In terms of mental illnesses (e.g., depression, schizophrenia, alcoholism).
Psychodynamic	Freud (1910/1967) Zilboorg (1937) Menninger (1938) Litman (1967)	In terms of unconscious conflicts, especially unconscious hostility toward the father; suicide is seen as unconscious murder.
Psychological	Murray (1938) Shneidman (1985)	In terms of psychological pain, produced by the frustration of psychological needs.
Constitutional	Roy (1986) Kety (1986)	As an expression of inborn (constitutional or genetic) factors.
Biological; biochemical	Bunney and Fawcett (1965) Asberg, Nordstrom, and Traskman-Bendz (1986)	As a result of biochemical imbalances in the body fluids (blood) or organs (brain).

same time as heightened suicidality) with causality (events that necessarily must precede the onset of a suicidal state). It is the causally related events that present us with reasonable avenues to effective prevention.

REFERENCES

Allport, G. (1937). *Personality: A Psychological Interpretation.* New York: Holt, Rinehardt & Winston.

———— (1942). *The Use of Personal Documents as Psychological Science.* New York: Social Science Research Council.

American Psychiatric Association (1987). *Diagnostic and Statistical Manual of Mental Disorders,* 3rd ed., rev. Washington, DC: American Psychiatric Association.

Asberg, M., Nordstrom, P., and Traskman-Bendz, L. (1986). Biological factors in suicide. In *Suicide,* ed. A. Roy, pp. 47–71. Baltimore: Williams & Wilkins.

Baechler, J. (1979). *Suicides.* Trans. B. Cooper. New York: Basic Books.

Battin, M. P. (1982). *Ethical Issues in Suicide.* Englewood Cliffs, NJ: Prentice-Hall.

Blaker, K. P. (1972). Systems theory and self-destructive behavior. *Perspectives in Psychiatric Care* 10:168–172.

Bunney, W. E., and Fawcett, J. A. (1965). Possibility of a biochemical test for suicide potential. *Archives of General Psychiatry* 13:232–239.

Choron, J. (1972). *Suicide.* New York: Scribner's.

Douglas, J. D. (1967). *The Social Meaning of Suicide.* Princeton, NJ: Princeton University Press.

Dublin, L. I. (1963). *Suicide: A Sociological and Statistical Study.* New York: Ronald.

Durkheim, E. (1897). *Suicide: A Study in Sociology.* Trans. J. A. Spaulding and G. Simpson. Glencoe, IL: Free Press, 1951.

Fowles, J. (1964). *The Aristos.* Boston: Little, Brown.

Freud, S. (1910). Comments on suicide. In *On Suicide,* ed. P. Friedman, trans. E. Fitzgerald, pp. 140–141. New York: International Universities Press, 1967.

Graunt, J. (1662). *Natural and political annotations . . . upon the bills of mortality.* London.

Hendin, H. (1964). *Suicide in Scandinavia*. New York: Grune & Stratton.

Hollinger, P. C., and Offer, D. (1986). *Sociodemographic, Epidemiologic and Individual Attributes of Youth Suicides*. Bethesda, MD: Department of Health and Human Services.

Iga, M. (1986). *The Thorn in the Chrysanthemum: Suicide and Economic Success in Modern Japan*. Berkeley: University of California Press.

Kelly, G. A. (1961). Suicide: The personal construct point of view. In *The Cry for Help*, ed. N. Farberow and E. S. Shneidman, pp. 255–280. New York: McGraw-Hill.

Kety, S. (1986). Genetic factors in suicide. In *Suicide*, ed. A. Roy, pp. 41–45. Baltimore: Williams & Wilkins.

Kraepelin, E. (1883). *Textbook of Psychiatry*. 1915.

Leenaars, A. A. (1988). *Suicide Notes*. New York: Human Sciences.

Lifton, R. J., Kato, S., and Reich, M. R. (1979). *Six Lives/Six deaths*. New Haven, CT: Yale University Press.

Litman, R. E. (1967). Sigmund Freud on suicide. In *Essays in Self-Destruction*, ed. E. S. Shneidman, pp. 324–344. New York: Science House.

Maris, R. (1981). *Pathways to Suicide: A Survey of Self-destructive Behaviors*. Baltimore: Johns Hopkins University Press.

Menninger, K. A. (1938). *Man Against Himself*. New York: Harcourt, Brace and World.

Miller, J. G. (1978). *Living Systems*. New York: McGraw-Hill.

Murray, H. A. (1938). *Explorations in Personality*. New York: Oxford University Press.

———— (1967). Dead to the world: the passions of Herman Melville. In *Essays in Self-destruction*, ed. E. S. Shneidman, pp. 7–29. New York: Science House.

Pepper, S. (1942). *World Hypotheses*. Berkeley: University of California Press.

Pfeffer, C. (1986). *The Suicidal Child*. New York: Guilford.

Richman, J. (1986). *Family Therapy for Suicidal Individuals*. New York: Springer.

Roy, A., ed. (1986). *Suicide*. Baltimore: Williams & Wilkins.

Runyon, W. M. (1982). *Life Histories and Psychobiography: Explorations in Theory and Method*. New York: Oxford University Press.

Shneidman, E. S. (1973). Suicide. In *Encyclopaedia Britannica*, 14th ed., vol. 21. Chicago: William Benton.

———— (1980). *Voices of Death*. New York: Harper & Row.

———— (1984). Aphorisms of suicide and some implications for psychotherapy. *American Journal of Psychotherapy* 38:319–328.

_____ (1985). *Definition of Suicide.* New York: Wiley.

_____ (1986). Some essentials of suicide and some implications for response. In *Suicide,* ed. A. Roy, pp. 1–16. Baltimore: Williams & Wilkins.

_____ (1987). A psychological approach to suicide. In *Cataclysms, Crises and Catastrophes: Psychology in Action,* ed. G. R. VandenBos and B. K. Bryant, pp. 147–183. Washington, DC: American Psychological Association.

_____ (1989). A multidisciplinary approach to suicide. In *Suicide: Understanding and Responding: Harvard Medical School Perspectives,* ed. D. Jacobs and H. Brown, pp. 1–30. Madison, CT: International Universities Press.

_____ (1990). A life in death: notes of a committed suicidologist. In *A History of Clinical Psychology in Autobiography,* ed. C. E. Walker, pp. 225–292. Pacific Grove, CA: Brooks/Cole.

Shneidman, E. S., and Farberow, N., eds. (1957). *Clues to Suicide.* New York: McGraw-Hill.

Süssmilch, J. (1741). *Die Göttliche Ordnung in den Veränderungen des Menschlichen Geschlechts, aus der Geburt, dem Tode, und der Fortflanzug desselben erwiesen.* Berlin: J. C. Spenser.

Tyler, L. (1984). *Thinking Creatively.* San Francisco: Jossey-Bass.

Zilboorg, G. (1937). Considerations in suicide with particular reference to that of the young. *American Journal of Orthopsychiatry* 7:15–31.

4

Suicide as Psychache

Nearing the end of my career in suicidology, I think I can now say what has been on my mind in as few as five words: *Suicide is caused by psychache* (sīk-āk; two syllables). *Psychache* refers to the hurt, anguish, soreness, aching, psychological pain in the psyche, the mind. It is intrinsically psychological—the pain of excessively felt shame, or guilt, or humiliation, or loneliness, or fear, or angst, or dread of growing old, or of dying badly, or whatever. When it occurs, its reality is introspectively undeniable. Suicide occurs when the psychache is deemed by that person to be unbearable. This means that suicide also has to do with different individual *thresholds* for enduring psychological pain (Shneidman 1985, 1992).

All our past efforts to relate or to correlate suicide with simplistic nonpsychological variables such as sex, age, race, socioeconomic level, case history items (no matter how dire), psychiatric categories (including depression), and so forth were (and are) doomed to miss the mark precisely because they ignore the one variable that centrally relates to suicide, namely intolerable psychological pain; in a word, psychache.

By its very nature, psychological pain is tied to psychological *needs*. In general, the broadest purpose of most human activity is to satisfy psychological needs. Suicide relates to psychological needs in that suicide is a specific way to *stop* the unbearable psychachical flow of the mind. Further, what causes this pain is the blockage, thwarting, or frustration of certain psychological needs felt by that person at that time and in those circumstances to be *vital* to continued life.

Suicide is not adaptive, but adjustive, in the sense that it serves to reduce the tension of the pain related to the blocked needs. Murray's monumental volume *Explorations in Personality* (1938) provides a comprehensive list of psychological needs and their definitions: abasement, achievement, affiliation, aggression, autonomy, counteraction, defendance, deference, dominance, exhibition, harmavoidance, infavoidance, inviolacy, nurturance, order, play, rejection, sentience, succorance, and understanding (see Table 3–2).

There is an integral relationship between suicide and happiness—or rather the absence of it. Genuine happiness—contrary to the nineteenth and twentieth century materialistic notions that narrowly identified happiness with the mere absence of pain and the presence of creature comforts—has a special magical quality (Spender 1988). There is the mundane happiness of comfort, pain avoidance, and psychological anesthesia. But genuine, magical happiness has relatively little to do with creature comfort; rather, it is the kind of ecstasy and consuming exuberance that one can experience best in a benign childhood. To the extent that suicide relates to happiness, it relates in people of *any* age—not to lack of mundane happiness but to the loss of childhood's magical joys.

A principal task for contemporary suicidology is to operationalize (and metricize) the key dimension of psychache. One way to begin is to ask the simple question, "How much do you hurt?" (Kropf 1990).

One trenchant way to understand any individual is to rank-order (or Q-sort) the prepotency among the twenty needs: that is, to define or characterize that individual's personality in terms of his or her weightings among all the needs. This can be done by assigning, for that individual, a number to each need, so that the total sum for the individual adds up to 100. This permits us to rate various individuals or a single individual over time by use of the constant-sum method. The task is simple and takes only a few minutes. (Try it by rating yourself; then rate a well-known public figure; have colleagues rate that same figure; rate your patients after each session; rate suicidal patients; non-suicidal patients.)

In relation to suicide, there are, within any individual, *two* sets of dispositions or sets of relative weightings among the twenty psychological needs. They are: (1) Those psychological needs that the individual lives with, that define his or her personality in its day-to-day intrapsychic and interpersonal func-tioning—the *modal* needs; and (2) those few psychological needs, the frustration of which that individual simply cannot tolerate; the needs that person would die for—the *vital* needs. Within an individual, these two kinds of needs are psychologically consis-tent with each other. The vital needs come into play when the individual is under threat or duress. This special disposition of needs can be elicited by asking an individual about his precise reactions to the failures or losses or rejections or humiliations—the dark moments—previously in his life.

By means of an intensive psychological autopsy (Shneidman 1977) it should be possible to identify (or label) every committed suicide in terms of the two or three prepotent needs, the frustration of which played a major role in that death. (With twenty needs, we have a possible taxonomy of a few hundred different types of suicide.)

The *prevention* of suicide (with a highly lethal person) is then primarily a matter of addressing and partially alleviating those frustrated psychological needs that are driving that person to suicide. The rule is simple: Mollify the psychache.

In the progression to a suicidal outcome, I believe that we can distinguish seven components. They are:

1. The vicissitudes of life; those stresses, failures, rejections, catabolic and social and psychological insults that are omni-present by virtue of living.

2. Various approaches to understanding human behavior. Suicidal behavior (as is all behavior) is obviously multidimensional—which means, in practice, that its proper explication has to be multidisciplinary. The relevant fields for suicidology include biochemistry (and genetics), sociology, demography-epidemiology, psychology, psychiatry, linguistics, and so on. The reader should appreciate that this chapter is limited to the psychological approach to suicide—without derogating the importance of other legitimate approaches.

3. The vicissitudes of life are perceptually funnelled through the human mind and apperceived (or appreciated) as ecstatic, pleasurable, neutral, inconsequential, or painful. If there is extreme psychache, a necessary condition for suicide is present. "I hurt too much."

4. Another necessary condition for suicide, in addition to psychache, is the perception of the pain as unbearable, intolerable, unacceptable. "I won't put up with this pain."

5. Still another necessary condition is the thought (or insight) that cessation of consciousness is the solution for the unbearable psychache. In a phrase: Death is preferable to living; death is a means of egression or escape. "I can kill myself."

6. A final necessary condition for suicide is a lowered threshold for enduring or sustaining the crippling psychache. A priori, people with more or less equal amounts of psychache might have radically different overt outcomes depending upon their different thresholds for tolerating or enduring psychological pain. (In life, pain is ubiquitous and inescapable; suffering is optional.)

7. The suicidal outcome: "I hurt too much to live."

About now, the alert and restive reader might be asking: What about depression? As everyone knows, depression is a serious psychiatric syndrome, well recognized and relatively treatable. But depression is not the same as suicide. They are quite different. For one thing, they have enormously different fatality rates. One can live a long, unhappy life with depression— not true of an acutely suicidal state. Theoretically, no one has ever

died of depression—it is not a legitimate cause of death on the
death certificate—but many people, too many, have died of
suicide. Vast numbers of people suffer from minor and major
depressions. Depression seems to have physiological, biochemical, and probably genetical components. The use of medications
in treatment is on target. It is, so to speak, a biological storm in
the brain. Suicide, on the other hand, is a phenomenological
event, a transient tempest in the mind. It is responsive to talk
therapy and to changes in the environment. Suicide is not a
psychiatric disorder. Suicide is a nervous dysfunction, not a
mental disease. *All* persons who commit suicide—100 percent of
them—are perturbed—but they are not necessarily clinically depressed (or schizophrenic, or alcoholic, or addicted, or psychiat-
rically ill). A suicidal crisis is best treated on its own terms. It is a
deadly serious (temporary and treatable) psychache. (See Table
4-1.)

TABLE 4-1.

Symptoms of Depression	Characteristics of Suicide
Depression	Suicide
1. Sadness	1. In great psychological pain (psychache)
2. Apathy	2. Cannot stand the pain (lowered threshold for suffering)
3. Loss of appetite or increased appetite	3. Sees ending life as an escape (death as solution)
4. Insomnia, or sleeping far more than usual	4. Sees no possibilities other than death (constriction)
5. Feeling physically agitated or slowed down	5. May or may not have symptoms of depression (suicide as a mental state)
6. Fatigue and lack of energy	
7. Feelings of worthlessness or great guilt	
8. Inability to concentrate or indecisiveness	
9. Thoughts of death or suicide	

Source (for Depression): *New York Times*, Aug. 6, 1992. Used by permission.

Depression never causes suicide; rather, suicide results from severe psychache—coupled with dysphoria, constriction of perceptual range, and the idea of death as preferable to life. By themselves, the clinical symptoms of depression are debilitating, but, by their nature, not deadly. On the other hand, severe psychache by itself may be life-threatening. Correlating suicide with *DSM* categories is irrelevant to the real action in the mind's main tent. Depression merits treatment for itself, but then to assert that suicide is essentially depression is either a logical mistake, a conceptual confusion, or a professional gambit. In any case, it is past time to make this correction.

Here, finally, based on over forty years of experience as a suicidologist, is a tight summary of my current beliefs about suicide:

1. The explanation of suicide in humankind is the same as the explanation of the suicide of any particular human. Suicidology—the study of human suicide—and a psychological autopsy of a particular case are identical in their goals: To nibble at the puzzle of human self-destruction.

2. The most evident fact about suicidology and suicidal events is that they are multidimensional, multifaceted, multidisciplinary—containing, as they do, concomitant biological, sociological, psychological (interpersonal and intrapsychic), epidemiological, and philosophic elements.

3. From the view of the psychological factors in suicide, the key element in every case is psychological pain; psychache. All affective states (such as rage, hostility, depression, shame, guilt, affectlessness, hopelessness, etc.) are relevant to suicide only as they relate to unbearable psychological pain. If, for example, feeling guilty or depressed or having a bad conscience or an overwhelming unconscious rage makes one suicidal, it does so only because it is painful. No psychache, no suicide.

4. Individuals have different thresholds for enduring or tolerating pain; thus the individual's decision not to bear the pain—the threshold for enduring it—is also directly relevant.

5. In every case, the psychological pain is created and fueled by frustrated psychological needs. These needs have been explicated by Murray (1938).

6. There are modal psychological needs with which the person lives and which define the personality and there are vital psychological needs whose frustration cannot be tolerated, which define the suicide. Within an individual these two kinds of needs are psychologically consistent with each other, although not necessarily the same as each other.

7. The remediation (or therapy) of the suicidal state lies in addressing and mollifying the vital frustrated needs. The therapist does well to have this template of psychological needs in mind so that the therapy can be tailor-made for that patient. Often, just a little bit of mollification of the patient's frustrated needs can change the vital balance sufficiently to save a life.

REFERENCES

Kropf, J. (1990). An empirical assessment of Murray's personological formulation of suicide. Ph.D. dissertation. California School of Professional Psychology. Fresno. CA.

Murray, H. A. (1938). *Explorations in Personality*, New York: Oxford University Press.

Shneidman, E. S. (1977). The psychological autopsy. In *Guide to the Investigation and Reporting of Drug Abuse Deaths*, ed. L. Gottschalk, et al. Rockville, MD: ADAMHA.

———— (1985). *Definition of Suicide*. New York: Wiley.

———— (1992). A conspectus of the suicidal scenario. In *Assessment and Prediction of Suicide*, ed. R. W. Maris, et al. pp. 50–64. New York: Guilford.

Spender, S. (1988). Introduction to second edition. *Memoirs of a Public Baby*, by Philip O'Connor, pp. 11–12. New York: Norton.

PART TWO

ANALYSES

5

Suicide among the Gifted

INTRODUCTION AND BACKGROUND

The two principal assertions in this chapter are (a) that discernible early prodromal clues to adult suicide may be found in longitudinal case history data, and (b) that it is useful to conceptualize these premonitory clues in terms of *perturbation* and *lethality*.

The data from which evidence for these assertions was obtained are those of the longitudinal study of 1,528 gifted people initiated by Lewis M. Terman in 1921.[1] Terman and his co-

---

[1]This study was conducted while the author was a Fellow at the Center for Advanced Study in the Behavioral Sciences, 1969–70. Arrangements were made for confidential access to the research records by Professor Robert R. Sears who, with Professor Lee J. Cronbach, is one of the two scientific executors of the Terman Study. The data themselves are the property of Stanford University. The author is especially grateful to Mrs. Melita Oden and Mrs. Sheila Buckholtz, longtime staff members

workers searched the public schools of the cities of California for exceptionally bright youngsters. His purposes were to discover what gifted children are like as children, what sort of adult they become, and what some of the factors are that influence their development (Oden 1968). That study, begun a half-century ago, continues to this day.

Of the original 1,528 subjects, 857 were males and 671 were females. The sample was composed of children (mean age 9.7 years) with Stanford-Binet I.Q.s of 140 or higher—the mean I.Q. was over 150—and an older group of high school students (mean age 15.2 years) who scored within the top 1 percent on the Terman Group Test of Mental Ability. The present analysis will be limited to male subjects, of whom approximately 80 percent were born between 1905 and 1914.

An enormous amount of data has been collected. At the time of the original investigation in 1921–22, the information included a developmental record, health history, medical examination, home and family background, school history, character trait ratings and personality evaluations by parents and teachers, interest tests, school achievement tests, and the like. Subsequently, there has been a long series of systematic follow-ups by mail or by personal field visits: in 1924, 1925, 1936, 1940, 1945, 1950, 1955, and 1960. In the field studies (1921, 1927, 1940, and 1950), subjects and their families were interviewed, and data from intelligence tests, personality tests, and questionnaires were obtained.

The Terman studies have catalyzed two generations of thought, research, attitudinal changes, and educational developments. Detailed descriptions of the subjects at various ages, as well as summaries of the important findings, are available in a series of publications authored by Professor Terman and his chief co-worker, Melita Oden (Oden 1968, Terman 1925, 1940, Terman and Oden 1947, 1959). Among longitudinal studies (Stone and Onque 1959) the Terman Study is unique in many ways, in-

---

of the Gifted Study, for their extensive help in preparing relevant data for his use and for advice and guidance along the way.

cluding the extent to which its staff has continued to maintain contact with the subjects for nearly half a century. As of 1960, only 1.7 percent of the 1,528 subjects had been lost entirely.

Almost everyone in the psychological and pedagogical worlds now knows the basic findings of the Terman Study: that intellectually gifted children—far from being, as was once thought, spindly, weak, and maladjusted or one-sided—are, on the whole, more physically and mentally healthy and successful than their less-than-gifted counterparts. An unusual mind, a vigorous body, and a well-adjusted personality are not incompatible.[2]

A mortality summary for the Terman gifted group is as follows: In 1960—when the median age was 49.6—there had been 130 known deaths, eighty-three male and forty-seven female. The mortality rate was 9.8 percent for males and 7.2 percent for females—8.6 percent for the total group. According to Dublin's life tables (Dublin, Lotka, and Spiegelman 1949), 13.9 percent of white males, 10.1 percent of white females, and 12 percent of a total cohort who survive to age 11 will have died before age 50. In 1960, the figures indicated a favorable mortality rate in the Terman group lower than the general white population of the same age.

By 1960, 110 of the 130 Terman group deaths—61 percent—had been due to natural causes. (Cardiovascular diseases ranked first with males, and cancer was first among females.) Accidents accounted for nineteen male deaths, while only five females died

---

[2]As part of the Terman Study of the Gifted, Catharine M. Cox (1926) completed a comprehensive retrospective study of the childhood intelligence of 301 historically eminent men born after 1450. Of the individuals discussed in her study, 119 were thought to have I.Q.s of 140 or higher. (As examples, here are some names—one person in each of the five-step I.Q. intervals from 140 to 190: Carlyle, Jefferson, Descartes, Hume, Pope, J. Q. Adams, Voltaire, Schelling, Pascal, Leibnitz, and J. S. Mill.) As to suicide among this extraordinary group, so far as can be ascertained, only one of the 301 eminent men died by killing himself—Thomas Chatterton, at age 17.

in accidents. Five men had lost their lives in World War II. There were no homicide victims. One death was equivocal as to mode and could not be classified. As of 1960, suicide was responsible for fourteen male and eight female deaths; by 1970 there were twenty-eight known deaths by suicide—twenty men and eight women.

An inspection of the listing of suicidal deaths (Table 5–1) suggested that there were several subgroups: student suicides, 30- and 40-year suicides, and middle-age suicides. Among the twenty-eight suicides—of both sexes, ranging in age from 18 to 63 (a forty-five-year span), year of death from 1928 to 1968 (forty years), using a variety of lethal methods (pills, poison, drowning, guns)—there was a subgroup of five persons—numbers 14 to 18— all of whom were male, Caucasian, with I.Q.s over 140, born about the same time (between 1907 and 1916), four of whom committed suicide within a year of each other (1965 or 1966), were in the "middle period" of their lives (ages at death 43, 50, 51, 53, and 58), and used the same method (all gunshot). This special subgroup seemed to offer a unique opportunity for an especially intensive investigation.[3]

A listing of all those subjects who had died indicated that there were ten other males, born about the same time (1910 to 1914) as the five suicides, who had died of natural causes (either cancer or heart disease) during the same years that four of the five suicides had killed themselves (1965–66). The opportunity for a natural experiment, using blind analyses, was evident.

_____

[3]In the technical literature on suicide, one does not find many anamnestic or case history reports for individuals who have *committed* suicide. (Materials for attempted suicides are another story; the data for them are far more plentiful.) Only four sources—spread over a half-century—come to mind: Ruth Cavan's (1928, pp. 198–248) extensive diaries of two young adults, Binswanger's (1958) detailed report of 33-year-old Ellen West, Kobler and Stotland's (1964, pp. 98–251) extensive reports of four hospitalized patients—ages 23, 34, 37, and 56—in a "dying hospital," all of whom committed suicide within the same month, and Alvarez's (1961) annotated bibliography.

Thirty cases were selected to include the five suicides, the ten natural deaths, and fifteen individuals who were still alive. The latter two subgroups were matched with the five suicides in terms of age, occupational level, and father's occupational level. That these three subgroups are fairly well matched is indicated by the information in Table 5-2. (The reader should keep in mind that all thirty subjects were male, Caucasian, Californian, middle- and upper-middle-class, had I.Q.s over 140, and were members of the Terman Gifted Study.) Each folder was edited by Mrs. Oden so that I could not tell whether the individual was dead or still alive. (Death certificates, newspaper clippings, and other "death clues" were removed.) The cases came to me, one at a time, in a random order. Although I was "blind" as to the suicide-natural death-living identity of each case, I did know the total numbers of cases in each subgroup.

RATING OF PERTURBATION (THE LIFE CHART)

The cases were analyzed in terms of two basic continua (by which every life can be rated): perturbation and lethality. Perturbation refers to how upset (disturbed, agitated, sane-insane, discomposed) the individual is—rated, let's say, on a 1 to 9 scale[4]—and the latter to how likely it is that he will take his own life. (Lethality is discussed in the next section below.) For each of the thirty cases a rough chart of the individual's perturbation in early childhood, adolescence, high school, college, early marriage, and middle life was made. Clues were sought relating to tranquility-disturbance, especially evidences of any *changes* and variations in the levels of perturbation. An attempt was made to classify the materials

---

[4]The following point must be strongly emphasized: A basic assumption in this entire scheme is that an individual's orientations toward his cessation are biphasic; that is, any adult, at any given moment, has (*a*) more or less long-range, relatively chronic, pervasive,

TABLE 5-1. The Twenty-eight Suicides in the Terman Study as of 1970

	Age at Suicide	Year of Birth	Year of Suicide	Marital Status	Education	Occupational Level*	Method of Suicide
Men							
1.	18	1910	1928	S	High School	S	Poison
2.	19	1916	1935	S	2 yrs. college	V	Gunshot
3.	24	1908	1932	S	AB+	Grad S	Drowning
4.	28	1910	1938	S	MA	II	Poison
5.	33	1913	1946	M,D,M	High school	III	Barbiturate
6.	34	1913	1947	S	2 yrs. college	III	Carbon monoxide
7.	35	1904	1939	S	Ph.D.	I	Gunshot
8.	37	1909	1946	M	1½ yrs. coll.	II	Poison
9.	42	1905	1947	M	2 yrs. college	II	Not known
10.	42	1916	1958	M,D,M,D	AB + 3 yrs.	I	Barbiturate
11.	45	1911	1956	M	3 yrs. college	II	Barbiturate
12.	45	1911	1956	M	AB,MA,LLB	IV	Carbon monoxide
13.	45	1913	1958	M	MD+	I	Poison
14.	43	1910	1953	M^4,D^4	2 yrs. college	II	Gunshot
15.	50	1916	1965	M,D	BS	Inc.	Gunshot
16.	51	1915	1966	M,D,M	High school	III	Gunshot
17.	53	1913	1966	M	LLB	I	Gunshot
18.	58	1907	1966	M^3,D^2	2 yrs. college	I	Gunshot
19.	61	1905	1966	S	MA	Ret (I)	Barbiturate
20.	63	1905	1968	M,D,M	Ph.D.	I	Barbiturate

Women

1.	22	1914	1936	S	2 yrs. college	S	Gunshot
2.	30	1905	1935	S	AB	A (librarian)	Carbon monoxide
3.	30	1913	1943	M	2 yrs. college	H	Gunshot
4.	32	1917	1949	W	3 yrs. college	A (physical therapist)	Barbiturate
5.	37	1916	1953	M[3],D[4]	2 yrs. college	A (writer)	Barbiturate
6.	40	1915	1955	M,D	3 yrs. college	H	Barbiturate
7.	44	1910	1954	M	MA	H	Barbiturate
8.	44	1910	1954	M,D	BS	A (social worker)	Barbiturate

*Occupational levels—Men: I. Professional; II. Official, managerial, and semiprofessional; III. Retail business, clerical, sales, skilled trades, and kindred; IV. Agricultural and related; V. Minor business, minor clerical, and semiskilled occupations.

Occupational groupings—Women: A. Professional and semiprofessional; B. Business (includes secretarial and office work as well as work in other business fields): H. Housewife.

TABLE 5–2. Occupations and ages for the suicide, natural death, and living subjects

	Suicide (N = 5)	Natural (N = 10)	Living (N = 15)
Occupational Level			
I—Professional	2	5	7
II—Official, managerial, semiprofessional	2	4	6
III—Retail business, clerical and sales, skilled trades	1	1	2
Father's Occupational Level			
I—Professional	–	2	5
II—Official, managerial, semiprofessional	4	6	6
III—Retail business, clerical and sales, skilled trades	–	1	4
IV—Agricultural and related occupations	–	–	–
V—Minor business or clerical and semiskilled	1	1	–
Year of Birth			
1907	1	–	–
1908	–	–	–
1909	–	–	–
1910	1	1	3
1911	–	3	3
1912	1	1	4
1913	–	2	1
1914	–	3	3
1915	1	–	1
1916	1	–	–

habitual, characterological orientations toward cessation as an integral part of his total psychological makeup (affecting his philosophy of life, need systems, aspirations, identification, conscious beliefs, etc.); and (b) is also capable of having acute, relatively short-lived, exacerbated, clinically sudden shifts of cessation orientation. Indeed, this is what is usually meant when one says that an individual has become "suicidal." It is therefore crucial in any complete assessment of an individual's orientation toward cessation to know both his habitual *and* his at-that-moment orientations toward cessation. (Failure to do this is one reason why previous efforts to relate "suicidal state" with psychological test results have been barren.)

under such headings as "Early prodromata," "Failures," and "Signatures"—each explained below.

A "life chart" was constructed for each case, roughly following the procedures developed by Adolf Meyer (1951, 1952). In each case the folders were examined more or less chronologically in an attempt to order the materials in a temporal sequence while keeping in mind a number of related skeins.

One example of perturbation (from an individual who turned out to be among the five homogeneous suicides): A high school counselor wrote about one young man that he was "emotionally unstable, a physical roamer and morally erratic, excellent to teachers who treat him as an adult but very disagreeable to others." At the same time, the home visitor wrote: "I like him tremendously; he is better company than many teachers." Ten years later the subject himself wrote: "My gifts, if there were any, seem to have been a flash in the pan."

Early Prodromata

Under this category were included early important interpersonal relationships, especially with the subject's father and mother. The folder materials contained ratings by the subject of his attitudes and interactions with each of his parents. Some information relating to relationships with parents may be of special interest. In the 1940 questionnaire materials—when the modal age of the male subjects was 29.8 years—there was a series of questions concerning earlier conflict and attachment to mother and father. The responses of the five individuals who, as it turned out, made up the homogeneous suicide group seemed to have three interesting features: (a) in answer to the question "Everything considered, which was your favorite parent—father, mother, had no favorite?" only one of the five answered "father"; (b) in answer to the question about the amount of conflict between the individual and his father and the individual and his mother, two of the five indicated moderate to severe conflict with the father, whereas none of the five indicated moderate or severe conflict with the mother; (c) the one suicide who was most obviously rejected by his father (and who indicated that he had had conflict with him) was the only one (of the five) to indicate that "there has been a person . . . who had had a profound influence on his life." He wrote: "My father, I think, has been responsible for a code of ethics stressing honesty and fair dealing in all relations." It was this man's father who insisted that he come into the family business and then called him stupid when he, for reasons of his own temperament, did not show the same amount of aptitude for business that his older brother demonstrated.

In general, for the five suicidal subjects, for reasons that are not completely clear, it seemed that the relationships with the father were more critical than the relationships with the mother. It may be that any exceptionally bright, handsome young child tends to be mother's darling and, for those same reasons, tends to be father's rival—hence the built-in psychological tendency for there to be more friction between father and son than between mother and son. (It all sounds vaguely familiar; every psychologist knows about this theme.)

In the perusal of the records, evidence of trauma or stress in early life was sought: the death of a parent, divorce of the parents, stress (either overt or subtle) between the parents, or rejection of the subject by either parent. In retrospect, I had in mind a continuum ranging from tranquil and benign at one end to stressful and traumatic at the other.

The folder materials indicated that at the time the study began, practically all of the subjects were described in essentially positive terms. For example, among the five subjects who, as it turned out, were the five homogeneous suicides, the following early descriptions by the home visitor appeared: "Attractive boy, well built, attractive features, charming." "Round chubby boy; very sweet face." "Winning little fellow, very fine all-around intelligence. The mother has excellent common sense and much is due to her." "Friendly, cheerful, freckled boy." "Tall for his age."

At the beginning, the psychological picture for most Terman youngsters was benign. However, in two of five homogeneous

suicide cases there were, at an early age, already subtle prodromal clues of things to come: "He is the constant companion of
his father but he is not his father's favorite." (A few years later,
when the child was 14, a teacher wrote about him: "This boy's
parents are of two minds; his mother is for college, his father
thinks that college is of no value to a person who expects to take
up the business. The boy does not show very much hardminded-
ness. His type is more the theoretical, he prefers ideas to matter.")
During the same year, his mother wrote that the child's worst
faults were "his lack of application and irresponsibility"—perhaps
not too unusual at age 14.

Another example: A child is ranked by his mother as
"average" in the following traits: prudence, self-confidence, optimism, permanence of mood, egotism, and truthfulness. We do
not know, of course, how much of this is accurate perception or
how much is self-fulfilling prophecy.

Still another example: When the boy was 14 there was a
series of letters from the head of his boarding school. (The parents
were away on an extended trip.) The headmaster wrote letters
having to do with the boy's veracity, perhaps revealing his own
special emphases: "We have every hope of making him a straight-
forward young man. We are people he cannot bluff, and with
consistent vigilance the boy will be able to overcome his difficulties." A few years later his mother wrote: "His success will
depend a good deal on his associates."

Least Successful

In Melita Oden's (1968) monograph she presented a number of
measures and comparisons between the 100 Terman subjects
ranked as most successful and an equal number adjudged to be
least successful. For each of the thirty cases that I have analyzed,
I tried to make some judgment along a success-failure continuum.
In the end, eight cases were labeled as conspicuous successes and
five cases as failures. As it turned out, none of those cases rated

by me as "most successful" subsequently committed suicide, whereas three of the cases rated as "least successful" killed themselves.[5]

An example: a very bright young boy (I.Q. 180) who did very well in high school, both academically and in extracurricular activities. When he was 15 years old Professor Terman wrote of him: "I think there is no doubt that he would make a desirable student at Stanford." Within a year, at age 16, he had entered Stanford and flunked out. Eventually, after working as a clerk, he returned to college after one year and graduated. He earned a law degree going to an evening law school. He then became an attorney in a large law firm. He was described as unsocial and shy. In his forties he says he was inclined to drink rather heavily, but not sufficiently to interfere with his work. His wife is described as vivacious and he as withdrawn. After a heart attack, his income suddenly became half of what he had been earning. He described himself as much less interested than his peers in vocational advancement or financial gain.

Signatures

In each case I looked for some special (albeit negative) indicators that might in themselves, or in combination, be prodromatic to suicide. For example, alcoholism, homosexuality, suicide threats, conspicuous achievement instability, depression, neurasthenia, and dyspnea could be listed. All five of the homogeneous suicides had one or more of these signature items. An additional eight (of the thirty cases) also had signature items. These items in themselves did not necessarily point to suicide, but when taken in

---

[5]Among the twenty men who committed suicide, at least three were considered outstandingly successful by gifted group standards: two in the 1960 study and one who died in 1938 who had a brilliant record until his death at the age of 28. Conversely, three were considered least successful: two in 1940 (they had died before 1960) and one in the 1960 evaluation (Oden, 1968).

combination with other features in the case, they constituted an important aspect of the total prodromal picture.

Another example, this one emphasizing the lifelong instability of the individual: When he was 7 his mother wrote that "he is inclined to take the line of least resistance." At the same time, the teacher rated him high in desire to excel, general intelligence, and originality; average in prudence, generosity, and desire to know; and low in willpower, optimism, and truthfulness. She indicated that, though he came from a good home, he was inclined to be moody and sulky. When he was 8 his mother said he was strongwilled and liked to have his own way, that school was easy, and that he was making excellent grades. When he was 10 his parents divorced. When he was 12 the teacher reported that he was not a very good student and was doing only fair work, that he had rather lazy mental habits. At age 16 he graduated from high school with a C average. He did not attend college. In his twenties he became an artist. He was married. During World War II he was in the army. After the service he was unemployed and was described by his wife as "immature, unstable, irresponsible and extravagant." Because of his many affairs his wife, although stating she was fond of him, left him. She called him impulsive, romantic, and unstable. In his thirties he worked for a while as a commercial artist. He wrote to Professor Terman: "I am a lemon in your group." He indicated, as a joke, that his "hobby" was observing women from a bar stool. He remarried. He wrote to Professor Terman in relation to his art work that he "received much acclaim from those in the immediate audience," but that his works had not yet been displayed in any shows. His life was a series of ups and downs, some impulsive behaviors, and lifelong instability, although his status improved markedly in the late 1950s.

Apropos "up and downs" in general, any sudden *changes* in life status or life-style can be looked upon as suspicious (i.e., prodromal to suicide), especially a change which marks a decline of status, position, or income. Generally, in suicide prevention work, one views any recent changes in life-style as possible serious indicators of suicidal potential.

RATING OF LETHALITY (THE PSYCHOLOGICAL AUTOPSY)

In addition to the life chart, the second procedure employed was one that I had some years before labeled "the psychological autopsy." This procedure is a retrospective reconstruction of an individual's life that focuses on lethality, that is, those features of his life that illuminate his intentions in relation to his own death, clues as to the type of death it was, the degree (if any) of his participation in his own death, and why the death occurred at that time. In general, the main function of the psychological autopsy is to help clarify deaths that are equivocal as to the *mode* of death—usually to help coroners and medical examiners decide if the death (which may be clear enough as to cause of death, for example, asphyxiation due to drowning or barbiturate overdose) was of an accidental or suicidal mode. Clearly, the *psychological* autopsy focuses on the role of the decedent in his own demise.

In the last few years, a number of individuals have written on this topic: Litman and his colleagues (Litman et al. 1963) have presented a general overview of its clinical use; Curphey (1961) has written of the use of this procedure from the medicolegal viewpoint of a forensic pathologist; and Weisman and Kastenbaum (1968) have applied this procedure to study the terminal phase of life. Elsewhere (Shneidman 1969b), I have indicated that three separate types (and uses) of the psychological autopsy can be discerned. Each is tied to answering a different primary question as follows: (*a*) Why did the individual commit suicide? (*b*) Why did the individual die at this time? and (*c*) What is the most accurate mode of death in this case? Given a death which is clear as to *cause* of death but which is equivocal as to *mode* of death, the purpose of this type of psychological autopsy is to clarify the situation so as to arrive at the most accurate or appropriate mode of death—what it "truly" was. This original use of the psychological autopsy grew out of the joint efforts of the Los Angeles County chief medical examiner-coroner (then Dr.

Theodore J. Curphey) and the staff of the Los Angeles Suicide Prevention Center as an attempt to bring the skills of the behavioral sciences to bear relevantly on the problems of equivocal deaths. In those 10 percent of coroner's cases where the mode of death is questionable or equivocal, this equivocation usually lies between the modes of accident and suicide. Here are three simplified examples:

1. *Cause of death:* asphyxiation due to drowning. Woman found in her swimming pool. Question: Did she "drown" (accident), or was it intentional (suicide)?
2. *Cause of death:* multiple crushing injuries. Man found at the foot of a tall building. Question: Did he fall (accident), or did he jump (suicide)? Or, even, was he pushed or thrown (homicide)?
3. *Cause of death:* barbiturate intoxication due to overdose. Woman found in her bed. Question: Would she be surprised to know that she was dead (accident), or is this what she had planned (suicide)?

An outline for a psychological autopsy is presented in Table 5–3.

In the usual application of the psychological autopsy, the procedure is to interview close survivors (relatives and friends) of the decedent in order to reconstruct his role in his own death. In the present study, I was, of course, limited to an examination of folder materials.

All the criteria that have been discussed above—perturbation, including early prodromata, failure, and signatures—were combined into one judgment of that individual's lethality, that is, the probability of his committing suicide in the present or the immediate future. In this process of judgment I was guided by two additional governing concepts: (a) the key role of the significant other and (b) the concept of a partial death (or chronic suicide or burned-out life).

TABLE 5-3. Outline for Psychological Autopsy

1. Identifying information for victim (name, age, address, marital status, religious practices, occupation, and other details)
2. Details of the death (including the cause or method and other pertinent details)
3. Brief outline of victim's history (siblings, marriage, medical illnesses, medical treatment, psychotherapy, previous suicide attempts)
4. "Death history" of victim's family (suicides, cancer, other fatal illnesses, ages at death, and other details)
5. Description of the personality and life-style of the victim
6. Victim's typical patterns of reaction to stress, emotional upsets, and periods of disequilibrium
7. Any recent—from last few days to last twelve months—upsets, pressures, tensions, or anticipations of trouble
8. Role of alcohol and drugs (a) in overall life-style of victim and (b) in his death
9. Nature of victim's interpersonal relationships (including physicians)
10. Fantasies, dreams, thoughts, premonitions, or fears of victim relating to death, accident, or suicide
11. Changes in the victim before death (of habits, hobbies, eating, sexual patterns, and other life routines)
12. Information relating to the "life side" of victim (upswings, successes, plans)
13. Assessment of intention, that is, role of the victim in his own demise
14. Rating of lethality
15. Reactions of informants to victim's death
16. Comments, special features.

The Crucial Role of the Significant Other

In an adult who is suicide prone, the behavior of the significant other, specifically the wife, seems either lifesaving or suicidogenic. My reading of the cases led me to feel that the wife could be the difference between life and death. In general, a wife who was hostile, independent, competitive, or nonsupporting of her husband who had some of the suicidal prodromata seemed to doom him to a suicidal outcome, whereas a wife who was helpful, emotionally supportive, and actively ancillary seemed to save a man who, in my clinical judgment at least, might otherwise have killed himself.

To the extent that these global clinical impressions of the important role of the spouse, in some cases, are correct, then, in those cases, there is an equal implication for suicide prevention, specifically that one must deal actively with the significant other. A regimen of therapy or a program of education must not fail to include the spouse; indeed it might be focused primarily on the wife and only secondarily on the potential suicide himself. Of course, the conscious and unconscious attitudes of the wife toward her husband must be carefully assessed. In a situation where the wife is deeply competitive (and might unconsciously wish him dead), using her as an auxiliary therapist would at best be an uphill climb. It is possible that in some cases a separation might be a lifesaving suggestion. All the above is not to impugn the wife; rather it is to involve her appropriately. It could very well be that, had the study focused on female suicides, the above prescription would be in relation to the complementary role of the husband.

The Concept of a Partial Death

Partial death is well known in suicidology. In the technical literature it was given its most well known presentation by Karl Menninger (1938) in *Man against Himself.* On valid psychological grounds it denies the dichotomous nature of psychological death and asserts that there are some lives that are moieties and only partial existences. Henry Murray (1967) expands this theme in his paper "Dead to the World":

When I chose the phrase "dead to the world," I was thinking of a variety of somewhat similar psychic states characterized by a marked diminution or near-cessation of affect involving both hemispheres of concern, the inner and the outer world. Here it is as if the person's primal springs of vitality had dried up, as if he were empty or hollow at the very core of his being. There is a striking absence of anything but the most perfunctory and superficial social interactions; output as well as intake is at a minimum. . . . I have been talking about a diminution or cessation of feeling, one component of consciousness, on the assumption that this condition is somewhat analogous to a cessation of the whole of consciousness. If the cessation of feeling is temporary it resembles sleep; if it is permanent (a virtual atrophy of emotional life) it resembles death, the condition of the brain and body after the home fires of metabolism in the cortex have gone out. In a feelingless state the home fires are still burning but without glow or warmth. [p. 9]

The last statement about the home fires burning led me to think of a burned-out person—a person whose whole life was a kind of chronic suicide, a living death, a life without ambition and seemingly without purpose.

In the lethality ratings of the thirty cases, those that gave me the greatest difficulty were the chronic, nonachieving, "partial death" lives. I decided that I would rate this type of person among the first twelve in lethality, but not among the first five. I did this with the conviction that this very style of living was in itself a kind of substitute for overt suicide; that in these cases, the *raison d'être* for committing overt suicide was absent, in that the truncated life itself was the significant inimical act (Shneidman 1963).

RESULTS OF BLIND CLINICAL ANALYSES

On the day that I completed the blind analysis of the thirtieth case I wrote a memorandum to Professor Sears that included the following:

My analysis of the data and possibly the data themselves do not permit me to state with anything like full confidence which five cases were suicidal. The best that I can do—from my subjective ratings of each individual's perturbation and lethality—is to rank order eleven of the cases as the most likely candidates for suicidal status. I should be somewhat surprised if any of the other nineteen individuals committed suicide. The rank order for suicide potential is as follows . . .

Then we—Mrs. Oden, Mrs. Buckholtz, and I—met to "break the key."

The facts revealed that the individual whom I had ranked as number 1 had, in fact, committed suicide, my number 2 had committed suicide, number 3 was living, number 4 had committed suicide, number 5 had committed suicide, and number 6 had committed suicide. Numbers 7 and 9 were living; numbers 8, 10, and 11 had died natural deaths. For the statistical record, the probability of choosing four or five of the five suicide cases correctly by chance alone is 1 out of 1,131 — significant at the .000884 level. Obviously, the null hypothesis that there are no discernible prodromal clues to suicide can be discarded with a fair degree of confidence.

Table 5-4 presents a summary of the blind analysis data in terms of a brief vignette, signature items, success-failure ratings, perturbation ratings, lethality ratings, and suicide probability ranking for all thirty subjects. (The "Postscript" information was not available to me when I made these ratings and was added to the chart after all the other ratings and rankings had been made.)

Much of my analysis of these thirty cases was inferential, sometimes even intuitive — which is to say that not every clue or cognitive maneuver can be recovered, much less communicated. But for what it is worth, I deeply believe that a number of experienced professional persons could have done as well. Indeed, I feel that the volumes of information generated in the past twenty years by suicidologists furnish the working concepts and the background facts for making precisely this kind of (potentially lifesaving) judgment every day of the year in the practical clinical situation. Knowledge of this sort is now an established part of the new discipline of suicidology.

One striking result was that among those who committed suicide in their fifties, the pattern of life consistent with this outcome seemed clearly discernible *by the time they were in their late twenties.* The data subsequent to age 30 served, in most cases, primarily to strengthen the impression of suicidal outcome that I had formulated at that point. Those relatively few cases in which this earlier impression was reversed in the thirties and forties had one or two specific noteworthy elements within them: *(a)* a psychologically supporting spouse or *(b)* a burning-out of the

TABLE 5-4. Blind Ratings and Outcomes for Thirty Matched Male Terman Study Subjects

No.	Notable Characteristics	Signatures	Life Success	Perturbation	Lethality	Suicide Rank	Postscript
1	NP hospitalization; divorced; great perturbation; talks of suicide at 15 and 20	Suicide threats	C –	7-8	High	1	Committed suicide
2	Deaf; professional; low drive for worldly success	Nonachiever	C	3-4	Low	12+	Living
3	Flunked out of college; obtained LLB; shy; ups and downs; drop in income; alcohol	Alcohol; ups and downs	C	6-7	High	2	Committed suicide
4	Insurance man in heart attack rut	–	B	3-4	Low	12+	Died – heart
5	Ambitious bank officer	–	B	3-4	Low	12+	Died – cancer
6	Brilliant professor of medicine; textbook author; good life	–	A	1-2	Low	12+	Died – cancer
7	Set back at adolescence by home stresses; obese; no college aspirations; withdrawn; low-level job; underachiever; stabilized	Underachiever; stabilized	C –	6-7	?	11	Died – heart
8	Physician; too high standards for people; tones down	–	B+	5-6	Low	12+	Died – heart

9	Hard-driving rancher; dominated by mother	–	B	5-6	Low	12+	Died–cancer
10	Stable geologist; steady life	–	A	1-2	Low	12+	Living
11	Lithographer; brilliant; no family back-up; underachiever	Underachiever	C	5-6	Low	12+	Living
12	Multimarried; emphysemic; inventor; ups and downs	Dyspnea; failure	C	6-7	High	4	Committed suicide
13	Scion of business fortune; straight success line; father helpful and supportive	–	A	4-5	Low	12+	Living
14	Quietly successful in own small business; tranquil life	–	B	3-4	Low	12+	Living
15	Had all advantages; did rather well but not superlatively	–	B	3-4	Low	12+	Living
16	Neurasthenic; esoteric mother; underachiever; chronic suicide	Depression; neurasthenia	C–	6-7	?	7	Living
17	Artist; unstable; flighty; impetuous; willful	Instability	B–	7-8	?	5	Committed suicide
18	Insurance man; stable life; interesting siblings	–	B	3-4	Low	12+	Living
19	Brilliant child and siblings; needed a father; stabilized by second wife	–	B	4-5	Low	12+	Living
20	Pleasant man; pleasant life; pleasant family; likes work	–	B	2-3	Low	12+	Living
21	Early genius; hiatus; never fully recovers; wife commits suicide	–	B	5-6	Mdn	12+	Died–heart

(continued)

TABLE 5-4. (continued)

No.	Notable Characteristics	Signatures	Life Success	Perturbation	Lethality	Suicide Rank	Postscript
22	Shy, depressed artist; multiple illnesses; making it	Depression; ill	B	6-7	?	9	Living
23	Unhappy; forced into father's business; rejected by father; always second to sibling; 4 divorces; unstable; downhill; alone	Depression; instability	B+	7-8	?	6	Committed suicide
24	Average school administrator; ordinary stresses	—	B	4-5	Low	12+	Living
25	Well-adjusted, stable attorney; great relationship with father; good life success	—	A	2-3	Low	12+	Living
26	Depressed engineer; hypomanic wife; his job holds him	Depression	B	6-7	Mdn+	8	Died—cancer
27	Scientist; brilliant beginning; wife drains him; good but not great	—	B+	3-4	Low	12+	Living
28	Engineer; overcame adolescent crisis and parents' divorce; good marriage; has grown steadily	—	B	4-5	Low	12+	Died—heart
29	Author; asthmatic; depressed; strong support from wife	Dyspnea; depression	A−	5-6	?	10	Died—cancer
30	Professional; stormy life; alcoholic; competing wife	Alcohol; instability	B−	6-7	?	3	Living

individual's drive and affect. In the latter cases, this condition of psychological aridity and successlessness seemed to be the price for continued life.

What were some of the main clinical impressions relating to adult suicide in this gifted male group? In the briefest possible vignette, my main overall clinical impression might be formulated in this way: The *father*, even in his absence, *starts* the life course to suicide; *school and work* (and the feelings of inferiority and chronic low-grade hopelessness) *exacerbate* it; and the *wife* can, in some cases, effect the *rescue* from it (or otherwise play a sustaining or even a precipitating role in it).

Among the five homogeneous suicides, three types of suicidal prodromata—relating to instability, trauma, and control—could be differentiated.

Instability

In general, suicide is more likely to occur in a life where there has been instability (rather than stability). As used here, instability is practically synonymous with perturbation.

Chronic Instability

Evidences of chronic, long-term instability would include neuropsychiatric hospitalization, talk or threat of suicide, alcoholism, multiple divorces, and any unusually stressful psychodynamic background—even though these bits of evidence occurred in as few as one of the five cases. Examples: Mr. A.: NP hospitalization, divorce, talk of suicide at 15 and at 20; Mr. B.: unstable personality, divorced, flighty behavior, few stabilizing forces; Mr. C.: unhappy man, rejected by father, always second-best, four marriages, highly perturbed.

Recent Downhill Course

A recent downhill change that occurs in a career marked by ups and downs, that is, a generally unstable life course, was characteristic of suicidal persons. Specifically, these changes include a marked sudden decrease in income, sudden acute alcoholism, a change in work, and divorce or separation, especially where the wife leaves the husband for another man. In general, a sudden, inexplicable change for the worse is a bad augury. This means that in an individual with an up and down history, the most recent bit of information can be singularly irrelevant, if not outright misleading. Examples: Mr. D.: highly recommended for university, flunked out of college, went back to school, earned an LL.B. degree, shy, alcoholic, sudden drop in income, up and down course, does not burn out; Mr. E.: inventor, multiple marriages, up and down course, severe emphysema. (NB: Dyspnea can be an especially incapacitating symptom and has been related to suicide in special ways [Farberow et al. 1966].)

Trauma

Early Childhood or Adolescent Trauma

Examples would include acute rejection by one or both parents, lack of family psychological support, and separation or divorce of the parents. A crisis in adolescence can turn a life toward lower achievement.

Adult Trauma

This includes poor health, such as asthma, emphysema, severe neurosis, obesity, and multiple illnesses. Another major type of adult trauma relates to the spouse, either rejection by the wife for another man or being married to a hyperactive (and competing) wife, who has changed from the woman he married. Examples: Mr. F., a depressed engineer whose top security job in aerospace holds him together; and Mr. G., who has a complicated, hypomanic, and successful wife toward whom he is deeply ambivalent.

Controls

Outer Controls

These are the compensations or stabilizing influences in individuals who, without these assets from other than within themselves, would be more perturbed than they are and might commit suicide. Examples: the stabilizing work of Mr. F., mentioned above; the stabilizing wife of asthmatic Mr. H., a woman who nurses him and keeps the world from inappropriately intruding upon him or exhausting him. She husbands his limited energies.

Inner Controls

These inner controls are not the usual strengths or positive features or assets of personality or character. They are the negative inner controls of default. One such is what occurs in some individuals who are perturbed early in their lives, who, if they survive, stabilize or simmer down or burn out in their fifties or sixties.

Examples: Mr. J.: He was psychologically traumatized during adolescence by home stresses. He has no hobbies, no college aspirations, is withdrawn, and works as a mechanic and caretaker.

Mr. K.: Extremely high IQ. He is neurasthenic, has a mother with esoteric tastes, experiences back and shoulder pains just like his father, and is unable to hold a job as a professional. He calls himself "an unsuccessful animal." He ends up working as a clerk in a large company. His stance is that—to use an example from Melville—of a contemporary Bartleby ("I prefer not to"), what Menninger (1938) has called a "chronic suicide," where the truncated life itself can be conceptualized as a partial death.

DISCUSSION

Whereas the clinical challenge is to be intuitive, to display diagnostic acumen, and to manifest therapeutic skill, the scientific challenge is to state theory and to explicate facts in a replicable way. I feel obligated to address myself to the theoretical side of this issue.

I shall begin with low-level theory, that is, an explication of the specific items that guided my thinking in choosing the individuals whom I believed had committed suicide. Some ten items were in my mind: (1) early (grammar school, adolescence, or college age) evidences of instability, including dishonesty; (2) rejection by the father; (3) multiple marriages; (4) alcoholism; (5) an unstable occupational history; (6) ups and downs in income; (7) a crippling physical disability, especially one involving dyspnea; (8) disappointment in the use of one's potential, that is, a disparity between aspiration and accomplishment; (9) any talk or hint of self-destruction; and (10) a competitive or self-absorbed spouse. In summary, this low-level theoretical explication states that a bright male Caucasian who committed suicide in his fifties was apt to be: rejected by his father, adolescently disturbed, multimarried, alcoholic, occasionally unsettled or unsuccessful, disappointed in himself and disappointing to others, unstable, lonely, and perturbed with a penchant for precipitous action.

At a somewhat deeper level, and thus more theoretical, are the elements of rejection, disparity between aspiration and accomplishment, instability, and perturbation. At a still deeper level (and even more theoretical) is the notion that the suicidal person is one who believes that he has not had his father's love and seeks it symbolically without success throughout his life, eventually hoping, magically, to gain it by a singular act of sacrifice or expiation. The most theoretical formulation might be stated as follows: Those gifted men who committed suicide in their fifties did not have that internalized viable approving parental homunculus that—like a strong heart—seems necessary for a long life.

It is interesting to reflect that the five gifted suicidal persons of this study constituted an essentially nonpsychotic group. This assertion is not to gainsay that each of them was severely perturbed at the time of the suicide, but they were not "crazy";

that is, they did not manifest the classical hallmarks of psychosis such as hallucinations, delusions, dereistic thinking, and the like. Their perturbation took the form—prior to the overt suicidal act—of alcoholism, other than one marriage (single, divorced, or multiple marriages), and chronic loneliness, occupational ups and downs, impetuosity and impulsivity, and inner (as well as overt) agitation. Although, as it is in most suicidal persons, one can suppose that their thought processes were circumscribed ("tunnel vision") and tended to be dichotomous ("either a happy life or death"), there was no direct evidence to indicate that they were psychotically bizarre (Shneidman 1969a).

As has been noted by Oden (1968), the "magic combination" for life success among the gifted is not a simple one. For suicide also the equation is a combination of obvious and subtle elements. Many factors, none of which alone seems to be sufficient, appear to coexist in a suicidal case. And, as in any equation, there are factors on both the positive (life-loving, biophilic, suicide-inhibiting) and the negative (death-loving, necrophilic, suicide-promoting) sides.

In the algebra of life and death, the wife may play an absolutely vital role, holding her spouse to life or, at the worst, stimulating or even provoking him to suicide. Every suicidologist knows that suicide is most often a two-person event, a dyadic occurrence, and for this reason, if no other, the management and prevention of suicide almost always has to involve the significant other. With high-suicide-risk gifted males, my impression is that the most important lifesaving task is not directly to the potentially suicidal person, but through the wife—especially in concert with the family physician.

Currently, there is a small number of retrospective studies seeking to establish some of the early precursors of suicide among special populations presumed to be intellectually superior, specifically physicians and university graduates. A few words about each.

Blachly and his colleagues (1968) have made an analysis of 249 suicides by physicians reported in the obituary columns of the *Journal of the American Medical Association* between May 1965 and

November 1967. Deaths from suicide exceeded the combined deaths from automobile accidents, airplane crashes, drowning, and homicide. The mean age of the suicidal group was 49. Blachly and his associates mailed questionnaires to the next of kin (usually the widow); about 30 percent of the inquiries were returned, many with extensive comments. The suicide rate varied greatly among the medical specialties, ranging from a low of 10 per 100,000 among pediatricians to a high of 61 per 100,000 among psychiatrists. A résumé of Blachly's main findings is presented in Table 5-5.

Paffenbarger and his associates (Paffenbarger and Asnes 1966, Paffenbarger, King, and Wing 1969) have completed analyses of over 50,000 medical and social histories (including physical and psychological evaluations) of former male students at the University of Pennsylvania and at Harvard covering a thirty-four-year period from 1916 to 1950. Their original focus was on individuals who subsequently died of coronary heart disease. The data drew their attention to those who had committed suicide—whom they then compared with their nonsuicidal cohorts. The 4,000 known deaths included 225 suicide deaths. Their findings relative to suicide point to paternal deprivation through early loss or death of the father, loneliness and underjoining in college, dropping out of college, and feelings of rejection, self-consciousness, and failure during the college years.

Dr. Caroline Thomas (1969)—like Paffenbarger, a cardiologist—is studying the causes of death among 1,337 former medical students of the Johns Hopkins University School of Medicine from 1948 to 1964. Her present project—as did Paffenbarger's—began as a study of the precursors of coronary heart disease but, in light of the data (fourteen suicides among the thirty one premature deaths) shifted to include precursors of suicide.

What may be of especial interest in Table 5-5 are the common elements or threads in the findings of these three projects and the clinical findings of this present study. To what extent these findings relate only to the intellectually superior and to what extent they are ubiquitous is a matter for further study;

TABLE 5-5. Summary of Findings of Three Studies of Precursors to Suicide among Intellectually Superior Subjects

Present Clinical Impressions*	Blachly's Tabular Results	Paffenbarger's Statistical Findings
a. early (before 20) evidences of instability, including dishonesty	a. mentally depressed or disturbed	a. college education of father
b. actual or felt rejection by the father	b. prior suicidal attempt or statement of suicidal intent	b. college education of mother
c. multiple marriages	c. heavy drinker or alcoholic	c. father professional
d. alcoholism	d. drug addiction or heavy drug user	d. father dead
e. an unstable occupational history	e. "inadequate" financial status	e. parents separated
f. ups and downs in income (not to mention ups and downs in mood)	f. death of close relative in decedent's childhood	f. cigarette smoker in college
g. a crippling physical disability, especially one involving dyspnea	g. suicide of relative	g. attended boarding school
h. disappointment in the use of potential, i.e., a disparity between aspiration and accomplishment	h. seriously impaired physical health	h. college dropout
i. any talk or hint of self-destruction		i. nonjoiner in college
j. a competitive or self-absorbed spouse		j. allergies
		k. underweight
		l. self-assessed ill health
		m. self-consciousness
		n. subject to worries
		o. feelings of being watched or talked about
		p. insomnia
		q. secretive-seclusiveness
		r. "anxiety-depression" index (including nervousness, moodiness, exhaustion, etc.)

*Of course, not all of these features occurred in any one suicidal case; conversely, some of these features occurred in as few as one suicidal case. It was the total impression that counted most.

nonetheless it is not premature to say that, on the basis of currently known data, it would appear that the common findings would seem to have general application.

REFERENCES

Alvarez, W. C. (1961). *Minds That Came Back.* Philadelphia: Lippincott.

Binswanger, L. (1958). The case of Ellen West. In *Existence*, ed. R. May, E. Angel, and H. F. Ellenberger, pp. 237–364. New York: Basic Books.

Blachly, P. H., Disher, W., and Roduner, G. (1968). Suicide by physicians. *Bulletin of Suicidology.* 1:1–18.

Cavan, R. S. (1928). *Suicide.* Chicago: University of Chicago Press.

Cox, C. M. (1926). *The Early Mental Traits of Three Hundred Geniuses.* (*Genetic Studies of Genius*, vol. 2.). Stanford, CA: Stanford University Press.

Curphey, T. J. (1961). The role of the social scientist in the medicolegal certification of death from suicide. In *The Cry for Help*, ed. N. L. Farberow and E. S. Shneidman, pp. 110–117. New York: McGraw Hill.

Dublin, L. I., Lotka, A. J., and Spiegelman, M. (1949). *Length of Life.* New York: Ronald.

Farberow, N. L., McKelligott, W., Cohen, S., and Darbonne, A. (1966). Suicide among patients with cardiorespiratory illnesses. *Journal of the American Medical Association* 195:422–428.

Kobler, A. L., and Stotland, E. (1964). *The End of Hope.* Springfield, IL: Free Press of Glencoe.

Litman, R. E., Curphey, T. J., Shneidman, E. S., et al. (1963). Investigations of equivocal suicides. *Journal of the American Medical Association* 184:924–929.

Menninger, K. A. (1938). *Man against Himself.* New York: Harcourt, Brace.

Meyer, A. (1951). The life chart and the obligation of specifying positive data in psychopathological diagnosis. In *The Collected Works of Adolf Meyer*, vol. 3, ed. E. E. Winters, pp. 52–56. Baltimore: Johns Hopkins Press.

———— (1952). Mental and moral health in a constructive school program. In *The Collected Works of Adolf Meyer*, vol. 4, ed. E. E. Winters, pp. 350–370. Baltimore: Johns Hopkins Press.

Murray, H. A. (1967). Dead to the world: the passions of Herman Melville. In *Essays in Self-Destruction*, ed. E. S. Shneidman, pp. 7–29. New York: Science House.

Oden, M. H. (1968). The fulfillment of promise: 40-year follow-up of the Terman gifted group. *Genetic Psychology Monographs* 77:3–93.

Paffenberger, R. S., Jr., and Asnes, D. P. (1966). Chronic disease in former college students. Part 3: Precursors of suicide in early and middle life. *American Journal of Public Health* 56:1026–1036.

Paffenberger, R. S., Jr., King, S. H., and Wing, A. L. (1969). Chronic disease in former college students. Part 4: Characteristics in youth that predispose to suicide and accidental death in later life. *American Journal of Public Health* 59:900–908.

Shneidman, E. S. (1963). Orientations toward death: a vital aspect of the study of lives. In *The Study of Lives*, ed. R. W. White, pp. 200–227. New York: Atherton.

———— (1969a). Logical content analysis: an explication of styles of "concludifying." In *The Analysis of Communication Content*, ed. G. Gerbner, et al., pp. 261–279. New York: Wiley.

———— (1969b). Suicide, lethality and the psychological autopsy. In *Aspects of Depression*, ed. E. S. Shneidman and M. J. Ortega, pp. 225–250. Boston: Little, Brown & Co.

Stone, A. A., and Onque, G. C. (1959). *Longitudinal Studies of Child Personality*. Cambridge, MA: Harvard University Press.

Terman, L. M. (1925). *Genetic Studies of Genius*. Vol. 1: *Mental and Physical Traits of a Thousand Gifted Children*. Stanford, CA: Stanford University Press.

———— (1940). Psychological approaches to the biography of genius. *Science* 92:293–301.

Terman, L. M., and Oden, M. H. (1947). *Genetic Studies of Genius*. Vol. 4: *The Gifted Child Grows Up*. Stanford, CA: Stanford University Press.

———— (1959). *Genetic Studies of Genius*. Vol. 5: *The Gifted Child at Mid-Life*. Stanford, CA: Stanford University Press.

Thomas, C. B. (1969). Suicide among us: can we learn to prevent it? *Johns Hopkins Medical Journal* 125:276–285.

Weisman, A. D., and Kastenbaum, R. (1968). The psychological autopsy: a study of the terminal phase of life. *Community Mental Health Journal Monograph* 4:1–59.

6

Suicide Notes Reconsidered in the Context of the Life

Almost without a flagging of interest, for over a quarter of a century, I have been keenly concerned with trying to unlock the mysteries of suicidal phenomena by using suicide notes as the possible keys. It is almost a basic tenet of suicidology that suicide notes are written in the context of the suicidal act, usually within a few minutes of the death-producing deed. On the face of it, suicide notes would seem to offer a special window, unparalleled among socio-psychological phenomena, into the thinking and feeling of the act itself. And yet, dozens of research studies by scores of qualified investigators over the past several years have not produced those new insights and information that that amount of focus and effort would have led us legitimately to expect. How to account for these essentially disappointing results? That question is the topic of this chapter.

Suicide notes are not like letters or diaries, which are written at leisure, often away from the scene of action. Suicide notes are comparable to battle communiqués, filled with the emotion of the current scene and describing some special aspects of the contemporary dramatic event.

And yet, as one reads dozens and hundreds of suicide notes, one finds that many of them tell pretty much the same story. What is most disappointing is that most suicide notes, written at perhaps the most dramatic moment of a person's life, are surprisingly commonplace, banal, even sometimes poignantly pedestrian and dull. It is obviously difficult to write an original suicide note; it is almost impossible to write a note that is really informative or explanatory.

Without a doubt, suicide notes are valuable and fascinating documents. They furnish extremely important data for the study of suicide. But they are not the royal road to an easy understanding of suicidal phenomena. The perusal of a suicide note is usually a disappointing process. The study of notes in large number, comparing groups of them, first one way and then another, has not yielded findings that have thrown completely new light on suicidal behavior in general.

Suicide notes are rather special documents. They obviously fall under the category of "personal documents" as discussed in the pioneer monograph of Gordon Allport (1942). It is interesting to reflect that in Allport's comprehensive listing of personal documents—autobiographies, confessions, diaries, memoirs, logs, letters, and the like—it apparently did not occur to him to include suicide notes. Allport's monograph is to be recommended to any serious student of personal documents, suicide notes included. In it, he lists over a dozen reasons why personal documents are written, including the following: special pleading, exhibitionism, desire for order, literary delight, securing personal perspective, relief of tension, assisting in therapy, redemption and social reincorporation, scientific interest, public service and example, and desire for immortality. One can see that the writing of a suicide note encompasses these reasons as well as such others as confession, attribution of blame, removal of guilt, pleading for understanding, coercive demand for action, and so forth.

The importance of the use of personal documents in psychological science is not to be underestimated. Indeed it may well be that we will learn more about suicidal phenomena from a close study of personal documents written over an extended period of time—diaries, journals, letters, and autobiographies—than from any other sources.

The study of suicide notes is a relatively recent occurrence although there is a nineteenth-century study of Brierre de Boismont (1856) in which he published his analysis of 1,328 suicide notes, expounding essentially moralistic viewpoints. In 1944, Curt Michael published a collection of 166 suicide notes written by known personalities from antiquity to modern times, emphasizing the ubiquitous human elements and focusing on the changes and attitudes toward life and death reflected in the prevailing culture. In 1945, Morgenthaler published a monograph on suicide notes in which he reproduced verbatim and in German forty-seven notes from Bern, Switzerland, dating from 1928 through 1935.

Shneidman and Farberow can be said to have begun the scientific study of suicide notes in 1957 by employing John Stuart Mill's methods of difference and residues, specifically by eliciting suicide notes from nonsuicidal persons and then analyzing substantial numbers of both genuine and simulated notes in blind studies. A set of thirty-three paired and matched genuine and simulated suicide notes—all sixty-six notes written by Protestant, Caucasian male adults in Los Angeles County in the period 1945 to 1955—has been used in a number of different studies.

There is a bibliography of studies of suicide notes, 1856–1979 (Shneidman 1979). As a whole, these studies indicate that it is possible to distinguish between genuine and simulated suicide notes, and, more importantly, genuine suicide notes are generally characterized by dichotomous logic, a greater amount of hostility and self-blame, more use of specific names and instructions to the survivors, less evidence of thinking about how one is thinking, and more use of the various meanings of the word "love."

But in general the results of all these studies have been fragmentary and not as illuminating as one would have wished. In almost every case, the results have reflected more the method of analysis than the suicidal state of man, and although some of the findings are interesting from several theoretical points of view, they have not provided an open-sesame into the understanding of human self-destruction. In a word, the results of these careful studies, taken as a whole, have been deeply disappointing.

When a person comes to commit suicide, his faculties of attention are constricted. There is a narrowing of focus of his perceptual field and he suffers from what may be called tunnel vision. Ringel (1976) has written about the "narrowing of the field of consciousness." Alvarez (1972) has called this "the closed world of suicide," which he describes in this way: "Once a man decides to take his own life he enters a shut-off, impregnable but wholly convincing world where every detail fits and each incident reinforces his decision." Further, he says: "Each of these deaths has its own inner logic and unrepeatable despair. . . . [Suicide is] a terrible but utterly natural reaction to the strained, narrow, unnatural necessities we sometimes create for ourselves" (pp. 283–284).

This narrowing of the field of consciousness, the "closed world of suicide," the constriction of focus of attention, or the tunnel vision that one finds during the actual moments of a suicidal deed are dramatically illustrated in the following excerpt of a an attractive, bright 25-year-old woman who, in a transient period of acute confusion and panic, jumped several stories from a hospital balcony and—sustaining only several fractures of one leg and hip, a pneumothorax and some organ ruptures—miraculously survived. Two days previously she had ingested fifty 100 mg sodium secobarbital tablets, had been brought to the hospital and treated in the emergency room, and had then been placed in a hospital room. She said about that attempt: "I was pretty isolated at that time. Precisely at the moment of my twenty-fifth birthday I sort of went into a panic state and things got worse and worse." She stated that she was angry that she had complicated everything by winding up in a hospital. I asked her what happened then. Here is a verbatim segment:

Well, after that I was out of danger more or less and at that point they pretty much let me wander around the hospital as I pleased. And there was some question about my husband letting me return home to the apartment, because he thought I was going to make another attempt and he couldn't bear to live with that. And it was all just up in the air, it was sort of like, well you go and find a place to stay and there was no place for me to stay. My sister wouldn't let me come and stay with her and I don't know anyone here, so it turned out that I was going to stay in some sort of welfare kind of arrangement which was going to be fixed or arranged by the social worker. All of a sudden I was out there in the middle of nowhere without any money, and my husband wasn't going to let me come back to the house and I was desperate. And then I went into a terrible state. So at this point I was supposed to be making these arrangements myself. I could barely even speak, you know, the social worker was calling various agencies and then turning the telephone over to me so that I could tell my story and I could even barely remember my name, let alone the date of birth or anything like that, and I thought my God in heaven, I can hardly even—and I was not functioning at all and these people are going to throw me into the street. And I didn't want to go to a psychiatric ward because I was really frightened that I would wind up—I could possibly have a psychotic episode or something like that. I was so desperate, I felt my God, I can't face this thing. Going out, and being thrown out on the street. And everything was like a terrible sort of whirlpool of confusion. And I thought to myself there's only one thing I can do, I just have to lose consciousness. That's the only way to get away from it. . . .

Writing of the suicide of several young poets, Boris Pasternak (1959), has stated:

A man who decides to commit suicide puts a full stop to his being, he turns his back on the past, he declares himself bankrupt and his memories to be unreal. They can no longer help him or save him. He has put himself beyond their reach. The continuity of his inner life is broken, and his personality is at an end. And perhaps what finally makes him kill himself is not the firmness of his resolve but the unbearable quality of this anguish which belongs to no one, of this suffering in the absence of the sufferer, of this waiting which is empty because life has stopped and he can no longer feel it. [pp. 88–89]

If this sense of personal emptiness is at all true of the suicidal person, is it any wonder that suicide notes, written at the very moment when an individual has lost touch with his own past, are concerned with the moment's minutiae and are relatively arid and psychologically barren?

One of the main functions of the personality is to protect itself from other aspects of itself. An individual cannot constantly stare into the horrors of his own life; he needs to view them only tachistoscopically, if at all. At best, the topic of death is psychologically threatening and needs to be intermittently denied in order to maintain one's mental balance and health. Denial is a necessary gyroscope in one's psychic life.

Now to take the step from death to suicide and to state my hypothesis about the reason for the relative barrenness of most suicide notes: In order for a person to kill himself he has to be in a special state of mind, a state of relatively fixed purpose (not gainsaying his ambivalence) and relative close-mindedness. It is a psychological state which, while it permits suicide to occur (indeed facilitates suicide), obviously militates against insight or good communication. In other words, that special state of mind necessary to perform the suicidal deed is one which is essentially incompatible with an insightful recitation of what was going on in one's mind that led to the act itself.

Suicide notes are often like a parody of the postcards sent home from the Grand Canyon, the Catacombs, or the Pyramids— essentially unimaginative, pro forma, and not at all reflecting the grandeur of the scene being described or the grandeur of the human emotions that one might expect to be engendered by the situation.

Actual suicide notes typically contain such phrases as "I love you . . . I am sorry . . . I am in pain (the central theme) . . . I have lost the way . . . don't blame yourself . . . you drove me to this . . . please be good to our child . . . fix the sparkplugs on the car . . . don't come into this room. . . ." For one who seeks deep insights into the reasons for human self-destruction, the profound reasons that individuals intentionally end their lives, these typical excerpts from genuine suicide notes are not very illuminating.

It is hypothesized that suicide notes cannot be insight

documents as suicidologists would hope they would be, mainly because they are written during a special psychological state, a state of focused purpose and narrow perception and psychodynamic denial. It is a state which, by its nature, precludes the individual's having access to the full ambivalent details of his own self-destructive drama, and thus diminishes the possibility of his sharing with others in a suicide note what is truly going on in his mind.

In order to commit suicide, one cannot write a meaningful suicide note. Conversely, if one could write a meaningful note, he would not have to commit suicide. It is almost as though one has to be, as it were, drugged or intoxicated in order to commit suicide, and it is well nigh impossible to write a psychologically meaningful document when one is in this special disordered state.

However, by no means are all suicide notes dross or barren. There are conspicuous exceptions in which the suicide note is filled with psychodynamic information, genuinely explaining the human reasons for the act and giving rather clear hints as to the unconscious reasons behind it. But they are rare; the clear exceptions.

A "good" suicide note would have to be written at least a fortnight before the act, in a more open frame of mind. But then, of course, it might not strictly be a suicide note but rather a journal or a diary. There are a few extensive diaries in the public domain of individuals who subsequently committed suicide. Two of them are reproduced in Ruth Cavan's book *Suicide* (1928). One is by a young woman of 26 who kept a diary of over 50,000 words over a seven-year period and who subsequently shot herself; the other is a diary kept by a young man, age 23, for a period of just over one-and-a-half years. His last entry was on the day of his death, before he drowned himself.

In Ponsonby's book *English Diaries* (1923) there is a remarkable diary by the nineteenth-century painter, B. R. Haydon, covering a period of twenty-six years, from 1820 to 1846, including an entry about an hour before he committed suicide by cutting his throat and shooting himself in the head. The most remarkable contemporary suicide diary is *The Inman Diary* edited by Daniel Aaron (1985). It is two volumes of extraordinarily intimate material by a rather loathsome but articulate man, who ends his life by gunshot.

These diaries are the real thing. They permit one to see the life in its longitudinal workings. They are serial glimpses over extended time into what William James, in his *Varieties of Religious Experience* (1902), called "the recesses of feeling, the darker, blinder strata of character which are the only places in the world in which we catch real fact in the making, and directly perceive how events happen and how work is actually done" (p. 501). We shall need to study these documents in greater detail to understand the psychological development of the suicidal drama.

Up to this point, I have spoken about persons who have committed suicide. But if one is being pushed toward death under the threat of a terminal disease or of execution, then apparently the psychological situation is quite different. Then one is forced from the outside to marshal one's psychic energies and, being so affected, can speak with passion and relevance. Witness the letters from the German concentration camps, and the letters written on the eve of their announced execution by John Brown, Fyodor Dostoevsky (who was reprieved), and Bartolomeo Vanzetti. Here is a relevant quotation from the Danish psychiatrist Frederik Wagner (1960):

It is interesting to note a striking difference between such letters and farewell letters of an entirely different category: letters from people who were convinced of facing an immediate, inevitable, unwanted death. In Brocher's *Letzte Briefe aus Stalingrad (Last Letters from Stalingrad)* (1954) the German soldiers openly express their feelings of despair and bitterness against their leadership, but even more often they dwell upon their "happy childhood," the "happy years" before the war or prior to the Hitler period, and first of all, their love for their relatives. In short: they stick to life. As an example of documents of particular high human quality can be mentioned the letters from members of the Danish resistance movement (1946) during the German occupation, written the night before their execution. These letters reveal a positive, dignified,

often religious attitude towards life and a warm attachment to family.
[p. 63]

This special insight-giving quality is especially noteworthy in
documents written by people who knew that they were dying of
a fatal disease and who openly addressed themselves to their
feelings about dying and death. What is to be noted about these
documents is the amount of psychological information that they
yield in contrast to suicide notes. This may be because they were
written over a period of time in which the individual has had an
opportunity to experience and to communicate a variety of
emotional states, including periods of denial. Whereas a level of
denial may characterize the entire brief period of writing a suicide
note, it may seem safe to assume that when a dying person is in
a period of denial, he or she simply does not turn to the
manuscript. Thus the dying person's manuscript is composed
during the more lucid periods. Recent articles of this genre
include an article by a dying housewife (Helton 1972), the
personal report of a psychiatric social worker dying of cancer
(Harker 1972), reflections of a dying professor ("Notes of a Dying
Professor" 1972), and an account by a 30-year-old psychiatrist
who discovered one day that he had acute myelogenous leukemia
(Trombley 1972). They contrast sharply, in tone and insight, not
to say length, with most suicide notes.

In relation to suicide notes, it seems as though we tend to
confuse the drama of the suicidal situation with our own expectations that there be some dramatic psychodynamic insights in
the communications written during the moments of that drama.
But the fact remains that memorable (authenticated) words ut-
tered *during* battle or *on* one's deathbed are relatively rare. It
seems to be true also of suicide notes. Understandably, however,
we continue to hope that any individual, even an ordinary
individual, standing on the brink of what man has always
conceptualized as life's greatest adventure and mystery, ought to
have some special message for the rest of us. Western civilization
has for centuries romanticized death (Shneidman 1971); we tend

to read with special reverence and awe *any* words, however banal, that are part of a death-oriented document and thus we tend to think of suicide notes as almost sacred and expansive pieces of writing. And then we are understandably disappointed when we discover that, after all, suicide notes are always secular and usually constricted.

Suicide notes have something of the fascination of a cobra: They catch our eyes, yet we are ever conscious that some serious threat may lurk in them. As guides for living, suicide notes are cryptic maps of ill-advised journeys. A suicide note, no matter how persuasive it seems within its closed world, is not a model for conducting a life. When one examines suicide notes, one can only shudder to read these testimonials to tortuous life journeys that came to wrecked ends. They fascinate us for what they tell us about the human condition and what they warn us against in ourselves.[1]

My own lifelong sustained study of suicide notes is admittedly a somewhat arcane pursuit. It would be like someone's contemporary fascination with alchemy, phlogiston, or the inheritance of acquired characteristics, or the notion that the world is flat, or that earth is the center of the universe, or the proof that Bacon really wrote Shakespeare's plays—all flawed ideas. The difference that may make my obsession with suicide notes seem legitimate is that I know that suicide notes—like the many schizophrenic diaries I have read—are flawed guides. I have never read a suicide note that I would want to have written.

But what can we actually learn about suicide from suicide notes? In the last twenty-five years my answers to this question have undergone some radical changes. I have held three different positions on the relationship of suicide notes to suicidal phenomena.

---

[1]Note: All the above is from an article, "Suicide Notes Reconsidered," (1973) published in *Psychiatry*. Seven years later, in 1980, in a chapter entitled "Suicide Notes and Tragic Lives," in *Voices of Death*, I had a rather different view of things. What follows is excerpted from that chapter.

My original view of the value of suicide notes dates from that special day in 1949 when I unexpectedly came across several hundred suicide notes in the vaults of a coroner's office. Since then, almost without a flagging of interest, I have been fascinated with suicide notes as perhaps the best available way of under-standing suicidal phenomena. I believed that it was possible to unlock the mysteries of suicidal phenomena by using suicide notes as the keys. When one addresses the question: "Why do people take this trip?" (i.e., commit suicide), one can reasonably look on suicide notes as psychological guides or maps and search them for clues as to how the tragic outcome of that life's voyage might have been averted. It would seem that suicide notes, written as they are in the very context of the suicidal act, often within minutes of the death-producing deed, would offer a special window into the thinking and feeling of the act itself. In no other segment of human behavior does there seem to be such a close relationship of document to deed. The golden road to the kingdom of understanding suicide was paved with suicide notes.

My subsequent counteraction to that view was a somewhat exaggerated jump to an almost opposite opinion (see the previous pages above). In that position I believed that suicide notes, written as they were by individuals in a state of psychological constriction and of truncated and narrowed thinking—made so by their psychological pain—could hardly ever, by virtue of the state in which they were composed, be illuminating psychological documents. Admittedly, that point of view had a touch of overkill in it.

I now believe that suicide notes, *by themselves*, are uniformly neither bountiful nor banal, but that they definitely can have a great deal of meaning under certain circumstances, specifically *when they are put in the context of a detailed case history* of the individual who both wrote the note and committed the act. In those instances—where we have both the suicide note and an extended life history—the note will then illuminate many aspects of the life history, and conversely, the life history can make many key words of the note come alive and take on special meanings that would otherwise have remained hidden or lost. My present view is thus an amalgamation, a synthesis, of my previous thesis and my subsequent antithetical view.

The remainder of this chapter is made up of an extended example of this notion that there is a vital reciprocity between suicide notes and the lives of which they are a part. In this situation, where we have *both* the suicide note and a *detailed* life history, the note will illuminate aspects of the life history, and details of the history will give special meanings to words and phrases in the note. It is close to the art of biography.

Here are five suicide notes written by one woman who committed suicide by barbiturate overdose, and many details of her life, to which these notes were but the penultimate acts and the final words.

In this case—Natalie, who killed herself at age 40—there were, in addition to her suicide notes, literally hundreds of separate personal documents and other records. They include the following: early school records, teachers' notes to her parents, school physicians' reports, school evaluations, college records, several psychological tests given since early childhood, numerous questionnaires, which she had completed at school, dozens of her letters to teachers and others, and miscellaneous personal documents by the score. A veritable treasure trove of case history data. (It took me many months to find them.)

We begin at the tragic end, with excerpts from the police report of her death:

On arrival, went through house into bathroom where victim was observed lying on the floor, head resting on a pillow, toward the west, feet pointed toward the east. Victim was dressed in a green bathrobe; was cold to the touch, rigor mortis having started to set in. On the pillow it was noted there was a stain, caused by a purge from the victim's mouth. Photographs of the scene were taken.

There was one small brown bottle with the label bearing prescription number and "One capsule at bedtime . . ." This bottle was empty. Also a small plastic container was received with the label inside the cover reading "One tablet 4 times daily, regularly . . ." This container was also empty.

Undersigned spoke to [name and address], who stated he was victim's father. He further said that approximately two weeks ago, victim told him that she was going to commit suicide. He said he talked her out of the notion at that time, and did not figure she would make any further attempt on her life. He further said victim had been in ill health since her divorce and had been treated by a psychiatrist, address unknown; also that the victim had filed a will which is currently in the possession of her attorney.

While at location, victim's husband, [name], who gave address same as victim's, employed at Eastern Steel Corp., arrived and stated he would take care of his two children, Betty, 15 years; and Nancy, 10 years.

The investigating officer reported finding five suicide notes. I have made a few changes in identifying details:

1. To her adult friend: "Rosalyn—Get Eastern Steel Co.—Tell them and they will find Bob right away. Papa is at his business. Betty is at the Smiths—Would you ask Helene to keep her until her Daddy comes—so she won't know until he comes for her. You have been so good—I love you—Please keep in touch with Betty—Natalie"

2. To her eldest daughter: "Betty, go over to Rosalyn's right away—Get in touch with Papa."

3. To her ex-husband, from whom she was recently divorced:

Bob—I'm making all kinds of mistakes with our girls—They have to have a leader and everyday the job seems more enormous—You couldn't have been a better Daddy to Nancy and they do love you—Nancy misses you so and she doesn't know what's the matter—I know you've built a whole new life for yourself but make room for the girls and keep them with you—Take them where you go—It's only for just a few years—Betty is almost ready to stand on her own two feet—But Nancy needs you desperately. Nancy needs help—She really thinks you didn't love her—and she's got to be made to do her part for her own self respect—Nancy hasn't been hurt much yet—but ah! the future if they keep on the way I've been going lately—Barbara sounds warm and friendly and relaxed and I pray to God she will understand just a little and be good to my girls—They need two happy people—not a sick mixed-up mother—There will be a little money to help with the extras—It had better go that way than for more pills and more doctor bills—I wish to God it had been different but be happy—but please—stay by your girls—And just one thing—be kind to Papa [*his* father]—He's done everything he could to try to help me—He loves the girls dearly and it's right that they should see him often—Natalie.

Bob—this afternoon Betty and Nancy had such a horrible fight it scares me. Do you suppose Gladys and Orville would take Betty for this school year? She should be away from Nancy for a little while—in a calm atmosphere.

4. To her ex-father-in-law:

Papa—no one could have been more kind or generous than you have been to me—I know you couldn't understand this—and forgive me—[The lawyer] has a copy of my will—Everything equal—the few personal things I have of value—the bracelet to Nancy and my wedding ring to Betty—But I would like Betty to have Nana's diamond—have them appraised and give Betty and Nancy each half the diamonds in the band. Please have somebody come in and clean—Have Bob take the girls away immediately—I don't want them to have to stay around—You're so good Papa dear—

5. To her two children:

My dearest ones—You two have been the most wonderful things in my life—Try to forgive me for what I've done—Your father would be so much better for you. It will be harder for you for awhile—but so much easier in the long run—I'm getting you all mixed up—Respect and love are almost the same—Remember that—and the most important thing is to respect yourself—The only way you can do that is by doing your share and learning to stand on your own two feet—Betty, try to remember the happy times—and be good to Nancy. Promise me you will look after your sister's welfare—I love you very much—but I can't face what the future will bring.

A number of sad observations can be made about these suicide notes. The despairing writer of them seems so pushed, so weary, so harried, so beaten by life. She has capitulated. Not atypically, the notes—especially the first two—contain directions, words like "get," "ask," "tell," "go." The disposition of affection is curious: It can be seen in different forms of the salutation and the complimentary close. The only use of "dear" or "dearest" is with her children and her ex-father-in-law. Words of love are reserved only for her neighbor-friend and for her children. There is no note to either of her living parents, both of whom resided nearby.

Her note to her ex-husband is a painful *mea culpa.* She takes all blame and pleads to him—a man who drank quite a bit and was impossible for her to live with—to be good to their children. In an amazing turnabout, she asks that the new stepmother and her ex-husband provide a stable home for her girls.

Her life can be retraced from the available materials. The conditions of her birth were noted as "absolutely normal." She was breast-fed until she was 2 months old. As an infant, she slept soundly.

At the age of 5½ she was given dancing lessons. There is a note that she was very enthusiastic and showed decided ability. When Natalie was 6, her mother wrote to a friend that "Edgar Guest's poems are her great favorites." In that same letter, the mother wrote: "I have tried to use a lot of common sense and have answered every question to the best of my ability because she is an understanding child and will listen to reason. I have not had to stimulate a desire to learn because she always wanted to know everything her older playmates knew and she would try to learn voluntarily."

She had a brother, who was eight years older than she. Later she would say about him that "he could never make a living."

When Natalie was 6 years old, in the first grade, she was given an individual intelligence test. One item that she missed— although she scored extremely high overall, with an IQ of over 153, which put her in the extremely superior category—was this one: "Yesterday the police found the body of a girl cut into eighteen pieces. They believed that she killed herself. What is foolish about that?" Her nonprophetic answer was "She wouldn't kill herself." The psychologist noted, however, her general alertness and her extremely logical mind.

A very important event occurred in Natalie's life when she was 7: her father deserted her mother. Later in her life, she noted, with obvious sadness, that *"My father never came to see me except once."*

The records of her childhood medical examinations are interesting. One, written by a school physician when she was 8, states that she was "somewhat nervous, bordering on irritability," and that she had some loss of hearing in her right ear. A school record when she was 11 notes that her last name had been changed to reflect the fact that her mother had divorced and remarried. The teacher's report states that she was a "youngster with an understanding and reasoning little mind that at times surprises her family" and that "her courtesy and tact are remarkable."

At age 12 there are several items of interest. She suffered from numerous headaches and had glasses prescribed. She reported that she still had disturbing eyestrain even with glasses. She experienced her menarche; she was a straight-A student (in the seventh grade) and indicated that she wanted to go to college and that she would also like to be a dancer. Her hearing loss had increased and she was somewhat sensitive about it; she would not admit this difficulty to any of her teachers. Her main teacher reported that although she was extremely bright, she "shrinks from opportunities for leadership." At about this time, she wrote a letter in which she indicated that her new stepfather was devoted and kind to her and her brother. Perhaps this helps to explain her unusual attitude to her girls' new stepmother (in the note to her ex-husband).

She finished high school and went on to college for three years but did not graduate. At college she developed a close, lasting student-teacher relationship with a distinguished professor; she wrote detailed letters to him for years. At the age of 25, having, in her own words, been "an unsuccessful secretary," her "ultimate goal" was to "be a successful homemaker." She married and in the two following years lived in five different cities. Understandably, she wrote that "it is hard to develop interests in any one place." She became pregnant almost immediately after getting married.

There is a gap in the records for five years. By age 30 she had two children and reports a "great tendency to worry and extreme nervousness." Her husband was drinking rather heavily. There was a dramatic change in her own physical and psychological state. She reported that she was "too tired even to wash the windows." She also reported a sharp pain in her side, which her doctor told her was due to "neurotic tendencies." She wrote that she was "chronically worn out and tired and very unhappy in the marriage."

There is a painful letter to her favorite college professor, written when she was about 35:

Until I was 25 I didn't know there were such things as problems in this world, but since then with the exception of my two lovely children and my perfect relationship with my mother, I've had just one struggle after another, made one blunder after another. My husband and I bicker constantly. I've wanted to divorce him a thousand times and still I know that is not the solution. We were both raised in broken homes and we both love our children too much. He comes home drunk at night far too often. He can't afford it. He refuses to look at the bills and says "Why haven't you saved money?" I have no one to talk to. I feel like I'm cornered. . . . My mother's youngest brother and my nearest neighbor both committed suicide in one month [about a year before].

In this same communication, writing about her misfortunes in general, she said this about her father: "I adored my father from afar. Our occasional meetings were unsatisfactory. My father is a very brilliant man—however *he has little use for me*—He lives twenty minutes away but has been in our home only once for a few minutes in the past two years." Those lines strike a key theme in her broken life. She said that she was reading Menninger's *Man Against Himself*—a book about suicide.

In another letter she wrote of her children: "Our little ones are nice, but the eldest still bites her fingernails and fights constantly with her younger sister. She is the result of my selfishness. . . . Well, I've poured out my heart and I'm a little ashamed. In my heart I've never doubted that I can be a happy, relaxed, useful human being, but it's taking such a long time to get there."

Four years later, when Natalie was 39, she separated from her husband, because—from another letter—of "his violent temper, his selfishness and his drinking." Nine months later she was divorced. Four months after the divorce was final (and he had already remarried), she was dead of suicide.

What deep psychological strains motivate such an act? When we read about her life, especially the subtleties of interaction with her father, we can see the malignant beginnings of her self-abnegating attitudes. At the end, she is so frantic that she will give anything, make any votive offering, including her life, to achieve the feeling of childhood love.

In her suicide she reenacted her own earlier life drama—the yearning for her parents to be together—and in this misdirected symbolic sacrifice, instead of giving her children a (seemingly) united home, she, in the most traumatic way possible, deprived them of their own mother. Her aspirations—to be her father's favorite, to be accepted and not abandoned, to care for and not reject her own children (as she had been rejected and not cared for), to be symbolically reunited with her father in a happy home, to sacrifice herself so that some of the problems of her children might be solved—were no better realized in her death than they were in her life.

Natalie's suicide note to her children is filled with contradictions and inconsistencies. (We remember that when she was tested as a child, the psychologist called her extremely logical.) In the suicide note, the implicit logical arguments flow back and forth, between assertion and counterassertion, never with any resolution. Here are some examples: She says, in effect, you will stay with your father, you should love your father, I know that you cannot love your father but at least you must respect him. She then almost free-associates to the word "respect" and argues, rather lamely, that love and respect are almost the same anyway, and in case that argument is not persuasive (which it is not), then one should, at least, respect one's self. The logic wanders.

Another sad example: She says to her children, "You must stand on your own two feet," but she also implies that the point of her removing herself from their lives is so that they can be reunited with their father—as, probably, she unconsciously yearns to be reunited with her father.

To tell one's children in a suicide note to remember the happy times certainly has some contradictory element in it, on the very face of it. "I love you so much," she says, but the end result of her actions is to make them orphans. She adds, "I can't face what the future will bring," but she then takes her life largely because of the haunting, inescapable past. And finally, there is her statement, "I'm getting you all mixed up," which obviously betokens the confusion not in their minds but in her own.

The connections between suicide notes and other aspects of a life seem inescapable with Natalie. The first has to do with Natalie's passivity, her fear of aggression, and her fear of violence. In her suicide note she says that the children have to have a leader; when she was 12, her teacher reported that she shrank from opportunities for leadership. It would appear that all her life she wanted love given to her; in her childhood, and as a wife and mother, she was afraid to stand up for her legitimate rights. She feared and hated quarreling. In the note she said, about the girls, that one afternoon they had "such a horrible fight it scared me." Indeed it must have—adding to her feelings of helplessness and hopelessness, feelings that are part of the suicidal scene.

Another connecting thread can be found between the poignant item contained in the letter she wrote around age 35 in which she says, "I adored my father from afar. . . . however *he has little use for me*," and all the pleading for her children in her suicide notes. In her note to her friend she says: "Please keep in touch with Betty"; and to her ex-husband: "Nancy misses you so . . . [and] needs you desperately . . . [and] really thinks you didn't love her . . . be good to my girls." If one substitutes her name for her girls', one can read the notes as though they were addressed to her own father, whom she could not bring herself— out of a mixture of hostility, rejection, and yearning—to contact. At the end, her love is expressed to her ex-father-in-law: "You're so good Papa dear." Finally, in a state of psychological bankruptcy, she tells her children: "Your father would be so much better for you." She is depleted, tired, exhausted, burned out. "I can't face what the future would bring," she says. For her, it would be more of the same. The notes *and* the life both tell us so.

It should now be evident that suicide notes, written, as they are, as part of the life that they reflect, can have a great deal of meaning (and give us a great deal of scientific and clinical information) when they are examined in light of the details of the full life history of which they are the penultimate act. By putting a suicide note within the context of the life history of the individual (who both wrote the note and committed the act), one can find that many words, ideas, emotional proclivities, styles of reaction, modes of thinking, and so on, which characterized that life are reflected in the specific details of the suicide note. And conversely, many words, phrases, ideas, passions, emphases, and the like, contained in the suicide note are extensions of those very same threads that had previously characterized the life. Living or dying, a particular individual has a certain consistency, a certain "unity thema," a certain "trademark," which he or she will show in work-style, in play-style, and in life-style, whether celebrating life in a poem of love or contemplating death in a note of suicide. We can now begin to appreciate the reciprocal relationship between suicide notes and the life itself.

REFERENCES

Aaron, D., ed. (1985). *The Inman Diary: A Public and Private Confession* (2 vols.). Cambridge, MA: Harvard University Press.

Allport, G. (1942). *The Use of Personal Documents in Psychological Science.* New York: Social Science Research Council.

Alvarez, A. (1972). *The Savage God: A Study of Suicide.* New York: Random House.

Cavan, R. S. (1928). *Suicide*. New York: Russell and Russell.

de Boismont, A. F. Brierre (1856/1965). *Du Suicide et de la Folie Suicide.* (On Suicide and Suicidal Insanity). Paris.

Harker, B. L. (1972). Cancer and communication problems: a personal experience. *Psychiatry in Medicine* 3:163–171.

Helton, L. (1972). Soon there will be no more me. *Los Angeles Times,* West Magazine, January 16, pp. 8–13.

James, W. (1902). *The Varieties of Religious Experience.* New York: Longman, Greens.

Michael, C. (1944). *Briefe und Auszeichnungen vib Epikur bis in Unseve Tage.* Zurich: Verlag Oprecht.

Morgenthaler, W. (1945). Letze Aufzeichnungen von Selbstmorden. *Beheift fur Schweizerischen Zeitschrift fur Psychologie und Ihre Anwendungen,* No. 1. Bern: Hans Huber.

Notes of a Dying Professor (1972). *Pennsylvania Gazette,* March, pp. 18–24.

Pasternak, B. (1959). *I Remember: A Sketch for an Autobiography.* New York: Pantheon.

Ponsonby, A. (1923). *English Diaries.* London: Methuen.

Ringel, E. (1976). The Presuicidal Syndrome. *Suicide and Life-Threatening Behavior* 6:379–394.

Shneidman, E. (1973). Suicide notes reconsidered. *Psychiatry* 36: 379–394.

——— (1979). Risk writing: a special note about Cesare Pavese and Joseph Conrad. *Journal of the American Academy of Psychoanalysis* 7:575–592.

——— (1980). *Voices of Death.* New York: Harper & Row.

Shneidman, E. S., and Farberow, N. L. (1957). Some comparisons between genuine and simulated suicide notes in terms of Mowrer's concepts of discomfort and relief. *Journal of General Psychology* 56:251–256.

Trombley, L. E. (1972). A psychiatrist's response to a life-threatening illness. *Life-Threatening Behavior* 2:26–34.

Wagner, F. (1960). Suicide notes. *Danish Medical Journal* 7:62–64.

7

The Suicidal Logic of

Cesare Pavese

In a previous publication on "risk writing" (Shneidman 1979), I discussed the role of writing fiction as a life-sustaining or death-facilitating process in certain authors' lives, citing Joseph Conrad and Cesare Pavese, respectively, to illustrate these two opposite effects. The present chapter is about Pavese only and is concerned with a quite different topic: the role of styles of *mentation*—ways of thinking, idiosyncrasies of reasoning, patterns of syllogizing, modes of "concludifying," peculiarities of logic—in relation to *suicide*. I begin with two general assertions: (1) that among any large number of individuals there are certain styles or patterns of mentation or logic that intensify the probability of a suicide, and (2) that within any one individual there is a range or armamentarium of styles of reasoning available to him, but that certain suicide-facilitating styles of reasoning appear during moments when he is perturbed (and thus may precede the suicide), including those moments when his level of disturbance is increased by his very thinking about suicide.

In addition, I wish specifically to describe Pavese's diary

writings in further detail, focusing on his styles of thinking (especially when he was thinking of self-destruction), which seemed almost inexorably to lead (or push) him to suicide.

SOME BARE FACTS ABOUT PAVESE

He was born in 1908 and died in 1950. He came from the Piedmont province of northern Italy, that lovely agricultural area between the Swiss Alps and the Italian Riviera. As a boy, he loved the verdant countryside. He went to a local school at his birthplace in St. Stefano Bello, attended secondary school at the regional capital in Turin, and then went to the university there to study literature.

Before he died, he was one of the most important novelists and poets in Italy. He won the Premio Strega, Italy's major literary prize. He is considered by some critics to be the most important postwar Italian novelist. He wrote nine novels, including *The Harvesters*, *The House on the Hill*, *Among Women Only*, and *The Devil in the Hills*, and several volumes of poems and short stories. He translated (into Italian) some works of several American authors, including Sinclair Lewis, Sherwood Anderson, John Dos Passos, and William Faulkner. His doctoral thesis was on Walt Whitman. He was especially drawn to Herman Melville and translated *Moby Dick* and *Benito Cereno*. (One critic has said that the death themes in Melville were the lode which especially attracted Pavese.)[1]

_____

[1]Frances Keene (in her introduction to Pavese's diaries) thinks so too: "Pavese was on intimate terms with death from his early stories. Even in his lifelong interest in American letters, he reflects the pull of this lode: It is Melville who, above all, fascinates and moves him." I am not sure what Keene meant by this line, but there is a great lode of death in the works of Melville—over 1,800 references to death in the eleven prose works alone. See my "The Deaths of Herman Melville" in *Melville and Hawthorne in the Berkshires*, Howard P. Vincent, ed. 1968. (Kent, Ohio: Kent State University Press, pp. 118–143); and in *Deaths of Man* (New York: Quadrangle/New York Times, 1973, and Penguin Books, 1974, pp. 161–177).

He edited a journal and later was an editor with the Giulio Einaudi publishing firm.

He kept a diary continuously from 1935 to the month of his death in 1950. It was published posthumously in Italian as *Il Mestiere di Vivere* and appears in English under two titles: *This Business of Living* and *The Burning Brand* (1961). My own opinion of Pavese's diary is that it is one of the most extraordinary personal documents in the world, especially for anyone who wishes—in William James' (1902) nonpareil phase—to "catch real fact in the making, and directly perceive how events happen and how [mental] work is actually done."

SOME LUGUBRIOUS FACTS ABOUT PAVESE

Pavese's childhood was, by his own account, a desolate experience. His father, who was a local judge, died of a lingering brain tumor when Pavese was six. His mother—who is described by a biographer as "spun steel, harsh and austere"—had already lost two young children, and from Pavese's point of view was not capable of giving him the love that he yearned for. He seemed haunted by death imagery and by a concern with rejection all of his life. Only eleven days before he took his life, he made this diary entry: "Today I see clearly that from 1928 [when he was 20] until now I have always lived under this shadow." In the first year of his diary (1935), he underlined the words "whispers of heavenly death," specifying the nature of the shadow.

From early childhood, Pavese had weak eyes and wore thick glasses to correct his vision, and severe asthma, which, for most of his adult life, he exacerbated by heavy smoking. He loved many women passionately, but had excruciatingly humiliating experiences with the physical expression of his passion. He had successes, as the world counts successes, but was obsessed over the fact that he was, in terms of his own standards for love and work, a dismal failure.

Even in his teens Pavese wrote about his own suicide:

You should know that I am thinking about suicide. . . . On a December evening I was walking along a small, lonely country road with my heart in turmoil. I was carrying a gun . . . I was figuring to myself the terrible pang I will give out in the night when my last illusions and fears will abandon me and I will stick it against my temple to blow my brains out (1926; age 18).

At the back of every exaltation of mine is the supreme exaltation of the thought of suicide. Oh, one day I'll have the courage for it. I long for it trembling from hour to hour (1927; age 19).

During that same year—in 1927, when he was 19—one of Pavese's schoolmates committed suicide. Again, Pavese went out into the countryside with a gun with the intention of shooting himself. At the last moment he fired the gun at some trees. But he did not dismiss the notion. The *idea* of suicide was to be his constant obsession—he called it his "syphilis"—for the rest of his life.

In 1935, the year he began his diary, Pavese was arrested by the Fascists (for publishing the journal *La Cultura*) and sentenced to prison at Brancaleone. The prison experience—a three-year sentence which was reduced to ten months—remained enormously important to him all his life. Further, on the day of his release, while waiting for a train, he was told that his inamorata had, just the day before, married someone else. He fainted dead away on the station platform.

Pavese seemed to have been tortured in his psychological relations with women and, as I have noted, many of his sexual encounters were humiliating disasters for him. He was, at times, either impotent or ejaculated quickly. It is evident from the entries in his diary that he suffered horribly over these events: "A man, unless he is a eunuch, can always achieve ejaculation with any woman . . . and a man who ejaculates too soon had better never been born. It is a failing that makes suicide worthwhile" (August 3, 1937).

There is also some suggestive evidence in his diary that he

was hypophallic and there are hints that he had some corrective surgery ["At three o'clock, an operation that will bring me peace again" (January 1, 1948)], but there are no indications of the success of any procedure.

In the last year of his life, Pavese had an intense and disastrous love affair with a young American movie actress, Constance Dowling, who was filming on location in Italy. When she left to return to America, not really having appreciated his special place in Italian letters, he was obsessed with thoughts about her and wrote constantly in his diary of his feelings of abandonment and worthlessness, and of his generalized anger toward (unattainable) women.

On August 27, 1950, Pavese committed suicide with an overdose of barbiturates in a hotel room in Turin. He was 42 years old.

LONELINESS, LOVE, SEX, SUFFERING, DEATH, AND SUICIDE IN PAVESE'S LIFE

There are several rather blatant recurring psychological themes — what Murray (1938) has called "unity thema" — in Pavese's life. In general, these relate to loneliness, love, sex, suffering, death, and suicide. These half-dozen themes dominated his life. His diary is replete with them. I shall attempt to illustrate certain aspects of some of them in the next section, where I discuss Pavese's logical styles, especially since these *ways* of thinking preselected, transmuted, transformed, and distorted the contents of his mind, and predisposed him to suicide.

PAVESE'S SUICIDE-FACILITATING STYLES OF LOGIC

I shall concentrate on three features of Pavese's mentational style which, it seems to me, were part and parcel of his suicidal life.

They are (1) an oxymoronic style of thinking; (2) an idiosyncratic mode of syllogistic thinking, specifically his way of misusing the middle term of the syllogism or reasoning in terms of attributes of the predicate (which I shall call *confused predicates*); and (3) a mentational tunneling or constriction of thinking.

Oxymorons

An oxymoron is a pairing of two words that mean the opposite of each other. It often has unusual epigrammatic effect. The best-known such passage in English literature is from Shakespeare's *Romeo and Juliet*, which contains such oxymorons as "Beautiful tyrant! fiend angelical!/heavy lightness, serious vanity/feather of lead, bright smoke, cold fire, sick health/sweet sorrow."

Pavese was especially keen about Herman Melville and may have known Melville's poem, "Art," filled with oxymoronic images:

In placid hours well-pleased we dream
Of many a brave unbodied scheme.
But form to lend, pulsed life create,
What unlike things must meet and mate:
A flame to melt—a wind to freeze;
Sad patience—joyous energies;
Humility—yet pride and scorn;
Instinct and study; love and hate;
Audacity–reverence. These must mate,
And fuse with Jacob's mystic heart
To wrestle with the angel—Art.

But there is a danger in an oxymoronic style of thinking. That danger occurs especially when the penchant for oxymoronic phrases is combined with sardonic and bitter twists. Oscar Wilde and Cesare Pavese show examples of this, while George Bernard Shaw—who could use oxymoronic cunning without the deep personal bitterness—does not. Pavese understood this (but could not save himself from it). His diary entry for November 8, 1943, on Shakespeare's style, reads: "The fool, full of dialectic wit, is later replaced by a leading character who is either mad or driven beyond endurance (Hamlet, Cleopatra, Lear, Macbeth) and then the witty speeches can become tragic without losing their pithiness. That is irony."

Certainly one key to Pavese's suicide lies in this peculiar aspect of his thinking style. Note, for example, the tone of the following diary entries:

There is something even sadder than falling short of one's ideals: to have realized them (December 18, 1937).

The women who are most careful to choose a rich lover are those who protest that money means nothing to them. Because, to despise money, one must have plenty of it (February 2, 1938).

One must have cunning, to gain tragic love. But it is precisely those who are incapable of cunning who thirst for tragic love (February 23, 1938).

The profession of enthusiasm is the most sickening of all insincerities (February 9, 1940).

We obtain things when we no longer want them (October 15, 1940).

The richness of life lies in memories we have forgotten (February 13, 1944).

The "unique event" which you find so exciting can only have its full value if it has never taken place (February 13, 1945).

If a man has not always had a woman he will never have one. . . . And the man who has a woman, looks for another (February 8, 1946).

Having regained their liberty, the liberals no longer know what to do with it (July 5, 1946).

What all these statements have in common is a subtle quality of combining sardonic opposites, of using ironic juxtaposition, assertions and denials, contradictory ideas—in other words, they contain a bitter oxymoronic quality. These ironies in Pavese's thoughts reflect, in my opinion, the deeper and more bitter ironies and contradictions in his life. Consider these ironic combinations in one man: that nature would combine in one person a large passion and a small phallus; a strong desire for women and a keen disdain of mankind; a feeling that a dramatic failure in life (like death by suicide) might make one a grand posthumous success; a need to write in order to feel alive and a belief that the printed text (of one's own works) gave one a kind of immortality so that one could then die; a great belief in the power of words and a deep need for complete and eternal silence; a gift for words about death and a special investment in those words so that they seem to become the facilitators of death itself.

Women and Failure

While a good deal of Pavese's diary reflects his concern with work and the failure attendant to it, a much greater portion of it touches on the theme of women and failure. Pavese's intense preoccupation with death, coupled with his zealous search for the love of a woman—both complicated by his incapacitating sexual dysfunctions—are among the main obsessive themes of his introspective musings. To Pavese, women are mysterious, unattainable, unsatisfiable, desirable, evil creatures. Consider these bitter statements:

3rd August, 1937. A woman, unless she is an idiot, sooner or later meets a piece of human wreckage and tries to rescue him. She sometimes succeeds. But a woman, unless she is an idiot, sooner or later finds a sane, healthy man and makes a wreck of him. She always succeeds.

27th September, 1937. Women have always been "bitter as death," sinks of iniquity, faithless jades, Delilahs. . . .

30th September, 1937. The only women worth the trouble of marrying are those a man cannot trust enough to marry.

21st January, 1938. A woman is adept at arousing a man's desire, but she is scandalized if this capacity of hers is recognized.

26th January, 1938. When women are God-fearing, people call them sanctimonious hypocrites. Other women claim intellectual freedom, which merely serves to increase their price.

13th October, 1938. If a woman does not betray you, it is because it does not suit her convenience.

27th October, 1938. It is possible not to think about women, just as one does not think about death.

15th October, 1940. Classification of women: those who exploit others, and those who let others exploit them. Classification of men: those who love the first type and those who love the second. . . . Both types confirm the impossibility of human fellowship.

9th September, 1946. Think the worst. You will not be wrong. Women are an enemy race, like the Germans.

Pavese's basic oxymoronic position—in which his own cleverness with words outdid him and trapped him—contains more than a superficial contradiction; it embodies a serious semantic confusion. Simply put, Pavese thought (believed, said) that one *lives through death:* "To want to kill oneself is to want one's death to be significant, a *supreme* choice, a deed that cannot be misunderstood" (January 8, 1938).

And this lethal clincher: "Is it conceivable to murder someone in order to count for something in this life? Then is it conceivable to kill oneself so as to count for something in one's own life?" (January 16, 1938).

In these thoughts, Pavese is confusing his "self" with his "post-self" (Shneidman 1973). He is behaving as though he were going to be alive after his death to experience the "counting for something." He is romanticizing his own death, as some writers do, thinking that death—and especially a *suicidal* death—somehow validates the writer's work and enhances the importance of his life. This sentimental notion, shared by fans of Sylvia Plath, Anne Sexton, and John Irving is that one has to kill oneself in order to be taken seriously.

Confused Predicates

In the past fifty years there has been an active interest in the logical styles of certain aberrant groups, especially those with brain damage and those diagnosed as schizophrenic (Pavese was neither). There is a string of distinguished names connected with these studies, including those of L. S. Vigotsky, Kurt Goldstein, J. S. Kasanin, Ellhard von Domarus, Silvano Arieti, and others. This is a topic that has interested me for some time (Shneidman 1969, 1982).

Two authors especially, Von Domarus (1944) and Arieti (1955), have discussed the idea of "paralogical" thinking, in which the individual (for whatever reasons) abrogates certain basic Aristotelian precepts relating to syllogistic thinking. Valid deductive logic depends on preserving the core identity of the *subject* of the premises: All *men* are mortal; *Socrates* is a man; therefore, *Socrates* is mortal. On the other hand, there are people who will habitually or occasionally reason (or syllogize or conclude) in terms of attributes of the *predicate*—and our logical ears are so trained and attuned that we think their reasoning peculiar (or weird or erroneous or fallacious) when they do so. An example: Certain Indians are *swift*; stags are *swift*; therefore, certain Indians are stags. The emphasis here is on the predicate, on the adjective, on the middle term. Another example: The Virgin Mary was a virgin; I am a virgin; therefore, I am the Virgin Mary. Or: A patient on a locked neuropsychiatric ward (quoted by Bleuler) announced that "I am Switzerland." Questions from the staff about his travels, his having been to Switzerland, his wishing to visit Switzerland, only served to agitate him. When someone suggested to him that he really wanted to be let off the locked ward, he indicated immediately that the person understood what he was saying. The latent syllogism (based on adjectival attributes of the predicate) went something like this: Switzerland loves freedom; I love freedom (and want to be off this locked ward); therefore, I am Switzerland. Never mind whether or not this is schizophrenic. Pavese, who was not schizophrenic, often reasoned in this same fashion, and it not only stemmed from his psychodynamics but it led him into greater confusions and (there is no doubt in my mind) played some role in the form of his suicidal thinking and eventually led—rather early, really, at 42—to his suicidal death.

An example:

You must confess you have thought and written many banalities in your little diary these past months. I agree but is there anything more commonplace than death? A lover's reasoning: If I were dead, she would go on living, laughing, trying her luck. But she has thrown me over and still does all those things. Therefore, I am as dead (February 25, 1938).

The argument embedded in this paragraph contains a blatant logical error—and gets Pavese into deep trouble. He reasons himself into hopelessness: Therefore I am as [good as] dead [and might as well be really dead]. It makes as much logical sense as his saying that he is Switzerland or the Virgin Mary. One has to watch carefully how one uses the word "therefore" (Shneidman 1982a).

Pavese's catalogical reasoning style—I call this pattern of thinking *catalogical* because it destroys the logician—linked suffering with death, death with suicide, and therefore the presence of suffering with (the necessity of) suicide. But first, here is Pavese's bitter (and frightening) definition of suffering, again linked to the need to break out of its spell by doing something. From clinical experience we know that committing suicide is often reduced to the need to do *something*—anything—to stop the flow of unbearable mental anguish:

30th October, 1940. . . . Suffering is a fierce, bestial thing, commonplace, uncalled for, natural as air. It is intangible; no one can grasp it or fight against it; it dwells in time—is the same thing as time; if it comes in fits and starts, that is only as to leave the sufferer more defenseless during the moments that follow, those long moments when one relives the last bout of torture and waits for the next. . . . The moment comes when he screams needlessly, just to break the flow of time, to feel that *something* is happening, that the endless spell of bestial suffering is for an instant broken, even though that makes it worse.

In this following diary entry we see how suffering was linked in Pavese's mind to death, and death linked to suicide.

10th November, 1938. The defense against things in general is silence as we muster strength for a fresh leap forward. But we must impose that silence on ourselves, not have it imposed on us, not even by death. To choose a hardship for ourselves is our only defense against that hardship. *This* is what is meant by accepting suffering. Not being resigned to it, but using it as a springboard. Controlling the effect of the blow. Those who, by their very nature, can suffer completely, utterly, having an advantage. This is how we can disarm the power of suffering, make it our own creation, our own choice; submit to it. A justification for suicide. Charity has no place in all this. Unless, perhaps, this act of violence is in itself the truest form of charity?

If Gandhi or any Buddhist had followed Pavese's logic, then they would all have committed suicide. To submit to certain onerous aspects of real life—to "will the obligatory," as Otto Rank and Henry Murray have discussed—is far from committing suicide. To die is obligatory; to commit suicide is not. Pavese slips a mental clutch in his reasoning and it throws all of him out of control. Interestingly, Pavese does not reason in this manner (in his diary) when he is discussing principles of poetry; he does so often when he is writing about his "cancers"—loneliness, women, impotence, rejection, and death—and then he makes these curious illogical moves over a flawed "therefore" to a suicidal conclusion.

In part, this was so because Pavese mythicized and philosophized the main themes of his life—love, work, festivals, and death—and was not able, in the ordinary way, to feel that he could participate in them in the reality of the daily course of his existence. He was psychologically removed from them—perhaps because his father and mother were remote from him—and seemed himself to be remote from what he wanted to touch most closely, not in his writings but in his life. In a letter about the village of his birth, he wrote, "I love S. Stefano madly, because I come from far away."

Constriction

Constriction is meant to describe the tunneling or narrowing of the mind's range of scanning and considering viable possibilities for effective, life-enhancing action. It is sometimes metaphorically called the tunneling of vision, a narrowing of the mind's eye. Boris Pasternak, in discussing the suicides of a number of young Russian poets, described this concept as a constriction of memory and associations that would ordinarily occur in the mind. One's ordinary thoughts and loves and feelings and responsibilities are simply not available to consciousness. One does not have to actually "forget" that he is married; rather the tie to the spouse is suddenly blocked and her lien disappears. The suicidal person, by virtue of his constriction, turns his back on his past and permits his memories to become unreal so that they cannot serve to tie him to life and save him. In this tunneled vision, the focus is on the unbearable emotion and on the way to escape from it — for that is, psychologically, what suicide is.

One important characteristic of constriction is dichotomous thinking. The suicidal person abandons the sense of life's innumerable continua and uses such polarized words as either/or, always, never, forever, nothing, totally, all, and, the most ominous of such words, only. Pavese's diary is replete with these. Some random examples will suffice.

The Relation of Love to Death

"How can there be, between a man and a woman, anything more important than love? . . . But if she disappears? . . . She will die and you will be lonely as a dog" (November 26, 1945).

Self-Abnegating Image

Pavese's diary is replete with references to a sense of failure in his work and of emptiness in his successes. Two examples:

. . . and then to realize that all this is nothing unless it is welcomed by some sign, some word of human appreciation. To lack that warming response is to die of cold, to be speaking in the wilderness, to be alone, night and day, like a dead man (June 27, 1946).

Today acclamation. They implore me to write, beg for my autograph. If you had known this when you were twenty! Does it mean anything to you now? I am sad, useless as a god (January 20, 1948).

The Price of Success

Roughly, the opposite of failure is success. But in Pavese's lugubrious logic, even success was not without its dangers and its toll. Life itself — just having been born — has its own heavy costs.

If you were born a second time you should be very careful, even in your attachment to your mother. You can only lose by it (January 22, 1938).

Every luxury must be paid for, and everything is a luxury, starting with being in the world (October 13, 1938).

You are alone. Having a woman to talk to is nothing. All that counts is the press of body against body. Why, why are you without that? "You will never have it." Everything has its price (February 8, 1946).

Women and Suicide

Can't you face the fact that one day soon, tomorrow perhaps, she will go off and you will never hear from her again. As if you were dead (January 26, 1938)!

What use has this love affair been? It has uncovered all my shortcomings, tested my quality, passed judgment on me. Now I see the reason why I isolated myself until '34. Subconsciously I knew that for me love would be a massacre. . . . The thing we secretly dread the most always happens. . . . When I was a little boy I used to tremble to think what it would be like to love someone and see her married to another. I exercised my mind with that thought. And you see (March 28, 1938)!

Pavese and Constance Dowling

In Pavese's life there was a special woman, Constance Dowling. She has been described as an American movie actress "who flowered briefly in the 1940s." Her screen credits include *Knickerbocker Holiday* (1944), *Up in Arms* (1944), and *The Flame* (1947). She was one of the first American actresses to make films on location in Italy—where she met Pavese—after World War II. Her sister, Doris, also an actress, was in Italy at the same time and Pavese knew them both. Constance was born in 1923 and died in Los Angeles in 1969.

There is an entry in Pavese's diary about Constance Dowling that reads: "25th March, 1950. One does not kill oneself for love of *a* woman, but because love—any love—reveals us in our nakedness, our misery, our vulnerability, our nothingness."

It is important to know something about this particular love affair and something about the sexual problems to which Pavese often alludes.

Throughout his adult lifetime, Pavese's love-style was a disaster. He was what one modern psychologist (Lee 1973, 1976) calls a *manic* lover—"obsessive, jealous, emotionally intense with a preoccupation with the beloved." It was a style that is calculated to scare off many women—especially if the love itself cannot be physically consummated.

The entire affair with Constance Dowling began and ended in 1950, the year of Pavese's suicide. She is first mentioned on January 14: "Thinking again of the sisters D." It is noteworthy that the sentence is preceded (in the entry for the same date) by this ominous line: "I am filled with distaste for what I have done, for all my works. A sense of failing health, of physical decadence. The downward curve of the arc. And your life, your loves, where are they?"

More entries about Constance:

Did I suffer like this before? Yes, then I suffered from the fear of death. There is always something to suffer (March 21, 1950).

The cadence of suffering has begun. Every evening, as dusk settles, my heart constricts until the night has come (May 8, 1950).

My happiness of '48–'49 is paid for in full. Behind that Olympian contentment lay my impotence and my refusal to become involved. Now, in my own way, I have gone down into the abyss: I contemplate my impotence, I feel it in my bones. . . . There is only one answer: suicide (May 27, 1950).

The Theme of Death

The death theme seems omnipresent in Pavese's diary and, one would reasonably extrapolate, in his life. His thoughts of death and his thoughts of suicide are quite distinguishable. There are twenty-five separate discussions of death—mostly about the allure of death—in Pavese's diary. The philosopher Spinoza has been called "a God-intoxicated man"; Pavese seems to have been a death-intoxicated man. For Pavese, the obsession with death did not stand by itself, but rather rested on (or grew out of) several factors: his sense of rejection by his mother; his suffering and loneliness; his notion that one had to pay a price for everything worthwhile—love, success, life itself; his view of women as frightening but desirable enigmas, before whom he stood naked and embarrassed; and his obsessional way of attempting to solve the problems of life, in which love and death became confused in his mind. All these perhaps reflect a deep unconscious wish to be joined with his mother. A key entry occurs on May 13, 1950, three months before his suicide (it is given in its totality; the elision marks and the italics are Pavese's): "Deep, deep, deep down, did I not grab at this amazing love affair, seize upon this undreamed of, fascinating thing, to make myself revert to my old thought—my long-standing temptation, to have an excuse for thinking of it again. . . ? Love and Death— *this* is the hereditary pattern."

In an earlier diary entry, Pavese begins by writing of the importance of love, but soon turns to thoughts of loss, death, and nothingness.

November 26th, 1945. How can there be, between a man and a woman, anything more important than love? . . . But if she disappears? . . . What remedy is there? Very well, then. But if you can accept death for yourself, how can you refuse anyone else the right to accept it? That, too, is charity. You can arrive at nothingness, but not resentment or hate. Always remember that nothing is owed to you. In fact, what do you deserve? Had you any claim on life when you were born?

The Final Entries

To the end (August 1950) Pavese retained the greatest fealty to his life-long image of himself as a self-destroyer, whose very self-destruction would give him the greatest significance he could achieve in his own eyes, even though he mollified this thought with thoughts of love and fears of sexual failure.

13th August, 1950. It's something very different. It is she, who came from the sea.

14th August, 1950. She, too, ends up in the same way. She, too. It's all right. By now we are all waves of this sea.

16th August, 1950. My dear one, perhaps you are really the best—my real love. But I no longer have time to tell you so, to make you understand—and then, even if I could, there would be the test—test—failure.

Today I see clearly that from '28 until now I have always lived under this shadow—what some would call a complex. Let them: It is something much simpler than that. . . .

And you are the spring, an elegant, incredibly sweet and lissom spring, soft, fresh, fugitive—earthy and good—"a flower from the loveliest valley of the Po," as someone else would say.

Yet, even you are only a pretext. The real fault, apart from my own, lies with that "agonizing disquietude, with its secret smile."

Why die? I have never been so much alive as now, never so young.

Nothing can be added to the rest, to the past. We always begin afresh.

One nail drives out another. But four nails make a cross.

I have done my part by the world, as best I could. I have worked; I have given poetry to men, I have shared the sorrows of many.

17th August, 1950. . . . In my work, then, I am king. In ten years I have done it all. If I think of the hesitations of former times. . . . In my life I am more hopeless, more lost than then. What have I accomplished? Nothing. For years I have ignored my shortcomings, lived as though they did not exist. I have been stoical. Was that heroism? No. I made no real effort. And then, at the first onset of this "agonizing disquietude," I have fallen back into the quicksand. . . . What remains is that now I know what will be my greatest triumph—and this triumph lacks flesh and blood, life itself.

I have nothing left to wish for on this earth—except the thing that fifteen years of failure bars from me.

August 18th, 1950. The thing most feared in secret always happens.[2]

All it takes is a little courage.

It seemed easy when I thought of it. Weak women have done it. It takes humility, not pride.

All this is sickening.

Not words. An act. I'll write no more.[3]

---

[2]There is an almost identical diary entry 12 years before (March 26, 1938): "The thing we secretly dread the most always happens."

[3]The last words in Pavese's diary are "Non scriverò più." I wonder if the words of his own translation of Chapter 30, "The Pipe," from *Moby Dick*, by his favorite American author were at all in the back of his mind? Captain Ahab is on the quarter deck, just having insulted his second mate. Smoking his pipe, he soliloquizes: "This smoking no longer soothes. Oh, my pipe! hard must it go with me if thy charm be gone! Here have I been unconsciously toiling, not pleasuring. . . . What business have I with this pipe? This thing that is meant for sereneness. . . . I'll smoke no more—" ("Non fumerò più"). And then Ahab tossed his lighted pipe into the boundless sea.

CAVEAT

A suicidologist could take this position about Pavese: Early in his life, when his self-abnegation and self-pity became irreversible, his suicidal death became inevitable. But that represents only part of the picture. Suicide is a complicated deed. It is not *due* to faulty logic. Each act of suicide has interwoven sociological, social, dyadic, anamnestic, psychodynamic, philosophical, and existential components—as well as elements of unfortunate cognitive style. The emphasis in this chapter on the mentational (cognitive, logical) characteristics of Pavese's life and death is simply the temporary use of one of the lenses of a multipowered microscope, where common sense demands that, for a full study, several turrets, lenses, and magnifications be employed.

When we look only through the "logical" lens, we can see that Pavese tended to process his emotionally-toned ideas through the filters of a cognitive style that exacerbated the irrational and tended consistently to lead him to the darkest conclusions and the gloomiest states of mind. Thus, we can still say that Pavese's style of thinking—granted that it was only part of his style of life and his psychodynamic history—directly predisposed him to making the fatal deductive leap into his own oblivion.

REFERENCES

Arieti, S. (1955). *Interpretation of Schizophrenia.* New York: Robert Brunner.

Bleuler, E. (1913). *Textbook of Psychiatry.*

James, W. (1902). *Varieties of Religious Experience.* New York: Henry Holt.

Lee, J. A. (1973). *Colours of Love.* Toronto: New Press.

———— (1976). *Lovestyles.* London: Dent.

Murray, H. A. (1938). *Explorations in Personality.* New York: Oxford University Press.

Pavese, C. (1961). *The Burning Brand: Diary 1935–1950.* Translated by A. E. Murch. New York: Walker.

Shneidman, E. S. (1969). Logical content analysis: an explication of styles of concludifying. In *The Analysis of Communication Content*, ed. G. Gerbner, et al., pp. 261–279. New York: Wiley.

———— (1973). *Deaths of Man*. New York: Quadrangle/New York Times Book Company.

———— (1979). Risk writing: a special note about Cesare Pavese and Joseph Conrad. *Journal of the American Academy of Psychoanalysis* 7:575–592.

———— (1982a). On "Therefore I Must Commit Suicide." *Suicide and Life-Threatening Behavior* 12:52–55.

———— (1982b). The Suicidal Logic of Cesare Pavese. *Journal of the American Academy of Psychoanalysis* 10:547–562.

Von Domarus, E. (1944). The specific laws of logic in schizophrenia. In *Language and Thought in Schizophrenia*, ed. J. S. Kasanin, pp. 104–114. Berkeley, CA: University of California Press.

PART THREE

RESPONSE

8

Psychotherapy with

Suicidal Patients

It seems logical that before we consider what the psychotherapy of a suicidal person ought to be, we have some common understanding of the suicidal state itself. Of course, everybody agrees that suicide is an enormously complicated term, encompassing a wide variety (and different ranges) of dysphoria, disturbance, self-abnegation, resignation, terror-cum-pain—to mention but a few inner states that are involved. But perhaps nowhere is there as insightful a description of suicide in as few words as that found in the opening paragraph of Melville's *Moby Dick:* "a damp and drizzly November in my soul." For that is what, metaphorically, most suicide is: a dreary and dismal wintry gale within the mind, where the vital issue that is being debated is whether to try to stay afloat in a stormy life or willfully to go under to nothingness.

Suicide is the human act of self-inflicted, self-intended cessation (i.e., the permanent stopping of consciousness). It is best understood as a bio-socio-psychologico-existential state of malaise. It is obviously not a disease, and just as obviously a number of kinds of trained individuals other than physicians can help individuals who are in a suicidal state.

If we are to escape many of the current somewhat simplistic notions of suicide (especially those which totally equate a disease called suicide with a disease called depression), then we need to explicate what the suicidal state of mind is like. Our key source in this can be the ordinary dictionary—eschewing any nomenclature of technical and, especially, technically diagnostic terms. In the dictionary there are words, for example, angered, anguished, cornered, dependent, frustrated, guilty, helpless, hopeless, hostile, rageful, shamed, that will help us in our understanding. For us, in this chapter, two less common (but ordinary) dictionary words—*perturbation* and *lethality*—will be the keystone words of our understanding.

Perturbation refers to how upset (disturbed, agitated, sane-insane, discomposed) the individual is—rated, let's say, on a 1 to 9 scale. Lethality refers to how lethal the individual is, that is, how likely it is that he will take his own life—also rated on a 1 to 9 scale.

At the outset, I need to indicate what kinds of suicidal states I am talking about in order to indicate what kinds of psychotherapy are appropriate for them. We can arbitrarily divide the seriousness (or risk, or lethality, or suicidality) of all suicidal efforts (actions, deeds, events, episodes)—whether verbalizations (ordinarily called threats) or behaviors (ordinarily called attempts)—into three rough commonsense groupings: low, medium, and high. In this chapter, I shall focus on the suicidal events or deeds of *high* lethality, where the danger of self-inflicted death is realistically large and imminent; what one might ordinarily call high suicide risks. Of course, a suicide act (deed, occurrence, event, threat, attempt) *of whatever lethality* is always a genuine psychiatric situation and should be treated without any iatrogenic elements. Thus, in the treatment of the suicidal person there is almost never any place for the therapist's hostility, anger, sardonic attitudes, daring the patient, or pseudo-democratic indifference.

By focusing solely on the *psycho*therapeutic approaches to

high suicide risks, it should be obvious at the beginning that this chapter is a moiety—omitting entirely (and advertently) the lively areas of treatment suicidal individuals receive by means of chemical, electrical, or institutional modalities.

Theoretically, the treatment of an acutely highly suicidal person is quite simple: It consists, almost by definition, of lowering his lethality level; in practice, this is usually done by decreasing or mollifying his level of perturbation. In short, we defuse the situation (like getting the gun), we create activity of support and care around the person, and we make that person's temporarily unbearable life just enough better so that he or she can stop to think and reconsider. The way to decrease lethality is by dramatically decreasing the felt perturbation.

Working intensively with a highly suicidal person—someone who might be assessed as 7, 8, or 9 on a 1 to 9 scale of lethality—as distinguished from someone of moderate or low lethality, is different from almost any other human encounter, with the possible exception of that of working intensively with a dying person—but that is another story. Psychotherapy with an intensely suicidal person is a special task; it demands a different kind of involvement. The goal is different—not that of increasing comfort, which is the goal of most ordinary psychotherapy, but the more primitive goal of simply keeping the person alive. The rules are therefore different, and it follows (or rather precedes) that the theoretical rationale is different.

At this juncture, I wish to make a distinction among *four* psychologically different kinds of human encounters: conversation (or "ordinary talk"); a hierarchical exchange; psychotherapy or a "professional exchange"; and, finally, clinical suicidology or working psychologically with a highly lethal person.

1. In ordinary talk or conversation, the focus is on the surface content (concrete events, specific dates, culinary details); on what is actually being said; on the obviously stated meanings; on the ordinary interesting (or uninteresting) details of life. Further, the social role between the two speakers is one in which the two participants are essentially equal. Each participant has the social right to ask the other the same questions which he or she

has been asked by the other. The best example of ordinary talk is two friends conversing with one another.

2. In a hierarchical verbal exchange the two participants are socially, and hence psychologically, unequal. This difference may be imposed by the situation, such as the exchange between a military officer and an enlisted person, or it may be agreed to by the two involved parties, such as between a physician and a patient. In either instance, the two are not psychologically equal. For example, an officer or a physician can ask an enlisted person or a patient, respectively, certain personal questions to which a rational response is expected, that the person of "lower status" could not ask the other person in return without appearing impertinent or aberrant. Yet most of the talk is still on the surface, concerning the real details of everyday life.

3. In a professional psychotherapeutic exchange the focus is on feelings, emotional content, and unconscious meanings, rather than on what is apparently being said. The emphasis is on the latent (between-the-lines) significance of what is being said more than on the manifest and obvious content; on the unconscious meanings, including double-entendres, puns, and slips of the tongue; on themes that run as common threads through the content, rather than on the concrete details for their own sake. Perhaps the most distinguishing aspect of the professional exchange (as opposed to ordinary talk) is the occurrence of transference, wherein the patient projects onto the therapist certain deep expectations and feelings. These transference reactions often stem from the patient's childhood and reflect neurotic patterns of reaction (of love, hate, dependency, suspicion, etc.) to whatever the therapist may or may not be doing. The therapist is often invested by the patient with almost magical healing powers, which, in fact, can serve as a self-fulfilling prophecy and thus help the interaction become therapeutic for the patient. In this paragraph, the use of the words therapist and patient already implies that, of the two parties, one has tacitly agreed to seek assistance and the other has agreed to try to give it. The roles of the two participants, unlike those in a conversation, are, in this

respect, not coequal. A therapist and a patient could not simply exchange roles.

4. In working as a clinical suicidologist with an individual who is highly suicidal, the focus is again different. In this situation, the attention is primarily on the lethality. Most importantly, what differentiates this modality of therapy from any other psychotherapy is the handling of the transference feelings. Specifically, the transference (from the patient to the therapist) and the countertransference (from the therapist to the patient)—especially those positive feelings of affection and concern—can legitimately be much more intense and more deep than would be seemly or appropriate (or even ethical) in ordinary psychotherapy where time is assumed to be endless and where it is taken for granted that the patient will continue functioning in life.

Working with a highly suicidal person demands a different kind of involvement. There may be as important a conceptual difference between ordinary psychotherapy with individuals where dying or living is not *the* issue and psychotherapy with acutely suicidal persons as there is between ordinary psychotherapy and ordinary talk.

The main point of working with a lethally oriented person—in the give and take of talk, the advice, the interpretations, the listening—is to increase that individual's psychological sense of possible choices and sense of being emotionally supported. Relatives, friends, and colleagues should, after they are assessed to be on the life-side of the individual's ambivalence, be closely involved in the total treatment process. Suicide prevention is not best done as a solo practice. A combination of consultation, ancillary therapists, and the use of all the interpersonal and community resources that one can involve is, in general, the best way of proceeding.

Recall that we are talking about psychotherapy with the highly suicidal persons—not one of low or even medium lethality. With this in mind—and keeping in mind also the four psychological components of the suicidal state of mind (heightened inimicality, elevated perturbation, conspicuous constriction of intellec tual focus, and the idea of cessation as a solution)—then a relatively simple formula for treatment can be stated. That formulation concentrates on two of the four psychological components, specifically on the constriction and the perturbation. Simply put, the way to save a highly suicidal person is to decrease the constriction, that is, to widen the range of possible thoughts and fantasies (*from* the dichotomous two—either one specific outcome or death—*to* at least three or more possibilities for an admittedly less-than-perfect solution), and, most importantly—without which the attempt to broaden the constriction will not work—to decrease the individual's perturbation.

How does a psychotherapist decrease the elevated perturbation of a highly suicidal person? Answer: by doing anything and almost everything possible to cater to the infantile idiosyncrasies, the dependency needs, the sense of pressure and futility, the feelings of hopelessness and helplessness that the individual is experiencing. In order to help a highly lethal person, one should involve others; create activity around the person; do what he or she wants done—and, if that cannot be accomplished, at least move in the direction of the desired goals to some substitute goals that approximate those which have been lost. Remember that life—and remind the patient of this fact (in a kindly but oracular way)—is often the choice among terrible alternatives. The key to functioning, to wisdom, and to life itself is often to choose the least terrible alternative that is practicably attainable.

Taken down to its bare roots, the principle is: To decrease lethality one puts a hook on perturbation and, doing what needs to be done, pulls the level of perturbation down—and with that action brings down the active level of lethality. Then, when the person is no longer highly suicidal—the usual methods of psychotherapy can be usefully employed.

As to how to help a suicidal individual, it is best to look upon any suicidal act, whatever its lethality, as an effort by an individual to stop unbearable anguish or intolerable pain by "doing something." Knowing this usually guides us as to what the treatment should be. In the same sense, the way to save a person's life is also to "do something." Those "somethings" include putting that information (that the person is in trouble with himself) into the stream of communication, letting others know about it, breaking what could be a fatal secret, talking to the person, talking to others, proferring help, getting loved ones interested and responsive, creating action around the person, showing response, indicating concern, and, if possible, offering love.

I conclude with an example—actually a composite of several actual highly suicidal persons I have known.

CASE STUDY

A young woman in her twenties, a nurse at the hospital where I worked, asked me pleadingly if I would see her teenage sister whom she considered to be highly suicidal. The attractive, younger woman—agitated and tearful but coherent—told me, in the privacy of my office, that she was single, pregnant, and determined to kill herself. She showed me a small automatic pistol she had in her purse. Her being pregnant was such a mortal shame to her, combined with strong feelings of rage and guilt, that she simply could not "bear to live" (or live to bear?). Suicide was the *only* alternative, and shooting herself was the *only* way to do it. Either she had to be unpregnant (the way she was before she conceived) or she had to be dead.

I did several things. For one, I took out a sheet of paper and—to begin to "widen her blinders"—said something like, "Now, let's see: You could have an abortion here locally." ("I couldn't do that.") It is precisely the "can'ts" and the "won'ts" and "have to's" and "nevers" and "always" and "onlys" that are to be negotiated in psychotherapy. "You could go away and have an abortion." ("I couldn't do that.") "You could bring the baby to term and keep the baby." ("I couldn't do that.") "You could have the baby and adopt it out." ("I couldn't do that.") "We could get in touch with the young man involved." ("I couldn't do that.") "We could involve the help of your parents." ("I couldn't do that.") and "You can always commit suicide, but there is obviously no need to do that today." (No response.) "Now first, let me take that gun, and then let's look at this list and rank them in order and see what their advantages, disadvantages and implications are, remembering that none of them is perfect."

The very making of this list, my fairly calm and nonhortatory and nonjudgmental approach already had a calming influence on her. Within 15 minutes her lethality had begun to deescalate. She actually rank-ordered the list, commenting negatively on each item, but what was of critical importance was that suicide, which I included in the total realistic list, was now ranked third—no longer first or second.

She decided that she would, reluctantly, want to talk to the father of her child. Not only had they never discussed the "issue," he did not even know about it. But there was a formidable obstacle: He lived in another city, almost across the country and that involved (what seemed to be a big item in the patient's mind) a long distance call. It was a matter of literally seconds to ascertain the area code from the long distance operator, to obtain his telephone number from information, and then—obviously with some trepidation and keen ambivalence for her—to dial his number (at university expense), and with the support of my presence to speak to him directly.

The point is not how the issue was practically resolved, without an excessive number of deep or shallow interpretations as to why she permitted herself to become pregnant and other aspects of her relationships with men, and so forth. What is important is that it was possible to achieve the assignment of that day: to lower her lethality.

In general, any suicidal state is characterized by its transient quality, its pervasive ambivalence, and its dyadic nature. Psychiatrists and other health professionals are well advised to minimize, if not totally to disregard, those probably well-intentioned but shrill writings in this field which naively speak of an individual's right to commit suicide—a right which, in actuality, cannot be denied—as though the suicidal person were a chronic univalently self-destructive hermit.

A number of special features in the management of a highly lethal patient—advertently repeated from Chapter 2—can be mentioned. Some of these special therapeutic stratagems or orientations with a highly lethal patient attend to or reflect the *transient, ambivalent,* and *dyadic* aspects of almost all suicidal acts.

1. A continuous, preferably daily, monitoring of the patient's lethality rating.
2. An active outreach; being willing to deal with some of the reality problems of the patient openly, where advisable; giving direction (sans exhortation) to the patient; actively taking the side of life. It relates to befriending and caring.
3. Use of community resources including employment, Veterans Administration (when applicable), social agencies, and psychiatric social work assistance.
4. Consultation. There is almost no instance in a psychiatrist's professional life when consultation with a peer is as important as when he is dealing with a highly suicidal patient. The items to be discussed might include the therapist's treatment of the case; his own feelings of frustration, helplessness, or even anger; his countertransference reactions generally; the advisability of hospitalization for the patient, and the like.
5. Hospitalization. Hospitalization is always a complicating event in the treatment of a suicidal patient but it should not, on those grounds, be eschewed. Obviously, the quality of care—from doctors, nurses, and attendants—is crucial.
6. Transference. As in almost no other situation and at almost no other time, the successful treatment of a highly suicidal person depends heavily on the transference. The therapist can be active, show his personal concern, increase the frequency of the sessions, invoke the magic of the unique therapist-patient relationship, be less of a *tabula rasa,* give transfusions of (realistic) hope and succorance. In a figurative sense, I believe that Eros can work wonders against Thanatos.

7. The involvement of significant others. Suicide is most often a highly charged dyadic crisis. It follows from this that the therapist, unlike his usual practice of dealing almost exclusively with his patient (and even fending off the spouse, the lover, parents, grown children), should consider the advisability of working directly with the significant other. For example, if the individual is male and married, it is important to meet his wife. The therapist must assess whether, in fact, she is suicidogenic; whether they ought to be separated; whether there are misunderstandings which the therapist can help resolve; or whether she is insightful and concerned and can be used by the therapist as his ally and cotherapist. The same is true for homosexual lovers, for patient and parent, and so forth. It is not suggested that the significant other be seen as often as the patient is seen, but that other real people in the suicidal patient's life be directly involved and, at the minimum, their role as hinderer or helper in the treatment process be assessed.

8. Careful modification of the usual canons of confidentiality. Admittedly, this is a touchy and complicated point, but the therapist should not ally himself with death. Statements given during the therapy session relating to the patient's overt suicidal (or homicidal) plans obviously cannot be treated as a "secret" between two collusive partners. In the previous example of the patient who opened her purse and showed me a small automatic pistol with which she said she was going, that day, to kill herself, two obvious interpretations would be that she obviously wanted me to take the weapon from her, or that she was threatening me. In any event, I told her that she could not leave my office with the gun and insisted that she hand her purse to me. She countered by saying that I had abrogated the basic rule of therapy, namely that she could tell me anything. I pointed out that "anything" did not mean committing suicide and that she must know that I could not be a partner in that kind of enterprise. For

a moment she seemed angered and then relieved; she gave me the gun. The rule is to defuse the potentially lethal situation. To have left her with a loaded gun would also leave her with a latent message.

9. Limitation of one's own practice to a very few highly lethal patients. It is possible to see a fairly large number of moderate and low-rated lethal patients in one's patient load, but one or two *highly* lethal patients seem to be the superhuman limit for most therapists at any given time. Such patients demand a great deal of investment of psychic energy and one must beware of spreading oneself too thin in his or her own professional life.

Working with highly suicidal persons borrows from the goals of crisis intervention: not to take on and ameliorate the individual's entire personality structure and to cure all the neuroses, but simply to keep him or her alive. That is the *sine qua non* of the therapeutic encounter with a suicidal person.

9

Implications for Prevention

and Response

Those readers who are looking under this heading for some simple prescription as to how to treat suicidal persons ("easy steps for little feet") have, I am afraid, missed the main message of this book. It should now be clear that we cannot hope to find a single cause for human phenomena as complex as self-destruction.

It also follows that there is, equally, a contextual implication for the *kind* of research efforts we should pursue. Specifically, we should abandon our use of oversimplified, two-term equations of cause and effect and instead use more applicable research designs employing procedures of path analysis and attention to the multiple variables in developmental changes over time.

I would protest that it is not I who obfuscates the issue; the phenomena of suicides themselves are complicated, and it is only responsible to report them so. Past methodologically oversimplified efforts have not worked because they were not methodologically relevant.

Not unexpectedly, there are also implications in this point of view for therapy with suicidal persons. I shall state a few of them.

The first implication is that I do not believe, in principle, in the individual private practice of suicide prevention. (I know that it is done and often done well, but I am speaking here in terms of a general rule.) And, of course, I am not speaking about one therapist seeing one patient. It is the setting I am talking about. Suicide prevention should optimally be practiced in consultation with a number of colleagues representing various disciplines. Suicide can best be understood in terms of concepts from several points of view. It follows that treatment of a suicidal individual should reflect the learnings from these same several disciplines.

A further implication for therapy, following from the above, is that, optimally, treatment of a suicidal person should be handled by more than one therapist. Here, I obviously have in mind the interdisciplinary Diagnostic Council at the Harvard Psychological Clinic directed by Dr. Henry A. Murray some years ago (roughly between 1930 and 1960). I propose that the treatment of a suicidal person would optimally be done by a *Therapeutic Council*. Such a council would be concerned with the biological, sociological, developmental, philosophical, and cognitive aspects of its patients. It might include a biologically oriented psychiatrist, a psychoanalytically oriented therapist, a sociologist, a logician-philosopher, a marriage and family counselor, and an existential social worker.

It may be that the skills of these several specialties can, on rare occasions, be found in one individual—the rare, so-called Renaissance Man. I believe I have known a few of them in my life: Drs. Henry A. Murray, Avery Weisman, James G. Miller, Franz Alexander. A Renaissance Man nowadays is hard to find. But the concept is that an individual therapist who gives deep interpretations of childhood memories, prescriptions for medications for depression, or a behavior modification regime is, by himself, not enough.

Practically (when working with suicidal persons), we do what we can. We see people in consultation. We make interpretations. We write prescriptions, and so on. We force the concept of suicide into the templates of our own theoretical bias about personality, its vicissitudes, and their remediation. That is not what it ought to be; but we also throw in our energies on the side of life, and that often seems to be lifesaving.

No efforts at remediation or therapy (however benignantly intended) can be effective unless there is some willing participation on the part of the individual who is defined as the patient. One implication of this is that we must now extend our previous definition of suicide to add the phrase (in our description of the suicidal person) ". . . in an ambivalent individual . . ." Granted there are some people who are, for all practical purposes, unambivalent (univalent) about killing themselves—we first hear about these people as coroner's cases—but most living people who are seen in consultation in relation to their "being suicidal" have the deepest ambivalences between wanting (needing) to be dead and yearning for possible intervention or rescue. The rescue often takes the form of improvement or change in one of the major details in the patient's world, such as the wish to be free of cancer, to be loved, and so on. In general, we can assume that a suicidal patient whom we are seeing, however lethally oriented, is deeply ambivalent about the crucial life-and-death issue. Obviously, the therapist should work with the life-directed aspects of the ambivalence (without, of course, being timorous to touch upon the death-oriented elements in that patient).

Having said the above, I do not think it a contradiction to indicate some further implications for individual psychotherapy, if individual psychotherapy is done. (We can assume that it will be.) Our definition of suicide (focusing on the problem-solving aspect of the act) implies that the therapist should try to understand not only the hurt that the patient is feeling but, centrally, the "problem" that the individual is trying to solve. Concomitantly, the therapist needs to appreciate what psychological needs the individual is trying to satisfy. The focus should not be on why suicide has been chosen as the method for solving life's problems, but rather on solving the problems, so that suicide—chosen for whatever reasons—becomes unnecessary (in that the problems are addressed and that the person sees some hope of at least partially satisfying, or redirecting, the urgently felt needs which were central to his suicidal scenario). In part, the treatment of suicide is the satisfaction of the unmet needs. One does this not only in the consultation room but also in the real world. This means that one talks to the significant others, contacts social agencies, and is concerned about practical items such as job, rent, and food. The way to save a suicidal person is to cater to that individual's infantile and realistic idiosyncratic needs. The suicide therapist should, in addition to other roles, act as an existential social worker, a practical person knowledgeable about realistic resources and aware of philosophic issues—a speciality which should be encouraged.

I have said that a clinical rule is to address the frustrated needs in order to decrease the patient's psychological discomfort. One does this task by focusing on the thwarted needs. Questions such as "What is going on?" "Where do you hurt?" and "What would you like to have happen?" can usefully be asked by a therapist helping a suicidal person.

The psychotherapist can focus on feelings, especially such distressing feelings as guilt, shame, fear, anger, thwarted ambition, unrequited love, hopelessness, helplessness, and loneliness. The key is the improvement of the external *and* internal situations just enough to make a difference. This can be accomplished through a variety of methods: ventilation, interpretation, instruction, behavior modification, *and* realistic manipulation of the world outside the consultation room. All this implies—when working with a highly lethal person—a heightened level of therapist-patient interaction during the period of elevated lethality. The therapist needs to work diligently, always giving the suicidal person realistic transfusions of hope until the perturbation intensity subsides enough to reduce the lethality to a tolerable, life-permitting level.

Another implication for individual therapy: The suicidal individual typically has a (transient) tunneling of perception manifested specifically in a narrowing or shrinking of the options for behavior which occur in his mind. The options have often been narrowed to only two: To live a certain specific way (with changes on the part of significant others) *or* to be dead. It follows that the therapist's task is to extend the range of the patient's perceptions, to widen his blinders, to increase the number of choices, including, of course, the number of viable options. I have, on more than one occasion, in the presence of a suicidal patient, written a list of things which might be done, including suicide. All of the items on the list are more or less onerous. But it is precisely in the adjectives (more or less) that lifesaving opportunities lie. The patient is then asked to rank, in order from least to most odious, this list of realistic options—including suicide—and then to discuss the least onerous ones.

The immediate antidote for suicide lies in reduction of perturbation. Suicide is best understood not so much in terms of some sets of nosological boxes (e.g., depression or any of the often sterile labels in *DSM-III*), but rather in terms of two continua of general personality functioning: perturbation and lethality. Everyone is rateable (by oneself or others) on how disturbed or distressed or upset (perturbation) he or she is and, additionally, on how deathfully suicidal (lethality) he or she is.

To say that an individual is "disturbed" and "suicidal" simply indicates that there is an elevation in that individual's perturbation and lethality levels, respectively. Experience has taught us the important fact that it is neither possible nor practical in an individual who is highly lethal and highly perturbed to attempt to deal with the lethality directly, either by moral suasion, confrontatory interpretations, exhortation, or whatever. (It does not work any better in suicide than it does in alcoholism.) The most effective way to reduce elevated lethality is by doing so indirectly; that is, by reducing the elevated perturbation. Reduce the person's anguish, tension, and pain and his level of lethality will concomitantly come down, for it is the elevated perturbation that drives and fuels the elevated lethality.

With a highly lethal suicidal person the main goal is, of course, to reduce the elevated lethality. The most important rule to follow is that *high lethality is reduced by reducing the person's sense of perturbation.* One way to do this is by addressing in a practical way those in-the-world things that can be changed, if ever so slightly. In a sensible manner, the therapist should be involved with such significant others as the patient's spouse, lover, employer, and government agencies. In these contacts the therapist acts as ombudsman for the patient, promoting his or her interests and welfare. The subgoal is to reduce the real-life pressures that are sustaining or increasing the patient's sense of perturbation. To repeat: In order effectively to decrease the individual's lethality, one does what is necessary to decrease the individual's perturbation.

In order to help a highly lethal person, one should involve others and create activity around the person; do what he or she wants done; and, if that cannot be accomplished, at least move in the direction of the desired goals to some substitute goals that approximate those which have been lost. Remind the patient that life is often the choice among undesirable alternatives. The key to well-functioning is often to choose the least awful alternative that is practically attainable.

The intermediate response to potential suicide is to increase awareness of other adjustment processes. The key to intermediate and long-range effectiveness with a suicidal person is to increase the options for action available to the person; in a phrase, to widen the angle of the blinders. We should keep in mind that the suicidal act is an effort to stop unbearable anguish or intolerable pain by the individual's "doing something." Knowing this usually guides us to what treatment should be. In the same sense, the way to save a person's life is by doing something.

The common characteristics of suicide (see Chapter 3) have direct implications for saving lives. Here are some practical measures for helping highly suicidal persons, following the previously presented outline:

1. Stimulus (unbearable pain): *Reduce the pain.*
2. Stressor (frustrated needs): *Fill the frustrated needs.*
3. Purpose (to seek a solution): *Provide a viable answer.*
4. Goal (cessation of consciousness): *Indicate alternatives.*
5. Emotion (hopelessness-helplessness): *Give transfusions of hope.*

6. Internal attitude (ambivalence): *Play for time.*
7. Cognitive state (constriction): *Increase the options.*
8. Interpersonal act (communication of intention): *Listen to the cry, involve others.*
9. Action (egression): *Block the exit.*
10. Consistency (with life-long patterns): *Invoke previous positive patterns of successful coping.*

An example may be clarifying: Given that the omnipresent action in committed suicide is to leave the scene (egression), then it follows that, when possible, the means of exit should be blocked. A practical application of this view is to "get the gun" in a suicidal situation where it is known that the individual intends to shoot himself and has a weapon. I have, admittedly on rare occasions, made an arrangement with a patient for him or her (and there have been instances of both) to bring the gun (in a bag or box) into the office for me to put in a safe place (including the local police station). Those guns were never reclaimed. The explosive situation had been defused and the person no longer had the need for a suicidal weapon.

Finally, I wish to say a few words about locus of action; that is, where (or between what) the suicidal drama is supposed to take place. Briefly: The early Christians, Saint Augustine (354–430) and Saint Thomas Aquinas (1225–1274), made suicide a crime and a sin; the site of the fault was in man's "heart," his soul. To jump a good bit, the French philosopher Jean Jacques Rousseau (1712–1778) emphasized the natural state of man and thereby transferred the blame from man to society, making man generally good (and innocent) and asserting that it is society that makes him bad. The disputation as to the locus of blame, whether in man or in society, is a major theme that dominates the history of suicidal thought. David Hume (1711–1776) was one of the first Western philosophers to discuss the topic in the absence of the concept of sin. His famous essay "On Suicide" (published posthumously in 1777) refuted the view that suicide is either a sin or a crime by arguing that suicide is not a transgression of our duties toward God or State. ("If it be no crime in me to divert the Nile or

Danube from its course, were I able to effect such purposes, where then is the crime in turning a few ounces of blood from their natural channel?") In the twentieth century, the two great suicidological theorists played rather different roles: Durkheim focused on society's inimical effects on the individual (without asserting that man was innately innocent), while Freud—eschewing the notions of either sin or crime—gave suicide back to man but put the locus of action in man's unconscious mind, for which man could hardly be blamed.

What are the implications of the view propounded in this volume in relation to the locus of action? It is certainly one of less unity than that of Rousseau, Hume, Durkheim, or Freud. Like them, it does not talk of crime or sin in relation to suicide, but it implies that the locus of action is in the individual—in *both* his conscious *and* unconscious mind—*and*—as he lives *within* his social surround—*with* his significant others, *in* his political and social times. Murray and Miller especially would not permit us to think of an individual not bathed in an environment, or of an organism that was not made up of smaller constituent systems behaving in the context of larger surrounding ones.

It is obvious that it is an *individual* who commits suicide, so that the locus of action can be said to be in his/her mind. (There are unconscious components in probably every conscious movement of the mind and each suicide contains both.) Furthermore, each mind interacts with other persons and is mightily influenced by them, and by social mores, folkways, fads, cults, injunctions, advertisements, importunings, and even transient events. Inasmuch as each suicide is a socially and interpersonally influenced intrapsychic event, efforts at individual prevention of a suicidal act are most effectively directed at transmuting the course of the mind and aided by making beneficent changes in the surroundings, where these changes are practical and can be made quickly.

The therapeutic message of this book is not to eschew the ordinary, common-sense gambits of response simply on account of their direct relationship to the nature of suicide itself. Of course, one should use *all* measures that work (for the therapist and the patient). These include support, psychodynamic interpretation, medication, the involvement of others including social agencies, and so on—all of which serve directly or indirectly to mollify one or more of the common characteristics of suicide.

In order to come back from a suicidal abyss and to stay on relatively firm ground, one needs to employ adjustment processes not prominent in one's armamentarium of techniques. In this regard I have a rather catholic view: I certainly embrace the suicide prevention centers of this country—you would hardly expect me to do otherwise; I endorse psychotherapy, counseling, outreach groups, and agencies. I have become tolerant of behavior modification techniques and role modeling—anything that increases the person's awareness of choosing between living with a variety of miseries (and possible unhappinesses) and the ambivalently viewed awful escape.

Of course, the actual practice of suicide prevention in the trenches is often not as clean as I have described it, for in dealing with the walking wounded and the desperately stricken, the situation—to quote from a personal communication of Robert E. Litman, perhaps the most experienced clinical suicidologist in the country—is often one of working "in the smoke and heat and hassle of everyday living, sometimes ourselves among the wounded, and in doubt of what is feasible, not to say what is optimal. We need to be reminded that to work in suicide prevention is risky and dangerous and there are casualties and that is to be expected." To which, without feeling at all inconsistent in my own mind, I can fully say, "Amen."

PART FOUR

FOLLOW-UP

10

Postvention:

The Care of the Bereaved

Grief and mourning are not diseases, but their deleterious and inimical effects can often be as serious as though they were. The recently bereaved person is typically bereft and disorganized. Longstanding habit patterns of intimate interpersonal response are irreversibly severed. There is a concomitant gale of strong feelings, usually including abandonment and despair, sometimes touching upon guilt and anger, and almost always involving a sense of crushing emptiness and loss. In light of these psychological realities it comes as no surprise that individuals who are acutely bereaved constitute a population at risk (Kraus and Lilienfeld 1959, Parkes 1964, 1970, 1971, 1972, Parkes and Fitzgerald 1969, Rees and Lutkins 1967, Stein and Susser 1969, Young, et al. 1963).

Excluding Freud's (1917) indispensable paper, "Mourning and melancholia," much of the important work on this topic has been done only since 1944 (Bowlby 1961, Caplan 1964, Lifton 1969, Lindemann 1944, Shneidman 1974, Silverman 1972, Weisman 1972). In general, these studies point out that grief and mourning may have serious physical and psychological concomitants (in the way of heightened morbidity and even a greater risk of death), and they explicate some of the dimensions of bereavement as well as ways of helping the bereaved.

This chapter will not be an attempt to replow the ground so fertilely turned by others, especially Parkes (1972) in his chapter "Helping the bereaved" in his book *Bereavement* in which he discusses the role of the funeral director, the church, the family doctor, and self-help organizations, among others. Instead, the discussion will be limited to what I know best, namely, my own work with bereaved persons.

A specific example will be useful at the outset. Here are some excepts from a taped session with a young adult widower whom I had seen for several months after his wife died. She was a university student (whom I came to know in a course on death and suicide that I taught). She died of scleroderma. This session is three years after her death.

DR. S.: Now to start with, your relationship with Edith was unusual in that you knew she was ill from the beginning.

MR. H.: That's correct, I first met her ten years ago, she was 18. It was just after her illness had been diagnosed and her parents, if I remember correctly, told me about it when they saw that we were becoming serious, after we had been courting for some time. And I really didn't know exactly what the disease was, I mean as far as life span was concerned. I wonder why I didn't try to find out more. Maybe I was afraid; I don't know. I knew her life would be shortened, but I don't think I really allowed myself to think about it or to find out exactly what it was. It was terminal about eight years after. I have thought about it, because it seems to me strange of my not pursuing it. She was the first girl I guess I really had a good meaningful relationship with, and I think I might have been very frightened to find out the truth. But I didn't want to know . . . The more I think of it the more I really realize I think I blocked a tremendous amount out.

Dr. S.: Her death was not totally unexpected to you. When she came into the hospital, she was struggling and you knew she was failing. How were you told that she was dead, and then what happened?

Mr. H.: The doctor that had been attending her told me when I came in that morning to see her, and he brought me aside. He took me somewhere. I think he gave me a tranquilizer. I was extremely impressed with him. I was probably in shock, but I remember the clear thing I did feel was some sense of relief that I don't have to wait any longer. That incredible waiting that I realized I had been going through was suddenly over. But then there was this, I don't know . . . I went home alone from the hospital, alone, really alone. I really don't recall what happened the rest of the day. I think that a good friend of ours stayed with me that night. I was feeling very freaked out. I must have gone around for maybe a week or so before I really began to feel the loneliness and her loss. I finally stopped running around taking care of everybody, and really felt the mourning, really felt her loss. It was a feeling inside of having an incredible emptiness. I felt sort of at a loss, kind of wondering how my life was going to continue. How it possibly could go on. Everything sort of like disintegrated. Sort of like a piece of me just was kind of lost.

Dr. S.: What helped you the most?

Mr. H.: I don't know that there's any one thing that helped me the most. Perhaps Susan probably has helped a lot. Even though it was after a year, she forced me to the issue of dealing with Edith, really moving her out of the apartment, and started showing me things. About six months after Edith died, I went around and grabbed everything that had anything to do with her and put them in boxes and shoved them in the closets; but still Edith was in the closet. She was still there. We moved things around the apartment to make it different. I started doing some of those things, but she just kept saying that she really felt it wasn't her place, that it was still Edith's. She wanted it to be hers. So she did force me a great deal.

Dr. S.: Did you get rid of all her things?

Mr. H.: Oh, no. As a matter of fact we have some pottery that Edith had made that we use, that I had never thought of using before.

Dr. S.: Do you sleep in the same bed that you had before?

Mr. H.: Yes, but I've moved the bed in the room and I sleep on the other side of the bed. I've told Susan that the bed used to be in a different location and I never made anything of it. I did this about six months after Edith died, before I met Susan. I did a few things, painted one of the walls, and a few things like this, rearranged the furniture. But there was still the other thing. It was very hard for me to commit myself to Susan. This was a big problem. This is over two years now. We've been married for several months and had been going together for two years. I took all that time to make a commitment.

Dr. S.: Why was that?

Mr. H.: I don't know. I searched in myself a lot for what it was. And I wasn't really able to grab it. I'm sure that part was really there. A part of it was the holding on. I'm sure that was also a large part of it. I don't think it was until Susan and I were married that we went through all the boxes in the closets, took all the stuff and decided either to throw it away or use it, to get it out of the closet, literally and figuratively.

Dr. S.: Did you make any inquiries as to Susan's state of health?

Mr. H.: Susan is very healthy. I don't recall. I might have asked her, but I'm conscious of the fact that I certainly noticed her health. She's also younger than I am by a few years, and I thought of that. You know what that means. I think part of that means that I don't want to live longer. I don't want her to die before I do. I'm sure that's there. I'd be surprised if it weren't.

Dr. S.: I knew Edith and then I knew you. How did that work out?

Mr. H.: Well, I think I came to you; I'm not sure if it was because you knew her. I think that was part of it, because you did know her and you knew me through her. But I think it was because of you yourself. I felt you were the type of person who could help me.

Dr. S.: In what way?

Mr. H.: I can't recall, whatever, but I think that some of the things that you said at the time helped me, helped to alleviate my desperation that I felt. A few times I did come in, I was feeling pretty desperate. Completely kind of lost and floundering. But that worked out . . .

PURPOSE OF POSTVENTION

I prefer to think of the work with the bereaved person as a process that I have called *postvention:* those appropriate and helpful acts that come *after* the dire event itself (Shneidman 1970, 1974). The reader will recognize prevention, intervention, and postvention as roughly synonymous with the traditional health concepts of primary, secondary, and tertiary prevention, or with the concepts of immunization, treatment, and rehabilitation. Lindemann has referred to "preventive intervention" (Lindemann and Vaughn 1972). It would be simpler to speak of postvention.

As I have described in *Deaths of Man* (Shneidman 1974) postvention consists of those activities that serve to reduce the aftereffects of a traumatic event in the lives of the survivors. Its purpose is to help survivors live longer, more productively, and less stressfully than they are likely to do otherwise. I will attempt to summarize my observations in the following paragraphs.

Reactions of Survivor Victims

It is obvious that some deaths are more stigmatizing or traumatic than others: death by murder, by the negligence of oneself or some other person, or by suicide. Survivor victims of such deaths are invaded by an unhealthy complex of disturbing emotions: shame, guilt, hatred, perplexity. They are obsessed with thoughts about the death, seeking reasons, casting blame, and often punishing themselves.

The investigations of widows by Parkes (1972) are most

illuminating. The principal finding of his studies is that independent of her age, a woman who has lost a husband recently is more likely to die (from alcoholism, malnutrition, or a variety of disorders related to neglect of self, disregard of a prescribed medical regimen or commonsense precautions, or even a seemingly unconscious boredom with life), or to be physically ill, or emotionally disturbed than nonwidowed women. The findings seem to imply that grief is itself a dire process, almost akin to a disease, and that there are subtle factors at work that can take a heavy toll unless they are treated and controlled.

These striking results had been intuitively known long before they were empirically demonstrated. The efforts of Lindemann (1944), Caplan (1964), and Silverman (1972) to aid survivors of "heavy deaths" were postventions based on the premise of heightened risk in bereaved persons. Lindemann's work, which led to his formulations of acute grief and crisis intervention, began with his treatment of the survivors of the tragic Coconut Grove nightclub fire in Boston in 1942, in which 499 people died. Silverman's projects, under the direction of Caplan, have centered around a widow-to-widow program. These efforts bear obvious similarities with the programs of "befriending" practiced by the Samaritans, an organization founded by the Reverend Chad Varah (1966) and most active in Great Britain.

Death a "Disaster"

A case can be made for viewing the sudden death of a loved one as a *disaster* and, using the verbal bridge provided by that concept, learning from the professional literature on conventionally recognized disasters—those sudden, unexpected events, such as earthquakes and large-scale explosions, that cause a large number of deaths and have widespread effects. Wolfenstein (1957) has described a "disaster syndrome": a "combination of emotional dullness, unresponsiveness to outer stimulation and inhibition of activity. The individual who has just undergone disaster is apt to suffer from at least a transitory sense of worthlessness; his usual capacity for self-love becomes impaired" (p. 77).

A similar psychological contraction is seen in the initial shock reaction to catastrophic news—death, failure, disclosure, disgrace, the keenest personal loss. Studies of a disastrous ship sinking by Friedman and Lum (1957) and of the effects of a tornado by Wallace (1956) both describe an initial psychic shock followed by motor retardation, flattening of affect, somnolence, amnesia, and suggestibility. There is marked increase in dependency needs with regressive behavior and traumatic loss of feelings of identity and, overall, a kind of "affective anesthesia." There is an unhealthy docility, a cowed and subdued reaction. One is reminded of Lifton's (1969) description of "psychic closing off" and "psychic numbing" among the Hibakusha, survivors of the atomic bomb dropped on Hiroshima:

Very quickly—sometimes within minutes or even seconds—Hibakusha began to undergo a process of "psychic closing off"; that is, they simply ceased to feel. They had a clear sense of what was happening around them, but their emotional reactions were unconsciously turned off. Others' immersion in larger responsibilities was accompanied by a greater form of closing off which might be termed "psychic numbing." [pp. 31–32]

POSTVENTION: AN ONGOING THERAPY

Postventive efforts are not limited to this initial stage of shock; they are more often directed to the longer haul, the day-to-day living with grief over a year or more following the first shock of loss. Typically, postvention extends over months during that critical first year, and it shares many of the characteristics of psychotherapy: talk, abreaction, interpretation, reassurance, direction, and even gentle confrontation. It provides an arena for the expression of guarded emotions, especially such negative affective states as anger, shame, and guilt. It puts a measure of stability into the grieving person's life and provides an interpersonal relationship with the therapist that can be genuine, in that honest feelings need not be suppressed or dissembled.

Parkes (1970) distinguishes four phases in the bereavement process: numbness, yearning/protest, disorganization, and reorganization—but in general we ought to view "stages" of recovery from death (and especially we need to view the so-called stages of the dying process) with a liberal and flexible mind.

Characteristics of the Postventive Session

In order to appreciate the nature of postvention, it is necessary to touch upon some important characteristics of the interaction between the bereaved victim and the therapist,[1] specifically the difference between a *conversation* (or "ordinary talk") and a *professional exchange*—recognizing that postventive efforts should be of the latter sort. This distinction is exceptionally elementary, but because this understanding is at the very heart of effective postventive work, these rudimentary ideas need to be made explicit. The differences between the two can be charted in the form of some contrasts between ordinary talk (e.g., "I'm so sorry to hear about the death." "Please accept my most sincere condolences." "Is there anything I can do?"), and a professional exchange. See Table 10–1.

Another retrospective example may be useful. Late one afternoon a beautiful 19-year-old girl was stabbed to death by an apparent would-be rapist in a government building. Within an hour her parents were shattered by the news given to them by two rather young, well-meaning, but inexperienced policemen. The victim was the couple's only child. Their immediate reactions

---

[1]The person who systematically attempts to help the bereaved individual is either a therapist or is acting in the role of a therapist. He cannot escape this role. This is not to say that many others—relatives, dear friends, organization (e.g., church) members, neighbors—do not play important, perhaps the most important, roles.

TABLE 10–1.

Conversation	Professional Exchange
1. Content	
Substantive content, that is, the talk is primarily about things, events, dates—the surface of the world.	Affective (emotional) content, that is, the exchange focuses (not constantly but occasionally) on the feelings and the emotional tone of the patient, sometimes minimizing the "facts."
2. Level	
Manifest level, that is, conversation focuses on what is said, the actual words that are uttered, the facts that are stated.	Latent level, that is, the professional person listens for what is "between the lines," below the surface, what is implied, not expressed, or only unconsciously present.
3. Meanings	
Conscious meanings, that is, in ordinary speech we deal with the other person as though what was said was meant and as though the person were "a rational man" and as though he "knows his own mind."	Unconscious meanings, that is, there is a whole flow of the mind that is not immediately available at any given moment to the person, and there are unconscious meanings and latent intentions in human exchanges. We listen for double entendre, puns, hidden meanings, latent implications, and so on.
4. Abstraction	
Phenotypic abstraction, that is, there is concern with the ordinary interesting details of life, where no set of details necessarily bears any relationship to any other set.	Genotypic abstraction, that is, the therapist is always looking for congruencies, similarities, commonalities, *generalizations* about the patient's psychological life. These constitute the understanding of the therapist (and are the reservoir of his possible interpretations to the patient).
5. Role	
Social role, that is, in a conversation or ordinary discourse people are coequals (like neighbors or friends) or depend on the prestige of age, rank, status, and so on, but essentially the relationship is between two people who have equal right to display themselves.	Transference, that is, a professional exchange that is not talk between two coequals. Rather it is a very special kind of exchange between one person who wishes help (and tacitly agrees to play the patient's role) and another person who agrees to proffer help (and thus is cast in the role of physician, priest, father, magician, witch doctor, helper). Much of what is effective in the exchange is the patient's "transference" onto the therapist. Some of the effectiveness of the therapeutic exchange lies in the power of the "self-fulfilling prophecy."

were shock, disbelief, overwhelming grief, and mounting rage, most of it directed at the agency where the murder had occurred.

A few days later, right after the funeral, they were in the office of a high official who was attempting to tender his condolences when the mother said in an anguished tone: "There is nothing you can do!" To which, with good presence of mind, he answered that while it was true that the girl could not be brought back to life, there was something that could be done. Whether he knew the term or not, it was postvention that he had in mind. He brought them, personally, to my office.

I began seeing the parents, usually together, sometimes separately. The principal psychological feature was the mother's anger. I permitted her to voice her grief and to vent her rage (sometimes at me), while I retained the role of the voice of reason: empathizing with the parents' state, recognizing the legitimacy of their feelings when I could, but not agreeing when in good conscience I could not agree. I felt that I was truly their friend, and I believed that they felt so too. I had insisted that each of them see a physician for a physical examination. A few months after the brutal murder, the mother developed serious symptoms that required major surgery, from which she made a good recovery. The situation raises the intriguing (and unanswerable) question in my mind whether or not that organic flurry would have occurred if she had not suffered the shock of her daughter's death (Rahe 1972). In the year following her daughter's death the mother had two extended hospitalizations. Several months after the tragedy the parents seemed to be in rather good shape, physically and emotionally, everything considered. They still had low-level grief and no doubt always will. Here is an edited verbatim portion of a session exactly one year after the death.

DR. S.: Is today a year?

MRS. A.: Exactly one year. And just about this time when she was killed . . .

DR. S.: Where are you both today? Can you sketch the course of your grief?

MRS. A.: Well, at first it was extremely intense. It was

actually a physical pain. For a couple of months I went around
and it hurt—it actually hurt in here. And I felt like I was carrying
the world on my shoulders and inside of me.

MR. A.: I don't think the pain was physical, it was . . .

MRS. A.: No, it wasn't. I mean I felt it physically, but it was
a mental pain too.

MR. A.: There are times when the pain is still there. It's hard
to describe it, it's just there, feeling of pain. I guess it's part of
sorrow. We had a very bad day yesterday, much more so than
today.

MRS. A.: You can't just cut off nineteen years in one day. It
was like losing an arm or a leg or a head or something. Or a head,
because you can do without an arm, and you learn to do, in a
way, without a daughter. It sounds trite when you say it that
way.

MR. A.: I think one of the things that has happened in the
past year is that, as far as I'm concerned, I don't think I've
discussed it too much, but I'm more capable of facing the
situation, of thinking about it. I used to try to put it out of my
mind. For a while there, the hardest thing I had to do was look at
her picture.

DR. S.: Do you still have that in your house, do you have it
displayed?

MRS. A.: Yeah.

MR. A.: We have one in our bedroom on the bureau. It stays
there all the time, but, uh, I don't get a shock anymore when I
look at her picture.

MRS. A.: I still turn around to look when I see blonde hair
bobbing up and down and I still turn to look, and then I realize
how stupid it is. She couldn't look like that anymore. A little girl
lives down the street, that I sometimes see, and she walks like she
walked. And it still plays tricks, I still look to see if it's her. And
sometimes the other children say or do something and it's always
in the back of our minds, always in the back of my mind anyway.
I think these meetings with you have been very good for us,
because there was someone we could talk to. And someone that
could show—in a way—take a different viewpoint. How can we

see beyond our noses when we're so griefstricken and, oh, I don't know.

Mr. A.: That's what I was trying to bring out a while ago, that is that you've helped us, me, in facing the truth.

Dr. S.: How was that done?

Mr. A.: I don't know; just the fact that I was discussing rather freely and maybe . . .

Mrs. A.: And we thought we could tell you anything and you wouldn't be angry or, I don't know exactly how to say it, but I always felt we could talk to you and we could tell you exactly what we thought and not face any recriminations or anything like that.

Dr. S.: Speaking of anger and recriminations, there was a time—isn't this so—that you were just terribly angry?

Mrs. A.: Yes.

Dr. S.: What has happened to that anger?

Mrs. A.: It's dissipated. At first, in the beginning, I was ready to kill everybody and anybody.

Dr. S.: Including me.

Mrs. A.: Including you because you represented the government to us.

Mr. A.: No, really?

Mrs. A.: Yes, in a way he did because I blamed the government for her death. I still feel that somebody here helped. Somebody here helped, and he must know. Whoever it is; who helped, did his part in getting her killed. By not patrolling the building, by not doing—a sin of omission is just as big as a big sin of commission. I mean they knew darn well that the building was not safe.

Dr. S.: So there are still certainly reservoirs of anger and blame.

Mrs. A.: At the time I wanted the murderer caught and killed. Now I would just like him stopped, but I don't want him killed. Will that bring her back? But people were afraid of us. They were afraid to talk to us.

Mr. A.: Some still are.

Mrs. A.: Some of them still are because they didn't know

what to say. It was a difficult thing; it's a difficult thing for most people to find words of sympathy. What do you tell parents whose daughter is killed like that? Another thing that in a way you taught me is to take one day at a time.

DR. S.: How did I teach you that?

MRS. A.: I don't know how, but that's what I've been doing, taking one day at a time. You were able really to show us in a proper perspective. That's one of the things you did; you were always the one to look at things in a straight manner. How could we when we were so prejudiced about anything—I mean about what happened to her. We are so close to the forest, we can't see the trees.

MR. A.: I think you've also managed to curtail her anger in general to a certain extent. Because she was mad at the whole world at the time—any reason. She'd get mad, get ready to prosecute her soup.

DR. S.: Have there been some changes in your general character?

MRS. A.: I think so, I've probably been a little bit more tolerant.

DR. S.: What do you think will happen now in the next year or two?

MRS. A.: We get more used to it. I suppose. He will become more resigned to it; that she isn't here, she won't come back, and that going to the cemetery won't hurt so much. But I try not to make this a special day because what's to celebrate? But it is in a way a special day.

DR. S.: It is an occasion to memorialize.

MRS. A.: It was sad to come home last night and find my husband was crying.

MR. A.: It was just a defense mechanism. I was crying to keep you from crying, so you would feel sorry for me for a change.

MRS. A.: I suppose in a way it made me less intolerant of other people. But what a price to have to pay. What a pity. All those years. There is something so final now. I used to feel that there was continuity, that she would have children and in a way live on. My husband is the last of his line. The last male of his line. The last one of his family.

MR. A.: It's the end of the name anyway.

DR. S.: There is a sense of being cut off from the future, isn't there?

MR. A.: I imagine there is going to be a lot of hurt when we have to attend weddings or births.

MRS. A.: Somehow it is very hard to think that when you die, that's the end. But it's not as bad as I used to be afraid of death. I am no longer afraid of death personally. It's no longer such a terrible thing. It was terrible, I suppose, because it was unknown. Another time I would have been afraid when I went into the hospital. I was so unafraid that I believed the doctor when he told me before the operation that it wasn't going to hurt. How naive can you be? I wanted to believe it. I don't think, I mean, I'm sure, I couldn't have gone through this past year without my husband.

DR. S.: I think you have helped each other in a marvelous way.

MRS. A.: I'm really sure that I could never have come through it.

MR. A.: Except for one time when she almost walked out on me.

MRS. A.: That's different. That didn't count. To get through the impossible days and even longer nights. We weren't perfect, and she was not perfect. Of course, no one will ever bring up any of her faults now.

DR. S.: That's so. One doesn't speak ill of the dead.

MRS. A.: No. Everybody, when they do talk about her, glosses over any of her faults. No one wants to talk about them. I don't know of anyone who has voluntarily brought up her name but you. Why is there such a taboo? It's been a whole year.

DR. S.: Do you feel more than a year older?

MR. A.: Very much. We were discussing this not too long ago, and we both felt we had missed out on middle age, that we went from youth to old people.

DR. S.: Really. You feel that way?

Mrs. A.: Most of the time I feel so old, and I caught myself talking to my brother and I said when we were young, and he said, "Hey, you are talking about a couple of years ago."

Dr. S.: Well, what we need to work on is to bring back the sense of youthful middle age.

Mrs. A.: I don't think that will ever come back. I always felt inside that I was about 19 or 20 and now I feel 60 years old. I said we could talk to you and tell you anything. You have taught us a great deal, and not to worry about recriminations.

Mr. A.: There were times when I felt that you were trying to make her mad at you.

Dr. S.: I never did that. I have always liked you.

Mrs. A.: I always felt that you liked me. It was that feeling. I remember the look on your face when I showed you her picture. I will never forget it.

Dr. S.: I can't describe what went through me.

Mrs. A.: You showed it. It was like hitting you, and you absolutely recoiled as though I had hit you. I miss you when I don't see you.

Dr. S.: How often do you think we ought to meet now? Should we make the next meeting in a month?

Mr. A.: They've been almost about a month apart.

Mrs. A.: I would hate to think about our meetings finishing, ending.

Principles of Postvention

What can be noted in this exchange are some general principles of postventive work:

1. In working with survivor victims of abrasive death, it is best to begin as soon as possible after the tragedy, within the first 72 hours if that can be managed.
2. Remarkably little resistance is met from the survivors; most are either willing or eager to have the opportunity to talk to a professionally oriented person.

3. Negative emotions about the decedent or about the death itself—irritation, anger, envy, shame, guilt, and so on—need to be explored, but not at the very beginning.
4. The postvener should play the important role of reality tester. He is not so much the echo of conscience as the quiet voice of reason.
5. Medical evaluation of the survivors is crucial. One should be constantly alert for possible decline in physical health and in overall mental well-being.
6. Needless to say, pollyannish optimism or banal platitudes should be avoided—this statement being a good example.
7. Grief work takes a while—from several months (about a year) to the end of the life, but certainly more than three months or six sessions.
8. A comprehensive program of health care on the part of a benign and enlightened community (or a first-rate hospital) should include preventive, interventive, and *postventive* elements.

REFERENCES

Bowlby, J. (1961). Processes of mourning. *International Journal of Psycho-Analysis* 42:317–340.

Caplan, G. (1964). *Principles of Preventive Psychiatry*. New York: Basic Books.

Freud, S. (1957). Mourning and melancholia. *Standard Edition* 14:243–258.

Friedman, P., and Lum, L. (1957). Some psychiatric notes on the *Andrea Doria* disaster. *American Journal of Psychiatry* 114:426–432.

Kraus, A., and Lilienfeld, A. (1959). Some epidemiologic aspects of the high mortality rate in the young widowed group. *Journal of Chronic Diseases* 10:207–217.

Lifton, R. (1969). *Death in Life: Survivors of Hiroshima*. New York: Vintage.

Lindemann, E. (1944). Symptomatology and management of acute grief. *American Journal of Psychiatry* 101:141–148.

Lindemann, E., Vaughn, W. T., and McGinnis, M. (1972). Preventive intervention in a four-year-old child whose father committed suicide. In *Survivors of Suicide,* ed. A. Cain, pp. 70–92. Springfield, IL: Charles C Thomas.

Parkes, C. (1964). Bereavement and mental illness. *British Journal of Medical Psychology* 38:1–26.

——— (1970). The first year of bereavement. *Psychiatry* 33:442–467.

——— (1971). Psychosocial transitions: a field for study. *Social Science Medicine* 5:101–115.

——— (1972). *Bereavement.* New York: International Universities Press.

Parkes, C., and Fitzgerald, R. (1969). Broken heart: a statistical study of increased mortality among widowers. *British Medical Journal* 1:740–743.

Rahe, R. H. (1972). Subjects' recent life changes and their near-future illness reports. *Annual of Clinical Research* 4:250–265.

Rees, W., and Lutkins, S. (1967). Mortality of bereavement. *British Medical Journal* 4:13–16.

Shneidman, E. S. (1964). Suicide, sleep and death. *Journal of Consulting Psychology* 28:95–106.

——— (1970). Recent developments in suicide prevention. In *The Psychology of Suicide,* ed. E. S. Shneidman, N. L. Farberow, and R. E. Litman, pp. 145–155. New York: Science House.

——— (1974). *Deaths of Man.* New York: Penguin.

Silverman, P. (1972). Intervention with the widow of a suicide. In *Survivors of Suicide,* ed. A. Cain, pp. 186–214. Springfield, IL: Charles C Thomas.

Stein, Z., and Susser, M. (1969). Widowhood and mental illness. *British Journal of Preventive Social Medicine* 5:106–110.

Varah, C. (1966). *The Samaritans.* New York: Macmillan.

Wallace, A. (1956). *Tornado in Westchester: An Exploratory Study of Individual and Community Behavior in an Extreme Situation.* Washington, DC: National Research Council.

Weisman, A. D. (1972). *On Dying and Denying.* New York: Behavioral Publications.

Wolfenstein, M. (1957). *Disaster: A Psychological Essay.* New York: Macmillan.

Young, M., Benjamin, B., and Wallis, C. (1963). The mortality of widowers. *Lancet* 2:454–456.

11

The Psychological Autopsy

It is probably best to begin by defining a psychological autopsy and its purposes, then to discuss some related theoretical background and ways of actually performing psychological autopsies. The words *psychological autopsy* themselves tell us that the procedure has to do with clarifying the nature of a death and that it focuses on the psychological aspects of the death. Two ideas, important to understanding the psychological autopsy, need to be discussed. The first is what I have called the NASH classification of deaths; the second is the idea of *equivocal* deaths.

From the beginning of this century (and with roots that can be clearly traced back to Elizabethan times), the certification and recordkeeping relating to deaths have implied that there are four *modes* of death. It needs to be said right away that the four modes of death have to be distinguished from the many *causes* of death listed in the current *International Classification of Diseases and Causes of Death* (World Health Organization 1957, National Center for Health Statistics 1967). The four modes of death are natural, accidental, suicide, and homicide; the initial letters of each make up the acronym NASH. Thus, to speak of the NASH classification of death is to refer to these four traditional modes in which death is currently reported. Contemporary death certificates have a category which reads "Accident, suicide, homicide, or undetermined"; if none of these is checked, then a "natural" mode of death, as occurs in most cases, is implied.[1]

It should be apparent that the cause of death stated on the certificate does not necessarily carry with it information as to the specific mode of death. For example, asphyxiation due to drowning in a swimming pool does not automatically communicate whether the decedent struggled and drowned (accident), entered the pool with the intention of drowning himself (suicide), or was held under water until he was drowned (homicide).

It so happens that a considerable number of deaths—the estimate is between 5 and 20 percent of all deaths that need to be certified—are not clear as to the correct or appropriate mode. These unclear or uncertain deaths are called *equivocal* deaths. The ambiguity is usually between the modes of suicide or accident, although uncertainty can exist between any two or more of the four modes.

The main function of the psychological autopsy is to clarify an equivocal death and to arrive at the correct or accurate mode of that death. In essence, the psychological autopsy is nothing less than a thorough retrospective investigation of the *intention* of the decedent—that is, the decedent's intention relating to his being dead—where the information is obtained by interviewing individuals who knew the decedent's actions, behavior, and character well enough to report on them.

Drug-related deaths can be among the most equivocal as to the mode of death. Proper certification often necessitates knowledge of the victim over and beyond standard toxicological information, including such questions as what dosage was taken (related to the exact time of death and the time at which autopsy blood and tissue samples were taken); the decedent's weight and build; the decedent's long-term drug habits and known toler-

---

[1]See U.S. Standard Certificate of Death, Figure 11-1 (p. 189).

ances; the possible synergistics of other ingested materials, notably alcohol, or the effects of certain combinations like hydromorphone (Dilaudid) and Methedrine; and the role of lethal action of drug overdoses, for example, morphine sulfate (morphine) as opposed to the quicker acting diacetyl morphine (heroin).

HISTORICAL BACKGROUND

In 1662 John Graunt, a London tradesman, published a small book of observations on the bills of mortality that was to have great social and medical significance. By this time the weekly bills were consolidated at the end of each year, and a general bill for the year was published. Graunt separated the various bits of information contained in these annual bills and organized them into tables. When the available data on deaths were believed accurate, Graunt then focused on individual causes of death. He next turned to the subject of population estimation. Finally he constructed a mortality table, the first attempt to organize data in this manner. Of greatest significance was his success in demonstrating the regularities that can be found in medical and social phenomena when one is dealing with large numbers. Thus, John Graunt demonstrated how the bills of mortality could be used to the advantage of both the physician and government (Kargon 1963).

In 1741, the science of statistics came into existence with the work of a Prussian clergyman, Johann Süssmilch, who made a systematic attempt to correlate political arithmetic, or what we now call vital statistics. From this study came what was subsequently termed the "laws of large numbers," which permitted extended use of the bills of mortality to supply important data in Europe as well as in the American colonies. Cassedy (1969) says that Süssmilch's "exhaustive analysis of vital data from church registers . . . became the ultimate scientific demonstration of the regularity of God's demographic laws" (p. 110).

For many years no provisions existed anywhere in the American colonies for anything comparable to the London bills of mortality (Cassedy 1969). At first there was no necessity for detailed records since communities were small, but something better than hearsay or fading memories was needed as towns grew larger. The birth of newspapers in the British sections of America, about the year 1700, provided a means of remedying this situation. Some editors went to the trouble of obtaining information from local church and town records. They accumulated long lists to which summaries were added, which together were loosely called "bills of mortality." Issued in a variety of publications, the bills became the earliest systematized American death certificates.

Meanwhile, back in England, "the London Bills of Mortality remained among the eternal verities for Englishmen" (Cassedy 1969, p. 118). Londoners were sure to find the bills on sale in each parish each week. Bills with lists of cases of various diseases printed on the back brought twice the price of the regular bills. The American colonists had relatives or friends send copies to them: "Just as John Graunt had found the English doing, the early Americans used the bills as grist for conversation if for nothing else" (Cassedy 1969, p. 118). Few in the colonies even knew of Graunt's statistical applications to the bills of mortality for years after his book was published. Not until William Douglass commented upon statistical method in his history of the British colonies in North America, published in 1751, did the colonists begin to make use of Graunt's methods.

The fact that no colonial bills were published during the seventeenth century may be attributed to printing priorities and especially to lack of legislative requirements. Though a printing press had begun operation in Cambridge, Massachusetts, in 1638, the next half century saw the introduction of only four more. These few presses were generally kept running at capacity turning out government documents. Though the government of each colony required the registration of all vital statistics, none of them made any provision for the information to be published.

Thus the publication of anything resembling the London bills was left to private enterprise. Despite the spread of colonial newspapers and the existence of a few church bills of mortality, British publications remained the colonists' best sources of vital statistical information (Cassedy 1969).

The use of such nonstandardized death records continued into the nineteenth century. Recognition of the need for informed medicolegal investigation in England led to a series of reforms aimed at improving the quality of death registration. In 1836 Parliament enacted a bill requiring the recording of all deaths. Under the terms of this act, notification of the coroner was not required unless the cause of death was one included in a special category. This system of death certification and registration was to ensure that those special deaths that came under the coroner's jurisdiction were in fact reported. The new certification system was designed to utilize the data on causes of death for statistical purposes as well as to prevent criminal practices. The medical explanation of the death was the essential information required for statistical determination. A curious aspect of the law, however, was that doctors were specifically enjoined to include no information on the mode of death on the death certificate.

The English 1836 registration act was amended in 1874 to require that personal information on the death be submitted to the registrar of the district within five days of its occurrence by the nearest relative of the deceased who was present at the death or in attendance during the last illness. A fine was to be levied for noncompliance. The new law also required a registered medical practitioner present during the last illness to complete a certificate stating the cause of death to the best of his knowledge and belief.

In 1893 a Select Committee on Death Certification of the House of Commons attempted to correct the shortcomings of the previous legislation, particularly "the carelessness and ignorance of the persons certifying, the absence of medical attendants during the last illness and the indefinite character of the disease itself" (Abbott 1901). That committee made a series of ten recommendations, the most important of which were the following:

1. That in no case should a death be registered without production of a certificate of the cause of death signed by a registered medical practitioner or by a coroner after inquest.
2. That in each sanitary district a registered medical practitioner should be appointed as public medical certifier of the cause of death in cases in which a certificate from a medical practitioner in attendance was not forthcoming.
3. That a medical practitioner in attendance should be required personally to inspect the body before giving a certificate of death.
4. That a form of a certificate of death should be prescribed, and that in giving a certificate a medical practitioner should be required to use such a form.

The United States Congress, trailing behind the British Parliament, enacted no standard registration act until 1903. Prior to that date, any attempts at standardization were left to the individual States.

In Massachusetts deaths were reported on sheets of paper measuring 18 by 24 inches, with approximately forty records to a page. Information asked for (but not always provided) included date of death, date of record, name of deceased, sex, marital status, age, residence, disease or other cause of death, place of death, occupation, place of birth, and names and birthplaces of parents. These questions are generally to be found on all records of that period. The California form added only a line for the signature of the attending physician or coroner. New Jersey requested the same information but asked for a more detailed explanation of the cause of death. This was optional, however, and the space provided for it was usually left blank. The New York form, the most comprehensive of its time, also required data concerning the burial.

These early death registrations lacked many significant data: cause of death and place of death were often omitted, and no questions were asked regarding an autopsy report or the time and manner of the death, relevant information needed for statistical purposes and criminal investigation.

When the United States Census Bureau was making its preparations for the 1880 census, it decided to rely upon registration records instead of mortality enumerations, wherever possible, and made a study of state and local forms to determine where these registration records were adequate to its purpose. Wide variation was noted in the ways in which items were worded and data recorded. The study revealed the inherent disadvantages of allowing each state to enact its own registration system without guidelines provided by some central authority (Colby 1965). Therefore, with the aid of the American Public Health Association, the Census Bureau developed what may be termed a model death certificate and prescribed its use by the states, but the use of a standard certificate for the registration of deaths was not approved by Congress until 1903.

THE DEATH CERTIFICATE

The impact of the death certificate is considerable. It holds a mirror to our mores; it reflects some of the deepest taboos; it can directly affect the fate and fortune of a family, touching both its affluence and its mental health; it can enhance or degrade the reputation of the decedent and set its stamp on his postself career. But if the impact of the death certificate is great, its limitations are of equal magnitude. In its present form the death certificate is a badly flawed document.

Today most states follow the format of the U.S. Standard Certificate of Death. Most relevant to our present interests is the item which reads: "Accident, suicide, homicide, or undetermined (specify)." When none of these is specified, a natural mode of death is, of course, implied. Only two states, Delaware and

Virginia, have made all four modes of death explicit on the death certificate (and have included a "pending" category as well). Curiously enough, Indiana included four modes of death on the death certificate form from 1955 to 1968, but then revised the form in 1968 and now provides no item for mode of death; nor, surprisingly, does the current Massachusetts death certificate contain an accident-suicide-homicide item.

In addition to the U.S. Standard Certificate, the International Classification of Diseases and Causes of Death plays a major role in determining the way a specific death may be counted—and thus in the apparent change in causes of death statistics from decade to decade. For example, the definitions of suicides and accidents were changed in the Seventh Revision (1955) and Eighth Revision (1965) of the International Classification, and the numbers of suicides and accidents changed along with the definitions. When the Seventh Revision was put into effect for the data year 1958, the death rate for suicides increased markedly over 1957. In part, one can find the explanation in this paragraph (National Center for Health Statistics 1965a):

About 3.3 percent of the total suicide rate for 1958 as compared with that for 1957 resulted from the transfer of a number of deaths from accident to suicide. In 1958 a change was made in the interpretation of injuries where there was some doubt as to whether they were accidentally inflicted or inflicted with suicidal intent. Beginning with the Seventh Revision for data year 1958, "self-inflicted" injuries with no specification as to whether or not they were inflicted with suicidal intent, and deaths from injuries, whether or not self-inflicted, with an indication that it is not known whether they were inflicted accidentally or with suicidal intent, are classified as suicides. The change was made on the assumption that the majority of such deaths are properly classified as suicide because of the reluctance of the certifier to designate a death as suicide unless evidence indicates suicidal intent beyond the shadow of a doubt. The magnitude of the comparability ratios for suicide varied considerably with means of injury, from 1.02 for suicide by firearms and explosives to 1.55 for suicide by jumping from high places.

It would seem that this redefinition led to an apparent 55 percent increase from one year to the next in suicides by jumping from high places. Even more interesting is the official observation that the death certifier would be reluctant to indicate suicide "unless evidence indicates suicidal intent beyond the shadow of a doubt." Clearly the certifier plays an important role in the process of generating mortality data. It is he who makes the subjective judgment of what constitutes conclusive evidence of the decedent's intent. The Eighth Revision (National Center for Health Statistics 1967), which made the category "Undetermined" available, introduced still further problems, apparently shifting many suicidal deaths to the Undetermined category.

What is urgently needed is an exploration and description of the current practices of certifying deaths, especially deaths by suicide. We need a uniform system that would eliminate such inconsistencies or confirm the differential unequivocally, as for example, 10.9 deaths by suicide per 100,000 population for Idaho versus 20.2 for Wyoming. What is required is a correctional quotient for each reporting unit—county, state, and nation. Until such information is obtained, available suicide statistics are highly suspect.

At the turn of the century, an early reference book of the medical science (Abbott 1901) urged reliable death registration bookkeeping and listed the following as "objects secured by a well-devised system":

1. Questions relating to property rights are often settled by a single reference to a record of death.
2. The official certificate of a death is usually required in each case of claim for life insurance.
3. Death certificates settle many disputed questions in regard to pensions.
4. They are of great value in searching for records of genealogy.
5. A death certificate frequently furnishes valuable aid in the detection of crime.
6. Each individual certificate is a contribution *causa scientiae*. Taken collectively, they are of great importance to physicians, and especially to health officers, in the study of

disease, since they furnish valuable information in regard to its causes, its prevalence, and its geographical distribution.

At least three more functions for the death certificate might be added to the half-dozen listed in 1901:

7. The death certificate should reflect the type of death that is certified—brain death (a flat electroencephalographic record), somatic death (no respiration, heartbeat, reflexes), or whatever type is implied.
8. The death certificate should include space for the specification of death by legal execution, death in war or military incursions, death by police action, and others of that sort.
9. Perhaps most importantly, the death certificate should abandon the anachronistic Cartesian view of man as a passive biological vessel on which the fates work their will. Instead, it should reflect the contemporary view of man as a psycho-socio-biological organism that can, and in many cases does, play a significant role in hastening its own demise. This means that the death certificate should contain at least one item on the decedent's intention vis-à-vis his own death.

In the Western world death is given its administrative dimensions by the death certificate. See Figure 11-1. It is the format and content of this document that determine and reflect the categories in terms of which death is conceptualized and death statistics reported. The ways in which deaths were described and categorized in John Graunt's day and earlier set deep precedents for ways of thinking about death, and they govern our thoughts and gut reactions to death to this day. Deaths were then assumed to fall into one of two categories: There were those that were truly adventitious—accidents, visitations of fate or fortune (called natural and accidental)—and there were those that were caused by a culprit who needed to be sought out and punished (called suicidal and homicidal deaths). In the case of suicide, the victim and the assailant were combined in the same person, and

STATE OF NEW HAMPSHIRE
DEPARTMENT OF HEALTH AND WELFARE
CERTIFICATE OF DEATH

LOCAL FILE NUMBER

STATE FILE NUMBER

DECEASED—NAME   FIRST   MIDDLE   LAST | SEX   DATE OF DEATH (MONTH, DAY, YEAR)

1.   2.   3.

RACE WHITE, NEGRO, AMERICAN INDIAN, ETC. (SPECIFY) | AGE—LAST BIRTHDAY (YEARS) | UNDER 1 YEAR MOS DAYS | UNDER 1 DAY HOURS MIN. | DATE OF BIRTH (MONTH, DAY, YEAR) | COUNTY OF DEATH

4.   5A.   5B.   5C.   6.   7A.

CITY, TOWN, OR LOCATION OF DEATH | HOSPITAL OR OTHER INSTITUTION—NAME (IF NOT IN EITHER, GIVE STREET AND NUMBER)

7B.   7C.

STATE OF BIRTH (IF NOT IN U.S.A., NAME COUNTRY) | CITIZEN OF WHAT COUNTRY | MARRIED, NEVER MARRIED, WIDOWED, DIVORCED (SPECIFY) | SURVIVING SPOUSE (IF WIFE, GIVE MAIDEN NAME)

8.   9.   10.   11.

SOCIAL SECURITY NUMBER | USUAL OCCUPATION (GIVE KIND OF WORK DONE DURING MOST OF WORKING LIFE, EVEN IF RETIRED) | KIND OF BUSINESS OR INDUSTRY

12.   13A.   13B.

RESIDENCE—STATE | COUNTY | CITY, TOWN, OR LOCATION | STREET AND NUMBER

14A.   14B.   14C.   14D.

FATHER—NAME   FIRST   MIDDLE   LAST | MOTHER—MAIDEN NAME   FIRST   MIDDLE   LAST

15   16.

INFORMANT—NAME | MAILING ADDRESS   (STREET OR R.F.D. NO., CITY OR TOWN, STATE, ZIP)

17A.   17B.

PART I   DEATH WAS CAUSED BY: [ENTER ONLY ONE CAUSE PER LINE FOR (A), (B), AND (C)] | APPROXIMATE INTERVAL BETWEEN ONSET AND DEATH

18.   IMMEDIATE CAUSE   (A)

CONDITIONS, IF ANY, WHICH GAVE RISE TO IMMEDIATE CAUSE (A), STATING THE UNDERLYING CAUSE LAST   DUE TO, OR AS A CONSEQUENCE OF: (B)

DUE TO, OR AS A CONSEQUENCE OF: (C)

PART II.   OTHER SIGNIFICANT CONDITIONS: CONDITIONS CONTRIBUTING TO DEATH BUT NOT RELATED TO CAUSE GIVEN IN PART I (A) | AUTOPSY (YES OR NO) | IF YES WERE FINDINGS CONSIDERED IN DETERMINING CAUSE OF DEATH

19A.   19B.

ACCIDENT, SUICIDE, HOMICIDE, OR UNDERTERMINED (SPECIFY) | DATE OF INJURY (MONTH, DAY, YEAR) | HOUR | HOW INJURY OCCURRED (ENTER NATURE OF INJURY IN PART I OR PART II, ITEM 18)

20A.   20B.   20C. M   20D.

INJURY AT WORK (SPECIFY YES OR NO) | PLACE OF INJURY AT HOME, FARM, STREET, FACTORY, OFFICE BLDG., ETC. (SPECIFY) | LOCATION   (STREET OR R.F.D. NO., CITY OR TOWN, STATE)

20E.   20F.   20G.

CERTIFICATION— MONTH DAY YEAR   MONTH DAY YEAR PHYSICIAN: TO | AND LAST SAW HIM/HER ALIVE ON MONTH DAY YEAR | I DID/DID NOT VIEW THE BODY AFTER DEATH | DEATH OCCURRED (HOUR) | AT THE PLACE, ON THE DATE, AND, TO THE BEST OF MY KNOWLEDGE, DUE TO THE CAUSE(S) STATED.

21A.   I ATTENDED THE DECEASED FROM   21B.   21C.   21D.   21E. M

CERTIFICATION—MEDICAL REFEREE: ON THE BASIS OF THE EXAMINATION OF THE BODY AND/OR THE INVESTIGATION, IN MY OPINION DEATH OCCURRED ON THE DATE AND DUE TO THE CAUSE(S) STATED. | THE DECEDENT WAS PRONOUNCED DEAD MONTH   DAY   YEAR   HOUR

22A.   22B. M   M.

CERTIFIER—NAME (TYPE OR PRINT) | SIGNATURE | DEGREE OR TITLE | DATE SIGNED (MONTH, DAY, YEAR)

23A.   23B.   23C.

MAILING ADDRESS—CERTIFIER | STREET OR R.F.D. NO.   CITY OR TOWN   STATE   ZIP

23D.

BURIAL, CREMATION, REMOVAL OR ENTOMBMENT (SPECIFY) | CEMETERY OR CREMATORY—NAME | LOCATION   CITY OR TOWN   STATE

24A.   24B.   24C.

DATE   (MONTH, DAY, YEAR) | FUNERAL HOME —NAME AND ADDRESS   (STREET OR R.F.D. NO., CITY OR TOWN, STATE, ZIP)

24D.   25A.

FUNERAL DIRECTOR—SIGNATURE | COUNTERSIGNED AGENT (CITY BD. OF HEALTH) | DATE

25B.   26A.   26B.

DATE REC'D BY TOWN OR CITY CLERK | CLERK'S OWN SIGNATURE | CLERK OF

27A.   27B.   27C.

A true copy, Attest: .... Clerk of .... Dated .... 19........

V. S. 16—68   S·68·25M

Figure 11-1. U.S. Standard Certificate of Death Form

the offense was designated as a crime against oneself, a *felo de se.* England did not cease to classify suicide as a crime until 1961, and in the United States it remains a crime in nine States.

The historical importance of certifying the mode of death— that is, of the coroner's function—can now be seen: It not only set a stamp of innocence or stigma upon the death, but also determined whether the decedent's estate could be claimed by his legal heirs (natural or accidental death) or by the crown or local lord (a suicide or a murder). That was certainly one important practical effect of the death certificate. The NASH categories of death were implied as early as the sixteenth century in English certification, and this submanifest administrative taxonomy of death has beguiled most men into thinking that there *really* are four kinds of death, which, of course, is not necessarily so at all.

Although it may be platitudinous to say that in each life the inevitability of death is an inexorable fact, there is nothing at all inexorable about our ways of dimensionalizing death. Conceptualizations of death are manmade and mutable; what man can make he can also clarify and change. Indeed, changes in our conceptualizations of death are constantly occurring, notwithstanding the NASH notions of death have held on for centuries after they became anachronistic. Each generation becomes accustomed to its own notions and thinks that these are universal and ubiquitous.

From the time of John Graunt and his mortuary tables in the seventeenth century, through the work of Cullen in the eighteenth century and William Farr in the nineteenth century, the adoption of the Bertillon International List of Causes of Death in 1893, and the International Conference for the Eighth Revision of the International Classification of Diseases as recently as 1965 (National Center for Health Statistics 1965b), the classification of causes of death has constantly been broadening in scope. The changes are characterized primarily by attempts to reflect additions to knowledge, particularly those contributed by new professions as they have developed—anesthesiology, pathology, bacteriology, immunology, and advances in obstetrics, surgery, and most recently, the behavioral sciences.

PURPOSES OF THE PSYCHOLOGICAL AUTOPSY

As long as deaths are classified solely in terms of the four NASH categories, it is immediately apparent that some deaths will, so to speak, fall between the cracks, and our familiar problem of equivocal death will continue to place obstacles in our path to understanding human beings and their dying. Many of these obstacles can be cleared away by reconstructing, primarily through interviews with the survivors, the role that the deceased played in hastening or effecting his own death. This procedure is called "psychological autopsy," and initially its main purpose was to clarify situations in which the mode of death was not immediately clear.

The origin of the psychological autopsy grew out of the frustration of the Los Angeles County Chief Medical Examiner-Coroner, Theodore J. Curphey, M.D., at the time of the reorganization of that office in 1958. Despite his efforts, which were combined with those of toxicologists and nonmedical investigators, he was faced with a number of drug deaths for which he was unable to certify the mode on the basis of collected evidence. As a result he asked the Los Angeles Suicide Prevention Center to assist him in a joint study of these equivocal cases, and it was this effort—a multidisciplinary approach involving behavioral scientists—which led to my coining the term "psychological autopsy" (Curphey 1961, 1967, Litman et al. 1963, Shneidman 1969, 1973, Shneidman and Farberow 1961).

In the last few years, especially with the interesting and valuable work of Litman and colleagues (1963), Weisman and Kastenbaum (1968), and Weisman (1974), the term "psychological autopsy" has come to have other, slightly different meanings. At present there are at least three distinct questions that the psychological autopsy can help to answer:

1. *Why did the individual do it?* When the mode of death is, by all reasonable measures, clear and unequivocal—suicide, for example—the psychological autopsy can serve to account for the reasons for the act or to discover what led to it. Why did Ernest Hemingway "have to" shoot himself (Hotchner 1966)? Why did former Secretary of Defense James Forrestal kill himself (Rogow 1963)? We can read a widow's explicit account of how she helped her husband, dying of cancer, cut open his veins in Lael Tucker Wertenbaker's *Death of a Man* (1957). Some people can under-

stand such an act; others cannot. But even those who believe they understand cannot know whether their reasons are the same as those of the cancer victim or his wife. What were their reasons? In this type of psychological autopsy, as in the following type, the mode of death is clear, but the reasons for the manner of dying remain puzzling, even mysterious. The psychological autopsy is no less than a reconstruction of the motivations, philosophy, psychodynamics, and existential crises of the decedent.

2. *How did the individual die, and when—that is, why at that particular time?* When a death, usually a natural death, is protracted, the individual dying gradually over a period of time, the psychological autopsy helps to illumine the sociopsychological reasons why he died at that time. This type of psychological autopsy is illustrated by the following brief case from Weisman and Kastenbaum (1968):

An 85-year-old man had suffered with chronic bronchitis and emphysema for many years but was alert and active otherwise. He had eagerly anticipated going to his son's home for Thanksgiving and when the day arrived he was dressed and ready, but no one came for him. He became more concerned as the hours went by. He asked the nurse about messages, but there were none, and he finally realized that he would have to spend the holiday at the hospital. After this disappointment the patient kept more and more to himself, offered little, and accepted only minimal care. Within a few weeks he was dead.

The implication here is that the patient's disappointment and his resignation to it were not unrelated to his sudden downhill course and his death soon afterward, that is, if his son had come to take him out for Thanksgiving, the old man would have lived considerably longer than he did. This man's death like some others— voodoo deaths, unexplained deaths under anesthesia, and self-fulfilling prophecy deaths, for example—must be considered subintentioned. There can be little doubt that often some connection exists between the psychology of the individual and the time of his death (Shneidman 1963).

There is, of course, a wide spectrum of applicability of this concept. When a person has been literally scared to death by his belief in the power of voodoo, the role of the victim's psychological state seems fairly obvious; and it is difficult to believe that there was no psychological connection between the fatal stroke of Mrs. Loree Bailey, owner of the Lorraine Motel in Memphis, and the assassination of Martin Luther King, Jr., at the motel 3 hours earlier. But in many other cases any relationship between the individual's psychological state and the time of his death seems difficult or impossible to establish.

As an example of the problems raised by this concept, consider the following case, reported in the *New York Times* of June 26, 1968:

WIDOW, 104, DIES IN COTTAGE
SHE ENTERED AS 1887 BRIDE

Mrs. John Charles Dalrymple, 104 years old, died here [Randolph Township, New Jersey] yesterday in the cottage to which she came as a bride in 1887.

Her husband brought her in a sleigh to the house, which she was to leave next week to make way for the new Morris County Community College. . . .

The main question here, as in Weisman and Kastenbaum's case of the old man who was left alone on Thanksgiving, is: might even this person have lived at least a little longer had she not suffered the psychologically traumatic threat of being dispossessed from the home where she had lived for eighty-one years? Or does the question in this particular case tax one's commonsense credulity?

3. *What is the most probable mode of death?* This was the question to which the psychological autopsy was initially addressed. When cause of death can be clearly established but mode of death is equivocal, the purpose of the psychological autopsy is

to establish the mode of death with as great a degree of accuracy as possible.

The typical coroner's office, whether headed by a medical examiner or by a lay coroner, is more likely to be accurate in its certification of natural and accidental deaths than of those deaths that might be suicides. Curphey (1961) says, "A major reason for this, of course, is that both the pathologist and the lay investigator lack sufficient training in the field of human behavior to be able to estimate with any fair degree of accuracy the mental processes of the victim likely to lead to suicidal death. It is here that the social scientists, with their special skills in human behavior, can offer us much valuable assistance" (p. 112).

The professional personnel who constitute a death investigation team obviously should hold no brief for one particular mode of death over any other. In essence, the members of the death investigation team interview persons who knew the deceased — and attempt to reconstruct his life-style, focusing particularly on the period just prior to his death. If the information they receive contains any clues pointing to suicide, their especially attuned ears will recognize them. They listen for any overt or covert communications that might illuminate the decedent's role (if any) in his own demise. They then make a reasoned extrapolation of the victim's intention and behavior over the days and minutes preceding his death, using all the information they have obtained.

CONDUCTING THE PSYCHOLOGICAL AUTOPSY

How is a psychological autopsy performed? It is done by talking to some key persons — spouse, lover, parent, grown child, friend, colleague, physician, supervisor, coworker — who knew the decedent. The talking to is done gently, a mixture of conversation, interview, emotional support, general questions, and a good deal of listening. I always telephone and then go out to the home. After rapport is established, a good general opening question might be: "Please tell me, what was he (she) like?" Sometimes clothes and material possessions are looked at, photographs shown, and even diaries and correspondence shared. (On one occasion, the widow showed me her late husband's suicide note—which she had hidden from the police!—rather changing the equivocal nature of the death.)

In general, I do not have a fixed outline in mind while conducting a psychological autopsy, but, inasmuch as outlines have been requested from time to time, one is presented below with the dual cautions that it should not be followed slavishly and that the investigator should be ever mindful that he may be asking questions that are very painful to people in an obvious grief-laden situation. The person who conducts a psychological autopsy should participate, as far as he is genuinely able, in the anguish of the bereaved person and should always do his work with the mental health of the survivors in mind.

Here, then, are some categories that might be included in a psychological autopsy (Shneidman 1969):

1. Information identifying victim (name, age, address, marital status, religious practices, occupation, and other details)
2. Details of the death (including the cause or method and other pertinent details)
3. Brief outline of victim's history (siblings, marriage, medical illnesses, medical treatment, psychotherapy, suicide attempts)
4. Death history of victim's family (suicides, cancer, other fatal illnesses, ages at death, and other details)
5. Description of the personality and life-style of the victim
6. Victim's typical patterns of reaction to stress, emotional upsets, and periods of disequilibrium
7. Any recent—from last few days to last twelve months—upsets, pressures, tensions, or anticipations of trouble
8. Role of alcohol or drugs in (a) overall life-style of victim, and (b) his death

9. Nature of victim's interpersonal relationships (including those with physicians)
10. Fantasies, dreams, thoughts, premonitions, or fear of victim relating to death, accident, or suicide
11. *Changes* in the victim before death (of habits, hobbies, eating, sexual patterns, and other life routines)
12. Information relating to the "life side" of victim (upswings, successes, plans)
13. Assessment of intention, that is, role of the victim in his own demise
14. Rating of lethality (described in the final section of this chapter)
15. Reaction of informants to victim's death
16. Comments, special features, and so on.

In conducting the interviews during a psychological autopsy, it is often best to ask open-ended questions that permit the respondent to associate to relevant details without being made painfully aware of the specific interests of the questioner. As an example: I might be very interested in knowing whether or not there was a change (specifically, a recent sharp decline) in the decedent's eating habits. Rather than ask directly, "Did his appetite drop recently?" a question almost calculated to elicit a defensive response, I have asked a more general question such as, "Did he have any favorite foods?" Obviously, my interest is not to learn what foods he preferred. Not atypically, the respondent will tell me what the decedent's favorite foods were and then go on to talk about recent changes in his eating habits—"Nothing I fixed for him seemed to please him"—and even proceed to relate other recent changes, such as changing patterns in social or sexual or recreational habits, changes which diagnostically would seem to be related to a dysphoric person, not inconsistent with a suicidal or subintentioned death.

In relation to a barbiturate death where the mode of death is equivocal (between suicide and accident), it might be callous to ask the next of kin, "Did your husband (wife) have a history of taking barbiturates?" A more respectful and productive question might be, "Did he (she) take occasional medication to help him (her) sleep at night?" If the response to this question is in the affirmative, one might then ask if the respondent knows the name of the medication or even the shape and color of the medication. If one determines that the deceased in fact had a history of taking sleeping medication, one might then ask if the decedent was accustomed to having some occasional alcoholic beverages prior to going to sleep. If these facts can be brought into the open, it may well be that one can then establish the quantity of the medication and alcohol content that the decedent was taking immediately prior to his death. The general method of questioning is one of "successive approaches," wherein the respondent's willingness to answer one question gives permission to ask the next one. That is the general way that one would inquire, if it were relevant, into, say, drug patterns of behavior. Where suicide or homicide is a possible mode of death, it is rather important to know whether or not the decedent was into drugs, a habitual user, or a dealer, on what terms he was with his dealer, and so forth.

FUNCTIONS OF THE PSYCHOLOGICAL AUTOPSY

The questions should be as detailed (and lines of inquiry pursued) only as they bear on clarifying the mode of death. All else would seem to be extraneous. And to do this depends, of course, on having established rapport with the respondent.

The results of these interviewing procedures are then discussed with the chief medical examiner or coroner. Because it is his responsibility to indicate (or amend) the mode of death, all available psychological information should be included in the total data at his disposal. Since a sizable percentage of deaths are equivocal as to mode precisely because these psychological factors are unknown, medical examiners and coroners throughout the country are robbing themselves of important information when they fail to employ the special skills of the behavioral scientists in cases of equivocal deaths. The skills of behavioral scientists should be employed in the same way as the skills of biochemists, toxicologists, histologists, microscopists, and other physical scientists. The time has long since passed when we could enjoy the luxury of disregarding the basic teachings of twentieth century psychodynamic psychology and psychiatry. Certification procedures (and the death certificates on which they are recorded) should reflect the role of the decedent in his own demise, and in equivocal cases this cannot be done without a psychological autopsy.

The retrospective analysis of deaths not only serves to increase the accuracy of certification (which is in the best interests of the overall mental health concerns of the community), but also has the heuristic function of providing the serious investigator with clues that he may then use to assess lethal intent in living persons.

And there is still another function that the psychological autopsy serves: In working with the bereaved survivors to elicit data relative to appropriate certification, a skillful and empathic investigator is able to conduct the interviews in such a way that they are of actual therapeutic value to the survivors. A psychological autopsy should never be conducted so that any aspect of it is iatrogenic. Commenting on this important mental health function of the psychological autopsy, Curphey (1961) has stated:

The members of the death investigation team, because of their special skills, are alert in their interviews with survivors to evidences of extreme guilt, serious depression, and the need for special help in formulating plans for solving specific problems such as caring for children whose parents committed suicide. Since we noted this phenomenon, the coroner's office has, in some few cases, referred distraught survivors of suicide victims to members of the team specifically for supportive interviews even when the suicidal mode of death was not in doubt. [p. 116]

This therapeutic work with the survivor-victims of a dire event is called *postvention* and has been presented in some detail elsewhere (Shneidman 1967, 1971, 1973).

A large university hospital in the East (which has asked not to be identified, but to which I am appropriately beholden) conducts what they call "psychiatric inquests" on those (rare) occasions when a patient commits suicide or makes a serious suicide attempt. A staff psychiatrist, emphasizing the therapeutic aspects of the psychological autopsy procedure, stated that "the inquest is a kind of postvention, designed primarily for the benefit of a shocked and grieving staff." He stated further that, for them, there are essentially three main purposes of such a procedure: "(1) To review with those responsible for the patient, the status of the patient prior to the act, and to determine what course of clinical management would more likely have led to its anticipation and prevention; (2) To facilitate expression of feeling appropriate to the event on the part of staff members; and (3) To determine whether dissemination of the results of the inquest would serve an educational purpose, and arrange for this (e.g., grand rounds) when appropriate." Further, he states that these meetings "should be small enough to exclude those interested primarily in the sensational aspects of the event in question, and should include only those whose presence would serve one of the above purposes."

Following, reprinted with permission, are verbatim reports (except for a few minor changes to disguise identity) of two psychiatric inquests from that university hospital setting.

Case 1. A 32-year-old male graduate student took his life by drug overdose. He had first been hospitalized in 1974 for treatment of strychnine poisoning and was discharged eight days later with a diagnosis of cyclothymic personality. He was readmitted late the same year with depression and paranoid delusions, both of which cleared rapidly on Triavil (a combination of the major tranquilizer–antipsychotic agent perphenazine—and the tricyclic antidepressant amitriptyline), was discharged after a two-week hospitalization, and was followed in the outpatient clinic by a resident who had undertaken his care only one week before the discharge date. Gradual improvement was reported, although the absence of the supervisor (who was aware of the suicide risk and would have questioned termination of treatment) leaves the reported improvement open to question. Two months later the patient said that he had discontinued his medications because they slowed him down and that he was confident about his work, feeling well, and would not try suicide again. He was discharged from outpatient treatment at his request, with the assurance that he could call back if he needed further help. He did not contact the clinic again, but three days before his death called his faculty advisor, made accusations against a fellow graduate student, and requested a departmental inquiry. He was advised to go on a vacation but went instead to another city, where it was reported that he spent two days praying in a chapel, returned to his boardinghouse, ate supper, and took a fatal drug overdose. Those commenting on the case stressed the questionable aspects of taking at face value the statements of the patient which led to his discharge from the clinic. Furthermore, the patient sent out danger signals in his last call to his faculty advisor.

Case 2. An 18-year-old male patient spent three months on the child psychiatry service two years prior to committing suicide. He had been evaluated for a mild aortic stenosis about which he and his family were greatly concerned. During his first admission, he showed fragmentation, loose associations, grimacing, and bizarre movements. Within three months of treatment with haloperidol (a major tranquilizer with antipsychotic properties), milieu therapy, and psychotherapy, he improved enough for discharge to outpatient treatment. Haloperidol was discontinued three weeks prior to his discharge from the hospital. He was carried as an outpatient for six months. About a month prior to readmission looseness of associations and paranoid ideation recurred, and he was reported by his family to have wandered nude out of his house. His school performance declined, and he said he had strange thoughts and could not trust anyone. He refused to take the haloperidol which was again prescribed for him. Upon readmission to the hospital he appeared disorganized, suspicious, and regressed. Two months later he had improved sufficiently to warrant a reduction of the haloperidol which he had been given since admission, but he again regressed and was placed on higher doses of haloperidol by a staff supervisor. His bizarre behavior, open sexual advances to staff and patients, and age combined to necessitate a transfer to a ward where he could be more appropriately managed. There it was reported that he accepted seclusion when required, seemed to respond to medications, but was in general withdrawn and regressed. He was angry at his therapist, who had informed him of his departure some months hence, and on the day of his suicide made known a desire to cut off his penis. Later that day he struck an attendant, spent some time in seclusion, and shortly after his release from seclusion left the ward undetected and went to the tenth floor where, finding an unguarded window, he jumped to his death. After the event it was revealed in a patient meeting that he had informed another patient of his intention and had given away his radio. The discussion pointed out the strong suicide potential of young disturbed males, the risks of multiple therapists and multiple absences, the hazards of disagreement about diagnosis, prognosis, and treatment method.

SUICIDE STATISTICS: SOME QUESTIONS

In relation to suicide statistics in the United States, we know that accurate figures do not now exist. There is widespread confusion and considerable difference of interpretation as to how to classify deaths. For example, what is considered suicide in one locality is often reported as accidental death in another. The factors that determine decisions of coroners and medical examiners must be made clearly visible as attempts are made to develop criteria for gathering vital baseline data in the area of suicide.

There is an urgent need to explore and describe present practices of reporting suicides and the degree of consistency or inconsistency of such reporting in the United States. Until such information is obtained, it will be impossible to interpret the available statistics. The coroners and medical examiners are the keys to the meaningful reporting of statistics on suicide.

It is believed that it is of the highest priority that an investigation be focused around the following questions directly related to this problem:

1. What percentage of all deaths are autopsied?

2. Who, at present, are the certifying officials, officers, or agencies? Are these medical examiners, physicians in the community, sheriffs, coroners? How are they selected? How trained?

3. What are the present official criteria given to certifying officials in various jurisdictions to guide them in reporting a death as suicide?

4. What are the present actual practices of certifying officials in reporting suicidal deaths? To what extent are these practices consistent with or different from the official criteria?

5. By what actual processes do the certifying officials arrive at the decision to list a death as suicide?

6. How often are autopsies performed? Who determines when an autopsy is to be performed? Are the services of a toxicologist and biochemist available?

7. What percentage of deaths are seen as equivocal, or undetermined, or as a combination of two or more modes (for example, accident-suicide, undetermined)?

8. What are the criteria for special procedures in an equivocal death?

9. How much of the total investigation of a death is dependent upon the police reports? What is the relationship of the coroner's investigation to the local police department?

10. When, if ever, are behavioral or social scientists involved in the total investigatory procedure of a death?

11. What percentage of certifying officials in the United States are medically trained? Does medical training significantly influence the way in which deaths are reported?

From data dealing with these questions, based on appropriate sampling from regions and taking into account rural-urban differences, size of municipalities, and so on, appropriate agencies could then address themselves to a number of important general questions, including the following:

- What local, state, regional, or other differences emerge in the practices of reporting the various modes of death?
- What are the general implications from the data for the accuracy of present death statistics, especially the statistics for each separate mode?
- What suggestions can be made for improvement in conceptualization, practice, and training which point toward more accurate and meaningful reporting?

SUGGESTIONS FOR THE CONCEPTUAL
IMPROVEMENT OF THE DEATH CERTIFICATE

The current NASH classification of death grew out of a seventeenth century way of thinking about man (as a biological vessel who was subject to whims of fate) and tended to leave man himself out of his own death. Twentieth century psychology and psychiatry have attempted to put man—conscious and unconscious—back into his own life, including the way in which he dies. The NASH classification of modes of death is not only apsychological but it tends to emphasize relatively unimportant details. For example, it is essentially a matter of indifference to a human being whether a light fixture above him falls and he is invaded by a lethal chandelier (accidental mode), or someone about him coughs and he is invaded by a lethal virus (natural mode), or someone shoots a gun at him and he is invaded by a lethal bullet (homicidal mode), if the fact is that he does not wish (intention) any of these events to occur.

In order to avoid the inadequacies of this conceptual confusion, it has been proposed that all human deaths be classified among three types: intentioned, subintentioned, and unintentioned (Shneidman 1963, 1973).

An *intentioned* death is any death in which the decedent

plays a direct, conscious role in effecting his own demise. On the other hand, an *unintentioned* death is any death, whatever its determined cause or apparent NASH mode, in which the decedent plays no effective role in effecting his own demise—where death is due entirely to independent physical trauma from without, or to nonpsychologically laden biological failure from within.

But most importantly—and, in a fashion I believe to be characteristic of a sizable percentage of all deaths—*subintentioned* deaths are deaths in which the decedent plays some partial, covert, or unconscious role in hastening his own demise. The objective evidences of the presence of these roles lie in such behavioral manifestations as, for example, poor judgment, excessive risk-taking, abuse of alcohol, misuse of drugs, neglect of self, self-destructive style of life, disregard of prescribed lifesaving medical regimen, and so on, where the individual fosters, facilitates, exacerbates, or hastens the process of his dying.

That individuals may play an unconscious role in their own failures and act inimically to their own best welfare and even hasten their own deaths seems to be well documented in the psychoanalytic and general clinical practice. This concept of subintentioned death is similar, in some ways, to Karl Menninger's concepts of chronic, focal, and organic suicide (1938). Menninger's ideas relate to self-defeating ways of continuing to live, whereas the notion of subintentioned cessation is a description of a way of stopping the process of living. Included in this subintention category would be many patterns of mismanagement and brink-of-death living which result in death. In terms of the traditional classification of modes of death (natural, accidental, homicide, and suicide), some instances of all four types can be subsumed under this category, depending on the particular details of each case.

Confusion also discolors and obfuscates our thinking in the field of suicide. Currently there is much overattention paid to the categories of attempted, threatened, and committed suicide. These categories are confusing because they do not tell us with what intensity the impulse was felt or the deed was done. One can attempt to attempt, attempt to commit, or attempt to feign, and so on. One can threaten or attempt suicide at any level of intensity. What is needed is a dimension which cuts across these labels and permits us to evaluate the individual's drive to self-imposed death. We propose a dimension called *lethality*, defined as the probability of a specific individual's killing himself (i.e., ending up dead) in the immediate future (today, tomorrow, the next day—not next month). A measure of the lethality of any individual can be made at any given time. When we say that individual is suicidal we mean to convey the idea that he is experiencing an acute exacerbation (or heightening) of his lethality. All suicide attempts, suicide threats, and committed suicides should be rated for their lethality. The rule of thumb would be that beyond a certain point one must be wary of the danger of explosion into overt behavior.

What is suggested is that, *in addition* to the present NASH classification, each death certificate contain a new supplementary item which reflects the individual's lethality intent. This item might be labeled *Imputed Lethality* (recognizing its inferential character) and would consist of four terms, one of which would then be checked. The terms are: *High, Medium, Low, Absent*, and would be defined as follows.

High lethality: The decedent definitely wanted to die; the decedent played a direct conscious role in his own death; the death was due primarily to the decedent's openly conscious wish or desire to be dead, or to his (her) actions in carrying out that wish (e.g., jumping rather than falling or being pushed from a high place; he shot himself to death; he deliberately interrupted or refused lifesaving procedures or medical regimen).

Medium lethality: The decedent played an important role in effecting or hastening his own death. Death was due in some part to actions of the decedent in which he played some partial, covert, or unconscious role in hastening his own demise. The evidences for this lie in the decedent's behaviors, such as his carelessness, foolhardiness, neglect of self, imprudence, poor judgment, provoking others, disregard of prescribed lifesaving medical regimen, active resignation to death, mismanagement of drugs, abuse of alcohol, tempting fate, asking for trouble, and so on, where the decedent himself seemed to have fostered, facilitated, or hastened the process of his dying, or the date of his death.

Low lethality: The decedent played some small but not insignificant role in effecting or hastening his own demise. The same as medium above, but to a much lesser degree.

Absent lethality: The decedent played no role in effecting his own death. The death was due entirely to assault from outside the body (in a situation where the decedent played no role in causing this to happen), or death was due entirely to failure within the body (in a decedent who wished to continue to live).

The item on the certificate might look like this:

IMPUTED LETHALITY (Check One):
High   Medium   Low   Absent
(See Instructions)

The reasons for advocating the suggestion are as follows: First, this classification permits reflection of the role that the dead individual played in his own dying, in hastening his own death; the ways in which he might have participated in his own death, and so on. Next, it is more fair. At present, individuals of higher social status who commit suicide are more likely to be assigned the mode of accidental or natural death than are individuals of lower social status who no more evidently commit suicide. If the term is to have any meaning at all, it should be fairly used across the board, measured by the individual's intention. Finally, the lethality intention item provides an unexampled source of information by means of which biostatisticians, public health officials, and social scientists could assess the mental health of any community. It is obvious that the number of deaths that are caused, hoped for, or hastened by the decedents themselves is a measure of the prevalence of psychological disorder and social stress. At present we do not have this measure, and we need it.

It might be protested, inasmuch as the assessments of these

intention states involve the appraisal of unconscious factors, that some workers (especially lay coroners) cannot legitimately be expected to make the kinds of psychological judgments required for this type of classification. To this, one answer would be that medical examiners and coroners throughout the country are making judgments of precisely this nature every day of the week. In the situation of evaluating a possible suicide, the coroner often acts (sometimes without realizing it) as psychiatrist and psychologist, and as both judge and jury in a quasi-judicial way. This is because certification of death as suicide does, willy-nilly, imply some judgments or reconstruction of the victim's motivation or intention. Making these judgments—perhaps more coroners ought to use the category of Undetermined—is a part of a coroner's function. But it might be far better if these psychological dimensions were explicit, and an attempt, albeit crude, made to use them, than to have these psychological dimensions employed in an implicit and unverbalized (yet operating) manner. The dilemma is between the polarities of the presently used oversimplified classification, on the one hand, and a somewhat more complex, but more meaningful classification, on the other. The goal should be to try to combine greatest usefulness with maximum meaningfulness.

In Marin County, California, the coroner's office assessed each death processed by that office in terms of *both* the traditional NASH classification of mode of death and the lethality intention of the decedent. For a two-year period, 1971–1972 (978 cases), the breakdown was as follows.[2]

Natural deaths (630): high lethality intent, none; medium lethality, 33 (5%); low, 37 (6%); absent, 560 (89%).

Accidental deaths (176): high lethality intent, 2 (1%); medium, 77 (44%); low, 40 (22%); absent, 57 (33%).

Suicidal deaths (131): high lethality intent, 131 (100%).

---

[2]I am especially grateful to Keith C. Craig, coroner's deputy, Marin County, for his interest and help in supplying these data.

Homicidal deaths (37): high lethality intent, none; medium, 20
(54%); low, 9 (24%); absent, 8 (22%).
Four deaths were of unknown origin.

The first thing we notice is that *some* natural, accidental, and
homicidal deaths were classified as having *some* degree of lethal
intention. If the medium-intention and low-intention categories
are combined, then over one-fourth (26%) of all natural, accidental, and homicidal deaths (216 in 843) were deemed to be
subintentioned. If one then adds the suicidal deaths, in which the
decedent has obviously played a role in his own death, then only
64 percent of all deaths (625 in 978) were deemed to have been
totally adventitious; conversely, 36 percent were deemed to have
had some psychological components.

Also of special interest in these Marin County data is the
finding that coroners can, with apparently no more difficulty than
they experience in assigning deaths to the NASH categories,
simultaneously (and by essentially the same process of inference
and induction) assign deaths to intentional categories as well. It is
an important pioneer effort and deserves widespread emulation.

In summary, the following points may be emphasized:

Causes. The classification of causes of death has been rather
well worked out and is consistent with contemporary knowledge.
There is currently an international classification which has wide
acceptance.

Modes. The modes of death have not been stated explicitly
and have not been too well understood. In general, four currently
implied modes of death—natural, accidental, suicidal, and homicidal—suffer from the important deficiency of viewing man as a
vessel of the fates and omitting entirely his role in his own
demise.

Intent. The addition of the dimension of lethal intention
serves to modernize the death certificate, just as in the past,
advances have been made from the teachings of bacteriology,
surgery, anesthesiology, immunology, and so forth. The time is
now long overdue for the introduction of the psychodynamics of
death into the death certificate. The addition of a single item on

imputed lethal intent (High, Medium, Low, Absent) would provide an appropriate reflection of the psychological state of the subject and begin, at last, to reflect the teachings of twentieth century psychology. In this way we might again permit the certification of death to reflect accurately our best current understanding of man.

REFERENCES

Abbott, S. W. (1901). Death certification. In *Reference Handbook of the Medical Sciences,* ed. Albert H. Buck. New York: William Wood.

Cassedy, J. H. (1969). *Demography in Early America.* Cambridge, MA: Harvard University Press.

Colby, M. (1965). The significance, evolution, and implementation of standard certificates. *American Journal of Public Health* 55:596–99.

Curphey, T. J. (1961). The role of the social scientist in the medicolegal certification of death from suicide. In *The Cry for Help,* ed. N. L. Farberow and E. S. Shneidman. New York: McGraw-Hill.

――――― (1967). The forensic pathologist and the multidisciplinary approach to death. In *Essays in Self-Destruction,* ed. E. S. Shneidman, pp. 110–117. New York: Science House.

Hotchner, A. E. (1966). *Papa Hemingway: A Personal Memoir.* New York: Random House.

Kargon, R. (1963). John Graunt, Francis Bacon, and the royal society: the reception of statistics. *Journal of Historical Medicine* 18:337–348.

Litman, R. E., Curphey, T. J., Shneidman, E. S., et al. (1963). Investigations of equivocal suicides. *Journal of the American Medical Association* 184:924–929.

Menninger, K. A. (1938). *Man Against Himself.* New York: Harcourt, Brace.

National Center for Health Statistics. (1965a). Mortality trends in the United States, 1954–1963. *Vital and Health Statistics.* PHS Pub. No. 1000. Series 20. No. 2. Public Health Service. Washington, DC: U.S. Government Printing Office.

――――― (1965b). Report of the U.S. delegation to the International Conference for the Eighth Revision of the International Classification of Diseases, Geneva, Switzerland, July 6–12. *Vital and Health*

Statistics. PHS Pub. No. 1000. Series 4. No. 6. Public Health Service. Washington, DC: U.S. Government Printing Office.

———— (1967). *Eighth Revision International Classification of Diseases, Adapted for Use in the United States*. PHS Pub. No. 1693. Public Health Service, Washington, DC: U.S. Government Printing Office.

Rogow, A. A. (1963). *James Forrestal: A Study of Personality, Politics and Policy*. Los Angeles: Boulevard Bookshop.

Shneidman, E. S. (1963). Orientations toward death: a vital aspect of the study of lives. In *The Study of Lives*, ed. Robert W. White, pp. 200–227. New York: Atherton.

———— (1967). Sleep and self-destruction: a phenomenological study. In *Essays in Self-Destruction*, ed. E. S. Shneidman, pp. 510–539. New York: Science House.

———— (1969). Suicide, lethality, and the psychological autopsy. In *Aspects of Depression*, ed. E. S. Shneidman and M. Ortega, pp. 225–250. Boston: Little, Brown.

———— (1971). Prevention, intervention, and postvention of suicide. *Annals of Internal Medicine* 75:453–458.

———— (1973). *Deaths of Man*. New York: Quadrangle.

Shneidman, E. S., and Farberow, N. L. (1961). Sample investigations of equivocal deaths. In *The Cry for Help*, ed. N. L. Farberow and E. S. Shneidman. New York: McGraw-Hill.

Weisman, A. D. (1974). *The Realization of Death: A Guide for the Psychological Autopsy*. New York: Behavioral Publications.

Weisman, A. D., and Kastenbaum, R. (1968). The psychological autopsy. *Community Mental Health Journal Monograph* No. 4. New York: Behavioral Publications.

Wertenbaker, L. T. (1957). *Death of a Man*. New York: Random House.

World Health Organization (1957). *Manual of the International Statistical Classification of Diseases, Injuries, and Causes of Death*. Based on the Recommendations of the Seventh Revision Conference, 1955. Geneva: World Health Organization.

12

An Example of an Equivocal

Death Clarified in a

Court of Law

PREFATORY NOTE

This chapter is an illustration of the principle of *res ipsa loquitur:* "The facts speak for themselves." In this chapter the documents—investigation reports, consultation reports, newspaper accounts, court testimony, letters—speak for themselves and convey their messages directly to the reader. In this sense, I hardly wrote this chapter; I merely assembled it. In this fascinating case, I was not so much the author as I was the amanuensis.

In all that follows, only the names of the attorney, Mr. Dan R. Hyatt, the consultant psychiatrist, Jerome A. Motto, M.D., and my own name are real. The others are fictitious. Also, all dates, places, and other identifying demographic details have been changed. I have obtained permission from the principal parties of the defense to write this account, and they have seen this text before it was printed.

THE CHARGE

A few years ago I received a long-distance telephone call from an attorney asking me if I might be interested to help in a court-martial case involving an army officer who had been charged with murdering his wife. The attorney's lucid presentation of the tenuous and questionable details in the official charges led me to agree, then and there, to testify for the defense. I shall begin by reproducing a local newspaper account—which I did not see until some time afterwards—which sets forth the serious charges brought against the officer.

Captain Charged in Death

ARMYVILLE, Sept. 22—A five-man court-martial panel was seated Wednesday in the trial of an army officer who is accused of slaying his wife in their Armyville apartment last July.

Capt. Joseph P. Campbell, 33, is charged with premeditated murder in the shooting death of Peggy Scott-Campbell on July 12. The 30-year-old woman was killed by a single blast from a 12-gauge pump shotgun.

The case, being heard before Judge (Col.) George D. Maris, is expected to last two weeks and involve dozens of witnesses and a trip to Los Angeles to hear testimony from an expert on suicide.

In his opening statement, Dan R. Hyatt, a civilian attorney who is representing Campbell, said he would prove that Scott-Campbell had suicidal tendencies. Also representing Campbell is Maj. James Purdich.

Prosecuting attorney Maj. Stanley Bates told the panel that the Campbells, who had been married about five years, were having marital problems and had discussed separation and divorce only hours before the shooting.

Bates said he would present evidence to show that following the argument, Scott-Campbell went to a nearby pizzeria where she was well known. She stayed late, he said, to help with the dishes. She left for home, but returned a few minutes later, telling the owner she had too much to drink. She asked that a cab be summoned to take her back to the couple's apartment.

Bates said he would introduce evidence that would indicate that Campbell beat her after she returned home and cut her five times with a knife. Bates told the court that Campbell later retrieved a shotgun from the bedroom, took her into the bathroom near the living room, and shot her in the chest.

Campbell woke up a neighbor and told him his wife had shot herself, Bates told the court.

In his opening statement, Hyatt said Scott-Campbell had made several prior suicide attempts. On the night she died, he said, Campbell had awakened to find her in the bathroom shower stall cutting her abdomen with a knife. His shotgun was sitting nearby, Hyatt said.

He said that when Campbell attempted to move the shotgun she grabbed the barrel with her right hand and pulled it toward her. The gun discharged.

Hyatt challenged the prosecution to prove that Campbell beat his wife. No witnesses, he said, ever saw Campbell strike his wife, although the bruises noted in the autopsy of the 130-pound woman could not be accounted for, he said.

Hyatt termed the cuts on Scott-Campbell's body as "hesitation marks" and said a doctor would testify that such marks are often inflicted by suicide-prone people.

"Why should he (Campbell) shoot his wife intentionally when she was trying to commit suicide?" Hyatt asked during his opening remarks.

Prosecutors told the court that the case would be based on circumstantial evidence from investigators and forensic experts.

In summary, the events were as follows: Peggy Scott-Campbell, age 30, is dead as a result of a shotgun wound to her chest. Her husband, army Capt. Joseph Campbell, age 33, asserts that the gun was accidentally discharged as he sought to take it from his wife who was in the process of attempting suicide by cutting herself in the abdomen (while seated in the shower of their apartment bathroom). The government charges that, following a domestic quarrel, he willfully murdered his wife by deliberately shooting her and then cutting her abdomen to make the event appear like a suicide attempt. He is being tried by a court-martial.

THE ISSUES

To either the ordinary observer or the trained investigator, the nature or mode of a death is usually self-evident. Each death falls into one of four modes: natural, accidental, suicide, or homicide (NASH). In some cases, however, the mode of death is not so clear; it is equivocal. Then what usually occurs is a more intensive investigation of the physical evidence of the case, including fingerprints, toxicological reports, and so forth. But sometimes the designation of the correct mode of death depends not on the physical evidence but on what the dead person had in mind. Did she take pills to die or just to sleep? Did he jump off the balcony, did he fall, or was he pushed? Did he mean to pull the trigger or was he just cleaning his gun? You can see that one has to distinguish between an investigation of the physical evidence in a case as opposed to a psychological investigation that focuses on the decedent's *intentions* vis-à-vis his or her own death. We shall be interested, in this case, to see whether or not the military investigator and the prosecuting attorney were able to make and maintain this distinction.

There is a further important distinction between a psychologically oriented report and a *psychological autopsy*. (Inasmuch as I coined the phrase "psychological autopsy," I feel that I am entitled to help define it).

The next section of this chapter contains the "Pre-Trial Report of the Military Special Investigator." In the first paragraph of that report, the investigator states: "This is in part a psychological autopsy because it attempts to use pertinent background information to arrive at an understanding of deceased's state of mind at the time of her death." Here, at the outset, he confuses a psychologically slanted report with a psychological autopsy. (This is only the first of several serious errors in this flawed report.) His report is *not* a psychological autopsy. He misunderstands what a psychological autopsy is.

A psychological autopsy is neither a procedure done exclusively from police or medical records nor a procedure conducted in an adversarial situation (where one sets out to prove one mode of death over another). A police officer or prosecutor cannot conduct a psychological autopsy. It would be as though one performed a physical autopsy with the bias of proving a homicidal mode of death, rather than ascertaining the facts and permitting those facts to lead one to an unbiased conclusion.

The psychological autopsy should always be done as an *amicus curiae*, specifically as an impartial consultant to the medical examiner-coroner. A hired gun cannot do it. The purported use of the psychological autopsy by either defense or prosecution in either criminal or civil trials is, as far as I can see, a misappropriation of the name of what is essentially a neutral scientific process, in which the self-announced expert witness tries to cloak himself with the honorific label of a procedure he did not conduct and probably does not understand.

The main function of the psychological autopsy (Curphey 1961, 1967, Clark and Horton-Deutsch 1992, Litman 1963, Shneidman 1969, 1973, 1977, Weisman 1974) is to clarify the *mode* of death in cases where the mode appears unclear. The usual uncertainties lie between Suicide and Accident. The logical setting for the psychological autopsy is the medical examiner-coroner's office where deaths are certified.

The psychological autopsy was developed in the late 1950s as a joint enterprise between the staff of the Los Angeles Suicide Prevention Center and Theodore J. Curphey, M.D., Chief Medical Examiner-Coroner of Los Angeles County. It was Dr. Curphey who recognized the direct relevance of behavioral science data in clarifying deaths that were equivocal as to mode. At his request, the LASPC assembled a multidisciplinary behavioral science team to conduct psychological autopsies of equivocal deaths.

By definition, the psychological autopsy focuses on the decedent's *intentions* in relation to his or her own death. By definition, all deaths, in addition to being classified in terms of the traditional NASH categories of death, may also be designated as intentioned, subintentioned, or unintentioned (Shneidman 1963, 1973). The psychological autopsy supplements the traditional autopsy, forensic findings, toxicological results, police reports, criminal investigations, and the like. It concentrates on the decedent's personality, character, behavior, history, habits, and self-destructive tendencies.

Putting the human drama aside, what we have in this case is a psychological enigma within a legal context. The goal is not only to establish what mode of death should appropriately be placed on the decedent's death certificate, but also (and primarily) to ascertain the guilt or innocence of an accused. In either way of conceptualizing this process, the issue is to rule out suicide and then render a decision between two modes of death: accident or homicide. If homicide, then there is a perpetrator and he should be punished; if accident, then there is no perpetrator and the individual accused in these proceedings is free of charges. The situation is made more complicated by the fact that the death in question occurred within a suicidal context, that is, the decedent was apparently attempting to take her own life (in an effort of unknown lethality) when the fatal event, homicide or accident, took place.

PRE-TRIAL REPORT OF THE MILITARY SPECIAL INVESTIGATOR

What follows in this section is a paraphrased and excerpted presentation of the "Report of Consultation in the Matter of Peggy Scott-Campbell (deceased) dependent wife of Capt. Joseph Campbell." The report was written by Perry N. Olds, a special agent of the Army Office of Special Investigation. The ten-page single-spaced typed report is divided into thirteen sections.

1. **Introduction.** This report was prepared for the Criminal Investigation Division to better understand the deceased's manner of death. The key issue is whether she was attempting suicide or whether she died from homicide that was subsequently reported otherwise. Materials used included photographs, witness statements, background information on both the decedent and the accused, correspondence, and so

forth. The investigator states: "This is in part a psychological autopsy. . . ." (I have already commented on this in the section above.) The investigator indicates the number of violent deaths he has previously analyzed—approximately 1,000 suicides and 460 homicides.

2. **Location and Date of the Incident.** The date, time, and place of the event are indicated. Neighbors' names—all Army officers—are indicated.

3. **The Presenting Event.** Witnesses stated that around 3:00 AM on the given date, Captain Campbell went to his neighbors and is reported to have said: "Peggy was hurt and he needed me to call an ambulance." "Peggy had tried to kill herself." "Peggy had shot herself." A neighbor ran to Campbell's place, where he found the deceased lying on the floor between the couch and the bathroom door. He could not detect a pulse. An ambulance was called. Medical and law enforcement personnel arrived soon thereafter.

4. **The Initial Story by Captain Campbell.** Witness reported that when Campbell came to his door, his eyes were red, he was crying and seemed confused. Another witness reported that Campbell said that Peggy "was trying to cut herself up" and he tried to get the shotgun (which she had put there by the shower stall) away from her, but "She grabbed it and pointed it toward herself and it went off."

During those early morning hours, after the death, Campbell told a military investigator about the events early that afternoon and evening. When he returned home in the late afternoon she was drinking a beer. She had spent the day watching rented videos. He prepared a barbecue while she continued watching TV. After eating, they watched some TV and played a computer game. While playing she drank some brandy and began to get intoxicated. She became angry with him and turned the computer off. He calmed her down and they talked about how they were not getting along. She told him that she felt trapped and wanted to return to school.

Around 10 P.M. he said he was tired and wanted to go to bed. She announced she was going out to a pizza parlor (which was a favorite place of hers). Some hours later, around 1 A.M., she returned. He did not want to get up, but she pulled the sheets off him. He then got up and went into the living room. It was obvious that she had been drinking.

He then went back to bed. A little later he heard her talking to herself. He got up to see what was happening. He looked through the house and saw the light in the bathroom. When he opened the bathroom door he saw her sitting in the shower stall. He noticed a cut on her abdomen and blood in the shower basin. He also noticed his shotgun. It was propped up against the shower ledge. When he tried to reach for the shotgun she grabbed it by the barrel, and, as she pulled the gun toward herself, it discharged.

Campbell took the shotgun into the living room, put it down by the couch, and ran next door, where he told his neighbors that he needed help. He then ran back to his house and moved Peggy from the shower stall to the living room, where he placed her on the floor. The gun was in the way, so he took it back to the back room. By this time, neighbors were attempting first aid on Peggy. The ambulance had been called. A neighbor suggested he step aside. He went into his bedroom where he changed his bloodsoaked shirt and pants.

5. **The Crime Scene.** The criminal investigation agents reported the crime scene as "a real mess." In the bedroom the agents observed what they believed to be bloodstains on the pillows, on the bedspread, on the fitted (bottom) sheet, and on the wall next to the bed. They also reported some damp washcloths with blood on the floor. In addition, they reported finding a trail of blood from the bedroom into the bathroom, and what they called "drag bloodstains" from the bedroom to the living room. They reported finding blood in places where Campbell denied having been subsequent to his contact with his wife's blood.

6. **The Autopsy.** An autopsy of the deceased was conducted by a forensic pathologist. He reported a number of findings, including a contact shotgun wound, which would indicate that the barrel was against her skin. The direction of fire was approximately level. On her lower abdomen there were four stab wounds. One of the cuts had numerous pricks around it. These the autopsy surgeon indicated might have been caused by "taunting" (tentative cuts on the body before a deep cut is made). In addition, there were multiple bruises on the extremities and the back of her head. He identified sixty bruised areas, with a majority being less than four hours old at the time of her death. There was a bruise on her chin. He also noted scars on both wrists and in each elbow. He reported her blood alcohol level was .10—actually it

turned out to be .17—and no other drugs in her body. "The manner of death was ruled homicide."

7. **Victimology.** The following information is given in this section: the place and date of the decedent's birth. There are indications that she had a somewhat dysfunctional childhood. Her stepfather describes her as "rebellious," "subject to mood swings," "high-strung," "unhappy," and stated that she had made several suicide attempts. Her military medical records indicate "a history of affective disorders since her early adolescence." Her symptoms reportedly included "severe dysphoria, sleep and appetite disturbance, tension and nervousness, irritability, anger with episodic aggression and suicidal ideation."

The marriage was apparently rocky. The stepfather reported that when alcohol was involved, "The situation could become very violent." For the three months preceding her death, Peggy had been seen by a military clinical psychologist for complaints of depression and stress. The psychologist indicated that Peggy needed regular contact with psychiatric and psychological services for her mood swings and depressive episodes.

When her husband was away on military maneuvers—once for a period of three months—she volunteered at a military hospital, but reportedly became bored and lonely and drank heavily. After his return her drinking continued, and he reportedly drank (sometimes heavily) on the weekends and was reportedly hot-tempered when he drank.

8. **Was Deceased Attempting Suicide on the Date of Her Death?** The key question is whether or not Peggy was attempting suicide when her husband discovered her. Four issues will be addressed: her mental status on the evening of her death, the fact that she was nude at the time of her death, the use of multiple methods in a suicide attempt, and the nature and extent of her injuries.

9. **Deceased's Mental Status.** There is a history of affective disorder, somatic complaints, and alcohol abuse. On the date of her death, three facts are undisputed: that she was at home with her husband on the fateful afternoon and evening except for her visit to the pizza parlor; that she did leave her home that evening driving her own car, and that she returned in the small hours, brought by taxi; and that at the time of her death she was intoxicated. There is no indication that she was in a

depressive mood swing during this period. Apparently the situation began to deteriorate when she became angry while they were playing a computer game in the early evening.

Would deceased have been sufficiently depressed to become suicidal? It seems unlikely that she was. She was unhappy in the marriage. It would not come as a surprise to her to be engaged with her husband in a discussion of the marriage and the possibility of their separating. This would argue against an impulsive suicide. In addition, a separation "would allow her to solve her problems." Based on all that is known . . . it is more likely that she would have been belligerent and hostile rather than retiring and self-punitive. In short, there is nothing to support a contention that she was in a mental state that would have led to self-destructive behavior; however, this remains an ambiguous issue.

10. **Deceased's Nudity at the Time of Her Death.** At the time of her death she was nude. What was the significance of this point? A review of 150-plus female active-duty and dependent suicides revealed none in which the person was nude at the time of her death. "Her reported nudity at the time she was reported to be attempting suicide is thus highly unusual and correspondingly improbable."

11. **Multiple Methods.** Suicides involving multiple methods—in this case, cutting and shooting—are not common. It does not make sense that she would have taken both the knife and the gun into the bathroom with her, "because if she had set aside the plan to kill herself in favor of a gesture, then why take the shotgun?" "If she anticipated the cutting to fail even before doing it (hence taking the shotgun into the bathroom), why did she not just go ahead and shoot herself first without attempting to stab herself to death?"

12. **The Nature and Extent of Her Injuries.** According to military records, suicide by cutting is rare, and when it occurs the cuts are on the wrists or throat. "Multiple wounds to the abdomen are noteworthy by their absence." Furthermore, "The use of a shotgun is . . . relatively rare among women." The pathologist reported that the wound was a contact wound, which means that the barrel of the gun was pressed against her body. "The circumstances described by Captain Campbell make this highly improbable." Finally, the large number of fresh bruises on the

deceased "clearly suggest aggressive contact within four hours of her death," something not accounted for by Campbell's report of the event.

13. **Summary.** "Taken in toto, Campbell's description of the fatal events appear to be contradicted by fact, logic, and probability. What is suggested is that on the evening (of the death), a violent contact occurred between deceased and Campbell during the course of which he shot her with the shotgun. The circumstances further suggest that following the shooting, Campbell placed deceased in the shower stall and staged the scene to conform to the story he intended to tell. He was favored in this design by virtue of her unstable personality and the fact that she had made suicide gestures in the past. Based on the foregoing, it is my professional opinion that Captain Joseph Campbell shot deceased with the shotgun and attempted to conceal the true facts of the event by staging the scene he subsequently reported."

/ signed /
Perry N. Olds
Special Agent
Office of Special Investigations
U.S. Army

REPORT OF PSYCHIATRIC CONSULTANT FOR THE DEFENSE

Captain Campbell's lawyer, Mr. Dan Hyatt, contacted two expert witnesses, Jerome A. Motto, M.D. and me. Dr. Motto is professor of psychiatry at the University of California at San Francisco and past president of the American Association of Suicidology. For a number of tactical and realistic reasons, Dr. Motto did not testify in person at the trial—held in another state. However, in my court testimony, I alluded to his report and read portions of it into the record, so that in this way, it figured in the trial. It is presented here with a few elisions. I consider it a model consultation report.

Consultation Report

The problem at hand is the determination of the mode of death of Peggy Scott-Campbell. The question addressed is whether her death on

July 23, 1990 was an accident in the course of thwarting her suicide attempt, or whether other issues played a role.

In order to form the basis for answering the question at hand, four preliminary questions are addressed: (1) Was Peggy Scott-Campbell the kind of person who would resort to suicide under adverse circumstances; (2) Was she being subjected to significant emotional stress at the time of her death; (3) Was there a precipitating event or circumstance that could reasonably have provoked a suicidal act at the time of her death; and (4) would Captain Campbell's character and behavior pattern be consistent with either premeditated or impulsive homicide?

1. **Was she vulnerable to suicidal impulses or behavior?** The record is very consistent as regards the emotional vulnerability of Mrs. Scott-Campbell. Her medical record indicates an ongoing affective disturbance since early adolescence. In 1984 she complained of severe dysphoria, anger with episodic aggressiveness, and suicidal thoughts. She was diagnosed at that time as suffering from a major depressive disorder with borderline personality traits. The recommendation that she have a psychiatric evaluation and follow-up treatment with anti-depressive medication was not implemented. Nor was the recommendation that she be seen for psychiatric and psychological treatment.

Mrs. Scott-Campbell is said to have exhibited outspoken suicidal behavior on at least four occasions. . . . These events are given varying dates by different informants, but the episodes themselves appear to be discrete and separate experiences. Some were related by Mrs. Scott-Campbell to confidants, and others are noted in Army medical records.

In addition to specific suicidal behaviors, there is virtual unanimity among those who knew her best that she was moody, emotionally volatile, prone to act impulsively and violently, and moved to intense feeling states by seemingly minor issues. The most provocative of these issues were apparently feelings of being criticized, ignored, or in some way devalued. Examples are numerous, such as Mrs. Scott-Campbell's own description (on tape) of the altercation with her friend Marlene, and the episode in which she is said to have kicked in the bathroom door after Capt. Campbell retreated there to escape her angry outburst.

2. **Was she under significant emotional stress?** Mrs. Scott-Campbell made no secret of her discontent with army life, with "not fitting in" with the separations entailed or with other army wives, or

with the "homebody" nature of her husband, leading to repeated consideration of divorce. Her persistently heavy drinking underscored her inability to find a stable adjustment; at the same time she apparently felt guilty about her behavior. She was heard to repeat "I'm sorry—I'm sorry—" when in an intoxicated state. She confided that Captain Campbell treated her well and that she wanted to reward him with a party. Though emotionally very immature, she was intelligent enough to know that sooner or later her repeated drunkenness and violent outbursts would catch up with her—that it was only a matter of time, and that time might be getting short. For a person with intense rejection sensitivity, the threat of being abandoned would constitute an ever-increasing emotional pressure in addition to her underlying insecurity and dissatisfaction with her life.

3. **Was there a precipitating event?** A recurrent theme in the available data regarding Mrs. Scott-Campbell's behavior is the sequence of (1) argument, (2) withdrawal by Captain Campbell, (3) drinking by Peggy Scott-Campbell, (4) guilt, depression, and contrition on the part of Mrs. Scott-Campbell. In one such previous sequence, Mrs. Scott-Campbell came home from a bar, told Captain Campbell she was going to cut her wrist, and when he tried to calm her down, she hit him with a chair. On the night of her death, this sequence seems to have been repeated. . . . Whatever the facts were, they went beyond the usual pattern of returning from a drinking episode feeling depressed, and calling someone to talk, or even making suicidal threats. Mrs. Scott-Campbell was unable to get Captain Campbell to respond to her that night, even to placate her, and combined with the progressive dissatisfaction of her life and the depression and guilt she was prone to express after drinking, this experience of "being ignored" could easily have triggered a characteristic violent act. In this instance the act was directed at herself, but her disorganization and ambivalence created only preparation for a lethal act (loaded gun, cutting of abdomen).

4. **Would his character be consistent with homicide?** Any effort to determine the likelihood of a given behavior by a given individual must take into account that person's behavioral history, as well as the characterological elements that contribute to that history. In short, the best predictor of behavior is past behavior.

In Captain Campbell's case, those who knew him on a day-to-day basis could hardly be more consistent in their impressions: "loving and supportive," "good natured," "least prone to violence," "Violence is not in him. He is not capable of violence," "Absolutely no way he could have done anything to hurt Peggy," and the like.

While it appears to be sophisticated to be skeptical of such unequivocal statements, it is difficult to document contradictory evidence. Mrs. Scott-Campbell's multiple bruises are only a mild example of what one sees in chronic heavy drinkers, as falls and bumping into objects are so common. Even cracked ribs, severe facial bruises, and head trauma are not uncommon. She stated that some bruises on her arm were from his trying to stop her from swinging a broken glass at him. In short, Captain Campbell's apparent need to be protective of his wife under the most provocative conditions, and to reflect this demeanor toward the rest of the world as well, is a virtually unanimous perception, and the record gives us nothing substantial to question it.

Comment on report of Investigator Olds. Investigator Olds recapitulates the events surrounding Mrs. Scott-Campbell's background and death, and then asks whether she would have been "sufficiently depressed to become suicidal." The question is irrelevant. The nature of her pathology is not depressive but characterological. This is familiar to persons engaged in the field of suicide prevention, although lay persons and even some professionals continue to consider suicide a function of depression rather than psychological pain.

Investigator Olds's subsequent three questions are based on epidemiological comparisons that are interesting but likewise irrelevant. Though some of the numbers can be challenged, the most important issue in this analysis is that such issues as nudity, methods used, and the nature and extent of injury are unique to each individual. The degree of ambivalence, clarity of cognitive functioning, how organized and obsessive the individual is, his or her state of turmoil and agitation, and so forth, are the determinants of behavior. What another or a thousand others have done plays no essential role in understanding a given individual's behavior. In the present instance, an intoxicated, frustrated, angry, disorganized individual is involved. Trying to create a scientific aura by judging how common a given pattern appears is simply sophistry.

In short, I believe Investigator Olds's data are interesting, as is his discussion, but they are of no significance whatever in the individual

instance under consideration. Thus an opinion based on such considerations is little more than speculation and fertile imagination.

Summary and Conclusions.
In summary, Mrs. Scott-Campbell was a person with a lifelong
emotional vulnerability, manifested by extremes of reactivity, a very low
threshold for psychic pain, and limited behavioral control. She required
a great deal of emotional support and in its absence had repeatedly
demonstrated a pattern of self-destructive behavior. In suicide prevention language, she would be regarded as "chronically suicidal," im-
plying that even at her best level of functioning she was vulnerable to
becoming suicidal in adverse circumstances, especially if a perceived
rejection was involved.

Captain Campbell demonstrated an inexplicable ability, perhaps a
need, to protect and nurture this emotionally vulnerable young woman.
The record is replete with observations documenting his consistency in
this regard. No evidence is available of traits that would contradict this.

The circumstances surrounding Mrs. Scott-Campbell's death are
entirely consistent with her patterns of behavior and with Captain
Campbell's efforts to protect her from her own lack of control. I find
nothing in the record to indicate otherwise, and regard undocumented
hypotheses to the contrary as speculative. Though the documented
record can mislead us, I feel that it provides a better basis for sound
judgment than hypotheses without documented support.

Jerome A. Motto, M.D.
Professor of Psychiatry
University of California, San Francisco

TWO CONSECUTIVE NEWSPAPER REPORTS OF THE TRIAL

These two accounts were written on the second and third days of
the court-martial and published (the following days) in the local
newspaper.

Testimony Given in Trial

ARMYVILLE, September 23— Murder defendant Capt. Joseph P. Campbell lowered his head Thursday while a criminal investigation agent testified about photographs he took where Campbell's wife died last July.

Special Agent Jerome Beach took the photos shortly after the death of Peggy Scott-Campbell on July 26. The 30-year-old woman died in the couple's Armyville apartment from a single shotgun wound to the chest. Her husband is being charged with premeditated murder.

The trial, before Judge (Col.) George D. Maris entered its second day Thursday and is expected to last into next week.

The defense plans to argue that Scott-Campbell's death could have been an accident or suicide.

In opening statements Wednesday, Campbell's attorney, Dan Hyatt, told the five-man court-martial panel that Campbell was attempting to take the sawed-off shotgun from his wife when it accidentally discharged.

Two photos introduced Thursday by the prosecutor, Major Stanley Bates, showed a shower basin half filled with blood and water. The bathroom was next to the living room in the couple's apartment. The government also offered into evidence the death weapon, a 12-gauge shotgun, a bloodstained blue T-shirt worn by Campbell, and an empty liquor bottle found in the living room. Beach testified that an empty bottle of Ativan, an anti-anxiety drug similar to Valium, was found on the couple's living room table.

In an opening statement Wednesday, Hyatt said his client awoke in the early morning of July 23 to find his wife in the bathroom shower stall cutting her abdomen with a knife. A shotgun was sitting nearby.

Oscar Christol, a fingerprint expert for the U.S. Army Criminal Investigations Laboratory, testified that it could not be determined if Scott-Campbell could have grabbed the gun barrel.

Christol said that when he received the shotgun, its barrel and grip were covered with paper sacks. That preservation method could have destroyed a palm print, he said.

In testimony late Wednesday, a key witness described Campbell as "a teddy bear."

"I have never seen him mad," said First Lieutenant William Lambert, referring to Campbell. "He was always telling jokes. He's the one who would always pick you up."

Lambert lived in the same apartment building where Scott-Campbell died. He testified that Campbell awakened him about 3 A.M. the night of the shooting.

"He was panicking," said Lambert, referring to the events of July 23. "He said, 'Peggy's hurt. Call an ambulance. She tried to kill herself.' "

Lambert testified that he accompanied Campbell to the couple's apartment, where he found the victim with a "quarter-sized hole in her chest." Lambert said he administered mouth-to-mouth resuscitation, but was unable to inflate the victim's lungs.

Lambert testified that Campbell, with the help of Captain Alice Adams, a friend of Lambert's, called an ambulance to the scene.

Later, Lambert testified, an emergency medical technician examined the victim and shook his head. Campbell then began crying, Lambert said.

Adams testified Wednesday that while waiting for the ambulance, Campbell told her that the weapon went off when he tried to pull the shotgun from his wife.

"I can't live without her. I can't believe my baby is gone," Adams said Campbell told her while waiting for the ambulance.

Antonio Mondello, owner of the pizzeria, testified Wednesday that Scott-Campbell, a regular customer, came into the restaurant, had several drinks, and left about 12:30 A.M.

"She was in an OK mood," Mondello testified. "She had a couple of beers."

The restaurant owner called for a taxi, he said. "She was the same old Peggy—cheerful. She helped me wash dishes," Mondello said.

Adams said that Scott-Campbell was in good spirits that evening and remembered her returning to the apartment building about 1 A.M.

"You could tell that she had been drinking," she said. "But she was in an OK mood and not angry."

Lambert testified that Campbell "appeared to be in shock" and "alternated from calm to crying," following the shooting.

According to Lambert, Campbell told him that he saw his wife holding a knife and the shotgun, and that he tried to take the shotgun away from her when it fired.

"He kept repeating, 'I did not murder her. I did not murder her,' " Lambert said.

Experts Testify in Trial

ARMYVILLE, Sept. 25—Two blood-spatter experts originally hired—but never called to testify—by the prosecution, testified late Thursday afternoon on behalf of an army officer accused of killing his wife last July.

Capt. Joseph P. Campbell, 33, is charged with premeditated murder in the July 23 death of Peggy Scott-Campbell. Scott-Campbell, 30, died in the couple's apartment from a single shotgun blast.

Leon Aron and Albert Hawkins, forensic blood-spatter specialists at the Minnesota State Crime Laboratory, testified that their analysis of bloodstains enabled them to reconstruct the shooting scene. They told the five-man court-martial panel that Campbell's statements to military investigators did not contradict their findings.

Campbell has maintained he awoke in the early hours of July 23 to find his wife in the bathroom shower, cutting her stomach with a knife. Witnesses testified earlier that Scott-Campbell had been drinking heavily that night. Campbell said he saw his 12-gauge pump shotgun nearby. Campbell told investigators he was attempting to remove the gun when his wife grabbed the barrel. It

discharged, striking her in the chest.

Campbell told Criminal Investigation Command agents he carried her into the living room, put her on the floor behind the couch, then summoned help.

"There were no inconsistencies in what we read in (criminal Investigation Command) reports," Aron said.

Aron said he and his colleague used the bathroom in the couple's apartment to stage a reenactment of the shooting. Aron said they used Campbell's statements to investigators to determine if the physical positions that Campbell and his wife were purportedly in at the time of the shooting were possible.

Aron and Hawkins testified that events can often be reconstructed by analyzing the shape, size, and distribution of bloodstains. Aron said, however, they could not determine if the shooting was a homicide.

Aron and Hawkins were first hired by the prosecution, which believed that Scott-Campbell was shot in the couple's bedroom before her body was carried into the living room. No evidence has been offered during the trial to support that theory.

The prosecution, led by Major Stanley Bates, continued to call witnesses Friday. The case, which began Wednesday, is expected to wind up next week.

On Friday, prosecution witness Perry N. Olds, investigative consultant from the Office of Special Investigations in Washington, testified he found nude suicides highly unusual. Olds said suicides involving multiple methods like knife and gun were also uncommon.

Olds said he was drawing on data from other military suicide cases. Those cases include service members and dependents, he said.

Prosecution and defense attorneys were expected to fly Saturday to Los Angeles to take a deposition from Dr. Edwin Shneidman, founder of the American Association of Suicidology.

A LETTER FROM THE DECEDENT'S MOTHER

Here is an unsolicited letter to the court from the mother of the decedent — the mother-in-law of the man charged with murdering her daughter. What, offhand, would one expect to find in it? I cannot forbear commenting that it is one of the most extraordinary suicidological documents I have seen in my professional career.

To Whom It May Concern:

It is probably not necessary to state that I have spent hundreds of hours thinking about the tragedy of my daughter's death and how such a thing could have occurred. I have been extremely reluctant to put any kind of statement into words for two reasons: First, any comprehensive picture of my daughter would fill a novel, and second, due to the necessity of brevity, I am concerned that something I say might be taken out of context of the entire picture. I cannot, however, see Joe's life go down the drain without making a statement about how his account of that night could be true. I, of course, not having been there, cannot know for certain what is true, nor can anyone but Joe himself. There are, however, some facts which are pertinent to the possibility of the truth of his statements.

In taking Joe's scenario at face value, it is likely that he thought Peggy was actually attempting suicide. It is my opinion that it is more likely that she was making another plea for help, not seeking to actually die. She would have, at least, have left a note for her mother if she had actually intended death to result from her actions. She was seeking help (relief from her unceasing emotional pain) in some form which would not require hospitalization/lock-up. She had resisted all Joe's efforts to persuade her to seek professional help because of this fear of being locked up in a mental ward. The fear was not irrational. It came about because I had admitted her to the mental ward of a major medical hospital after a similar (but milder) "show" of suicide attempt when she was in her late teens.

Self-infliction of abdominal stab/slash wounds is a pretty dramatic and unusual method of gaining attention, however, each successive "plea" must be different and more dramatic than those preceding it, since said preceding attempts have obviously failed to bring relief. Peggy had a relatively high physical pain threshold, although low emotional pain threshold, which, together with the alcohol level and possibility of pills, could very well explain the bizarre nature of this particular plea for help.

It was very difficult for me to admit Peggy to the hospital that time they locked her up, and she was very angry with me for a long time. It was my thinking at the time that the experience would deter her from ever seeking attention in such a dangerous way again. In retrospect, she should have been referred for professional psychological counseling, not treated with fear tactics. This was not recommended nor done and the long-term result has been her subsequent unnecessary death and the possible complete ruin of her husband's life. I believe Joe loved her deeply and sought, to the best of his ability and knowledge, to help her and to protect her from herself.

Joe had no idea of the depth or duration of depression and social maladjustment with which he was attempting to deal. He knew only what she told him and what he, an untrained observer, could see for himself. She could not tell him what she did not herself know or understand. I myself, although I tried, was never able to understand what made her tick and I think it would have taken an extremely sensitive, experienced psychologist, with great gifts of insight and wisdom, to figure it out.

Joe's entire life is on the line here and, unless there's something significant I don't know, I think unfairly. He loved Peggy deeply. He put up with a great deal, and did it with unbelievable patience and acceptance. He stayed with her when any other man would have thrown his hands up in despair and walked out long ago. He gave her the only real happiness she ever had in her life. I think that frightened her. She could never understand how he could love her since she was never able to love herself, but Joe saw, knew and loved the depth, intrinsic goodness, and love of all creation that was the true Peggy beneath the surface of terrible depression and inability to cope with life, with which she suffered her entire life. She had a desperate need to be loved and accepted because of her inability to understand her own self worth. She was convinced she wasn't worth loving. This is what made her go to such desperate measures to prove otherwise, at any cost. The cost was great indeed.

There is nothing that can bring my daughter back. The *only* solace is that she is at peace now in God's love—the first peace she has ever known. My sister wrote me that as she was praying her rosary, she felt Peggy's presence, bringing her an overwhelming sense of joy such as she had not felt in years. She said she thought that Peggy wanted to share *her* joy with us. I was very moved by this and, at first, concerned that I had not felt her presence. In thinking about it, I believe it is because I have not worked through my grief yet, particularly all the guilt I feel over what I might have done differently to have kept this terrible tragedy from happening. I have a lot of thinking and praying to do over this yet, but there is one thing I do know. I don't want to add a second tragedy to the oppressive burden of guilt I already have, and condemning Joseph unjustly for Peggy's death would do just that.

I, frankly, don't think there should even be a trial. I don't think Joe is guilty of anything except negligence in handling the gun in trying to take it away from her. It is regrettable and he knows better, but how many of us would have done any better under such circumstances? A larger negligence may have been in somehow not getting her professional help, or at least telling me of the seriousness of what was going on. I might have been able to discern the urgency of the situation and done something about it. Then again, I may not have understood the gravity at all. I'm sure Joe would have sought help if he had understood how serious the situation was becoming and the possible repercussions. Hindsight is always 20/20.

I have been under a great deal of pressure from my family not to get involved, to just "wait and see what happens." In fact, I just received a letter from my mother in which she clearly stated her feelings that to say anything in defense of Joe would be a betrayal of Peggy. So, against all advice and in the knowledge of possible repercussions, I am writing this letter for two reasons. First, I feel I know Joseph very well and I do not believe that he would hurt Peggy, let alone kill her, even in anger, *no matter what she had done*. I do not say this naively. I know they have gotten into it a few times, when both had been drinking, and there were some blows meted out from both sides. What I'm saying is that he could not coolly, maliciously hurt her. And the idea of premeditation is so preposterous as to not even be worthy of comment. Second, Peggy loved Joe very much, despite what she may have done that might make it appear otherwise. She was driven by emotional problems that were not her fault and which she could not control. I do not believe that Peggy would want Joe's life ruined. He has suffered enough already for any unwitting part he played in this tragedy. To lose his military career, for which he spent many years in preparation, is a severe blow. He has lost his wife he loved and misses her desperately. He is suffering untold pain from the guilt he feels over what he should or should not have done differently at the time, as well as not having somehow forced her to get help before it came to what it did. Is this not enough? I think it is.

Respectfully,
/ signed /
Maria E. Scott

EXCERPTS FROM MY TESTIMONY, WITH COMMENTS

The following is an excerpt of my responses to questions from Mr. Dan Hyatt, counsel for the defense.

HYATT: The army investigator, Mr. Olds, has testified earlier in this case. He offered an opinion that it was unusual to see two instrumentalities when either attempting or committing suicide. Do you have an opinion with respect to that statement?
ESS: Yes. In a picayune way he is right. But in an overall way he is howlingly wrong. I'll tell you about each of those if I may.
HYATT: Please.
ESS: Suicide itself, fortunately, is an event of infrequent

occurrence. So that you can make tabulations of methods and all sorts of things. A lot of events are infrequent, but if the incontrovertible evidence is that the person has done it, then you can't say that the person has not done it simply because it is infrequent. Using two methods is much more infrequent than using one. That's true. But then to argue from that to this particular case is a tyro's error. It's a mistake that freshmen, undergraduates in my Death and Suicide course at UCLA, make of going from statistics to an individual case. Statistics are an interesting background for a case but they don't tell you about *that* case. Here we are talking about *this* case.

HYATT: Mr. Olds also testified that he thought it was very rare based on his study of army personnel and their dependents, his data base, that it was very rare to find a dependent female to commit suicide or attempt to commit suicide in the nude. Do you have an opinion about that?

Ess: Yes. Well, I would say to him, "That's true. That's absolutely true. But you're really not seriously making an argument that that has a bearing on *this* case, are you?" And if he said "Yes," my already low opinion of him would drop precipitously.

HYATT: What value do you see of statistical information such as that offered by Mr. Olds in determining the cause of death?

Ess: In a particular case?

HYATT: Yes.

Ess: None. It's background material.

HYATT: Is the utilization of statistics in the manner testified to by Mr. Olds a scientifically acceptable method, or is that data reasonably relied upon by other experts in your field as a means of drawing a conclusion?

Ess: If your question is, is it a scientifically credited method the way he has done it, the answer is no.

HYATT: And why would that be?

Ess: The technical response is that in these matters, in suicidology, the confusion of statistical-demographic-epidemiological-numerical data with the etiology or outcome of any particular individual case, to make a judgment about that individual case on the basis of statistics is a methodological error.

HYATT: Why is it a methodological error?

Ess: Because it has things backwards. It isn't that the statistics generate the case; it is that the cases taken in long series or large numbers generate the statistics. To say that it is rare is not to say that it did not occur.

HYATT: What do you say when you hear that Peggy Campbell was nude on the evening of her death?

Ess: I would say, "Gee whiz, isn't that unusual." But then to argue as he did that it couldn't be suicide on that account is a howler. It boggles the mind. Where did his logic go?

HYATT: And would you have the same opinion as to the use of two instrumentalities?

Ess: Yes, sure. What is persuasive is the whole history of her lifetime. . . .

My courtroom exchanges with Maj. Stanley Bates, the deposing counsel for the prosecution, had, in my mind, a somewhat eerie quality. Against all the evidence that I could see, he held firmly to the view that Captain Campbell had murdered his wife in the bedroom and dragged her body into the bathroom and then cut her abdomen to disguise the deed. He completely endorsed Mr. Olds's report—the heart of the prosecution's case. In addition, there was what seemed to me a mildly bizarre twist: He insisted on meeting with me privately before he cross-examined me. Mr. Hyatt and I acceded to this request. But in that private session, in response to a question from me about his marital status—I had said, "Tell me something about yourself," and instead of finessing or parrying my somewhat impertinent question, as I expected him to do, considering the circumstances—he told me about his recent divorce. He then pressed me to believe his view of the case. He seemed to me to be muddleheaded, not too well prepared, and curiously immature for an Adjutant General officer.

Back in the courtroom, I was not very sympathetic to his flawed view of the case. He saw the accused as guilty and wanted to convict him. But he had neither the facts on his side nor the tools in his head, but he had the fervor of his convictions and confusions. I could see him carrying contaminated water in some other cases, and that troubles me. Of course—as I have stated and implied in my testimony above—I consider Mr. Olds's crucial investigation report to be badly flawed, bordering on incompetence.

Here is a brief verbatim excerpt of the exchanges between Major Bates and me.

BATES: For the record also, I would like to back up to where we started to do this. And I'll log an objection to this for the reasons that we've just discussed. Doctor, a physical autopsy is something that you make by gathering facts to render a professional judgment on the mode of death. Is that correct?

ESS: I beg your pardon. You said a physical autopsy.

BATES: No sir. I said a psychological autopsy.

ESS: No. For the record, you said physical, if I may say so.

BATES: My question is that is it your testimony that in a psychological autopsy you gather facts to make a professional judgment on the mode of death?

ESS: Yes.

BATES: And that psychological autopsies are sometimes undetermined?

ESS: Yes.

BATES: And that they can be an accurate determination of the mode of death?

ESS: I didn't hear you. Did you say accurate or inaccurate?

BATES: Can be an accurate determination of the mode of death.

ESS: Yes.

BATES: Is it your testimony that the psychological autopsy can always be correct?

ESS: No. It is just more information.

BATES: Would it be important to rely upon . . . strike that. Is it not important to have accurate facts in relying upon, to rely upon accurate facts to make a psychological autopsy?

ESS: Yes.

BATES: And if these facts were inaccurate, it could significantly affect the determination through the psychological autopsy?

Ess: Well, the psychological autopsy stands alongside the investigation of the physical facts. It doesn't rest upon them. I think that is part of the confusion here.

Bates: I would like to object at this point. And see if you can perhaps just answer the question. Would you like for me to restate it, sir?

Hyatt: What is the basis for your objection?

Bates: He's not answering the question.

Ess: Well, you don't understand the psychological autopsy, Major. You truly don't.

Bates: I would object to this also. Is it not important in making a psychological autopsy . . . I'll strike that. Doctor, did you generate a written report in this case?

Ess: No.

ADDITIONAL NEWSPAPER ACCOUNTS

Deposition Offered in Trial

ARMYVILLE, Sept. 30—A noted authority on suicide described a military wife who was shot to death last year as "terribly unhappy," and suicide-prone.

A videotape featuring Dr. Edwin Shneidman, founder of the American Association of Suicidology, was played Thursday in the premeditated murder trial of Capt. Joseph P. Campbell. The defendant, 33, is charged with slaying his wife, Peggy Scott-Campbell, in the bathroom of their apartment July 23. The 30-year-old woman died of a chest wound from a 12-gauge pump shotgun.

Campbell told military investigators that he found his wife of five years in the shower stall, cutting her abdomen with a knife. His shotgun was nearby.

Witnesses have testified that Campbell said his wife grabbed the barrel of the gun when Campbell tried to remove it. It discharged, striking her in the chest.

The defense is trying to prove that Scott-Campbell was shot accidentally while attempting suicide.

Shneidman's deposition was taken in Los Angeles on Monday. A court-martial panel of five officers is hearing evidence in the courtroom of Judge (Col.) George D. Maris.

Shneidman evaluated the psychological autopsy report of Dr. Jerome Motto, a psychiatrist and professor at the University of California in San Francisco. Motto is a consultant for the defense.

Shneidman said he believed Scott-Campbell was attempting to kill herself on the night she died.

"If she had survived that episode—this is a terrible thing to say about a fellow human being—she would be dead by her own hands in a year or two," he testified.

Shneidman said he based his conclusions in part on a letter written by Scott-Campbell's mother on her son-in-law's behalf.

Earlier this year, Maria E. Scott wrote a "To whom it may concern" letter to the court stating that when her daughter was a teenager, she had admitted her to a hospital mental ward.

"She had resisted all Joe's efforts to persuade her to seek professional help because of this fear of being locked up in a mental ward," Scott wrote. "He loved Peggy deeply," the letter also said.

Although only portions of the letter were admitted into evidence, Scott also added, "I, frankly, don't think there should be even a trial. I don't think Joe is guilty of anything except negligence in handling the gun in trying to take it away from her."

"In forty years, I never read a document like this," Shneidman said, referring to the letter.

Shneidman disputed prosecution testimony offered last week by Perry N. Olds, an army criminal investigator. Olds testified that statistics show that nude suicides and suicides involving two instruments of destruction were highly unusual.

Shneidman agreed, but told the court that statistics cannot be applied to individual cases.

Also played Thursday was the videotaped deposition of Beverly Simkins, a former counselor at the Armyville education center.

For a time, Simkins said, Scott-Campbell worked with her. Simkins said the woman experienced wide mood swings and eventually quit her job at the center and became almost reclusive. Scott-Campbell also drank excessively, she testified. She described the victim's husband as a peaceable man who was devoted to his wife.

Prior to deploying to Panama, Simkins said, Campbell came to her office and asked that she look out for his wife.

Winifred LeClerq, who described herself as a close friend of the Campbells, testified Thursday that Scott-Campbell would sometimes telephone her at night to discuss personal problems.

"She felt like she wasn't worth anything or had no reason for living," LeClerq said.

The defense rested Thursday afternoon. Prosecution rebuttal witnesses were scheduled to begin testifying later Thursday.

Tape Reveals Wife's Anguish

ARMYVILLE, Oct. 2—"I was playing with the shotgun the other day. . . ."

The voice belonged to Peggy Scott-Campbell, a military spouse who has been dead since July 23. Her words, laughter, and song filled a courtroom Thursday afternoon and brought tears to the eyes of the man accused of killing her.

For Capt. Joseph Campbell, it was a voice from the grave.

Campbell sobbed quietly as he listened to a cassette tape she had made months before when he was in Panama. The tape, however, was never mailed, and Campbell, who returned to the United States in May, had never heard it.

Until Thursday at his murder trial.

The tape became an unusual and spellbinding piece of evidence. . . .

The 33-year-old officer was charged with premeditated murder in the shotgun death of his 30-year-old wife. Scott-Campbell was fatally wounded in the bathroom of the couple's apartment.

The shotgun is the same one to which she referred in the tape recording.

Campbell claimed he found his wife, a woman with a history of mental problems, in the bathroom, cutting herself with a knife. His sawed-off shotgun was nearby. He told authorities that when he tried to remove the gun, she grabbed the barrel and pulled it to her chest, causing it to discharge.

Military investigators confiscated the tape, along with other evidence, shortly after the shooting. Campbell's attorney said his client has had access to the recording, but found it too painful to hear.

On Thursday, the 45-minute tape spoke to the court. It portrayed a lonely, frightened woman who missed her husband and feared he might be killed. Her words also revealed an angry, depressed personality that was having trouble coping with life.

At the same time, the tape unveiled a side of Scott-Campbell that was fun loving and playful.

On the tape she tells Campbell repeatedly that she loves him and, at one point, she mentions the shotgun. She also asks where he keeps the shells.

But Scott-Campbell doesn't dwell on the gun. She talks about many other things, like their dog getting into the garbage, her trip to a Chinese restaurant, the laundry, and a possible vacation when he returns from Panama.

"You've only been gone a little over two weeks," she says on the tape. "It seems like a year."

"I'm doing better than some of these other women. They're freaking out or crying all the time."

"Oh, babe, I can't wait until you get home."

"It's no fun going to bed. Nobody to tuck me in. Nobody to turn out the lights."

"I'm lonely. I'm miserable without you. I'm scared."

"It's hard being here without you. It's hard being anywhere without you."

"I did make the bed once since you were gone, but mostly the sheets are up around my ears. I want to reach out and touch your foot, but there's no foot."

"At least my heart is with you. My heart is with you every second, every moment of every day and minute you're over there. I just hope you understand."

She asks what Bible passage Campbell was reading before he was deployed to Panama, adding, "I really want to know."

"I have not been sleeping that great, honey, and when I do sleep, it's horrible."

Suddenly she puts on some music, a collection of songs from the 1960s. She mentions that she tries not to watch the television news. Against a backdrop of Sonny and Cher singing "I Got You Babe," she talks of a television special she watched, dedicated to servicemen in Panama.

"I cried during the whole thing. It was really moving."

"I just want you home now. I'm so scared of losing you."

Her voice is pleading, almost a cry.

"Joe, I swear I'll never take you for granted again."

"Come home to me. You've got

to come home to me."

She stops the music and sings a song to her husband. It's a strange song to come from a troubled woman, but she sings it with feeling.

It's titled "I'm the Happiest Girl in the Whole U.S.A."

NEWSPAPER ACCOUNT OF THE VERDICT

Captain Acquitted in Trial

ARMYVILLE, Oct. 1—An officer charged with the shotgun slaying of his wife last July was found innocent Friday by a five-man court-martial panel.

The panel's verdict came after about three hours of deliberation that brought to an end a court-martial that lasted more than a week.

Capt. Joseph Campbell had been charged with premeditated murder in the death of Peggy Scott-Campbell on July 12. Campbell had told investigators that he walked in on his wife while she was trying to kill herself in the bathroom of their apartment. Campbell said he found her cutting her abdomen with a knife. He said he saw his shotgun lying nearby.

When he attempted to remove the gun, Campbell said she grabbed the barrel and put it to her chest, causing it to discharge.

When Judge (Col.) George Maris read the verdict, Campbell threw back his head and emitted an audible sigh. His mother, Elizabeth Campbell, began crying loudly.

Campbell first hugged his two attorneys, Dan Hyatt, a civilian from Portland, Oregon, and Major James Purdich, a military attorney.

When Campbell embraced his mother, he broke into tears.

"I'm glad it's over. It's been a long time," he said. "It kind of restored my faith in the system. I loved my wife very much. I'm sorry she had to be dragged through this, too."

Chief prosecutor Maj. Stanley Bates would not comment on the verdict.

In closing arguments Friday

morning Bates told the panel that Campbell was anything but a peaceful "teddy bear" as defense witnesses sometimes characterized him.

"She (Scott-Campbell) was not greeted by a teddy bear. She was greeted by a bear with fangs."

He later referred to Campbell as a "grizzly bear, a peaceable person like most who can be pushed into violence."

Citing Scott-Campbell's drinking problems, her belligerent attitude, and her habit of ignoring housecleaning, Bates argued that she had pushed her husband over the brink.

"He's angry. He tolerated a lot for a long time," he said.

Bates said that the couple had an argument the evening prior to Scott-Campbell's death about separation and divorce, during which the woman mentioned returning to school.

Scott-Campbell later went out alone to a nearby pizzeria. Bates told the panel an angry Campbell waited up for his wife. When she returned, he charged that Campbell beat her and then took her into the bathroom and shot her.

After pulling the trigger, Bates said that Campbell attempted to cover up the crime by cleaning the bathroom and changing clothes. Bates argued that under the circumstances it would have been impossible for the woman to grab the gun and pull it to her chest.

Hyatt, in his closing arguments, said the charges brought against Campbell were unwarranted.

Regarding the murder charge, Hyatt remarked, "Why would you kill someone who is in the process of killing themselves?"

Hyatt said that a tape recording made by Scott-Campbell proved the couple loved each other very much. The defense attorney said the government had failed to prove that Campbell was guilty.

"They proved beyond a reasonable doubt this man is innocent," he said.

Hyatt described Scott-Campbell as a "very fragile human being." Evidence established that while a teenager, she had been locked up in a hospital mental ward. In a letter, her mother told the court that Scott-Campbell was reluctant to seek professional help for fear of being locked up again.

At the time of her death her blood alcohol content tested .17. Campbell's blood tested zero alcohol.

The trial began September 21 and involved a trip by attorneys to Los Angeles where a deposition was taken from Edwin Shneidman, a noted authority on suicide.

NEWSPAPER ACCOUNT OF SUBSEQUENT
DEVELOPMENTS

Top Army Lawyer Called Irresponsible by Defense

ARMYVILLE, Oct. 8—The civilian attorney of an officer acquitted last week of killing his wife has accused the Corps' top lawyer of being irresponsible by bringing a premeditated murder charge against his client.

Dan Hyatt, a lawyer from Portland, Oregon, also accused Col. Robert Bakersfield, the staff judge advocate of the Corps, of refusing to consider evidence that surfaced following an Article 32 investigation of Capt. Joseph Campbell. The evidence could have altered the charges, Hyatt said.

A Corps spokesman said that Bakersfield would not respond to the accusation.

Campbell, 33, was charged with the killing of Peggy Scott-Campbell, 30, with a 12-gauge shotgun inside their off-base apartment. A five-member court-martial panel acquitted the ten-year army veteran following a seven-day trial. The trial involved travel by prosecution and defense lawyers to both U.S. coasts to obtain videotaped depositions.

Hyatt asserted that Bakersfield ignored Article 32 investigation findings that recommended a charge of involuntary manslaughter be filed.

"Given the evidence as to Captain Campbell's intent, I felt it extremely unlikely that premeditation existed or could be proven by the government," wrote Lt. Col. George R. Pasteur, the investigating officer who conducted the Article 32.

An Article 32 investigation is similar to a civilian grand jury investigation.

Pasteur, after listening to three days of testimony concluded in the Article 32 report that "the charges and specifications are not in the proper form. The government barely produced minimum evidence which would indicate premeditation on the part of Captain Campbell."

Pasteur, an artillery officer, stated that the evidence warranted a charge of involuntary manslaughter instead.

Hyatt, citing trial costs that he said would exceed $250,000, claimed that filing the charge of premeditated murder constituted an "irresponsible exercise of power" by Bakersfield and Major Stanley Bates, who was chief prosecuting attorney.

Bates was unavailable Friday for comment.

Hyatt accused Bakersfield of failing to consider new evidence which included:

• Testimony from two blood-spatter experts that proved Scott-Campbell was shot in the bathroom of the couple's apartment, not the bedroom as the government believed. Hyatt said the experts, originally hired by the government for $25,000, were never called to testify by the prosecution.

• Answers from Campbell to thirty-five additional questions posed by the Criminal Investigation Command.

• A letter from Mrs. Maria Scott, Scott-Campbell's mother, outlining her daughter's psychological history, which included a stay in a mental ward. She said her son-in-law loved her daughter and would not have killed her.

"The idea of premeditation is so preposterous as to not even be worthy of comment," she wrote.

Campbell has said that he found his wife in the bathroom cutting her abdomen with a knife and that the shotgun was lying nearby. He said that when he tried to remove the shotgun, his wife grabbed the barrel and put it to her chest, causing it to discharge.

Hyatt said Bakersfield would not even look at the new evidence.

"He refused to take (the evidence) to the General (Corps Commander, Lt. Gen. Jonathan M. Faubus), and that was irresponsible," Hyatt said. "I think he's got a duty to the general to keep him apprised of continuing developments in the case. That shows a real bias."

Faubus was the convening authority.

"In my fifteen years of practice, I haven't seen a case that was such a gross overstatement of the charge," said Hyatt, a Vietnam veteran who specializes in military law. "There is no more serious charge than premeditated murder, and there was not evidence to support it."

In the military, a premeditated murder conviction carries an automatic sentence of life imprisonment.

Hyatt said that the military justice system is fair. "But it's also a system where abuse of power occurs with regularity."

"With Joseph, you've got basically a grieving widower," Hyatt said. "Can you imagine the horror of facing the prospect of having to spend the rest of your life in prison because this one person (Bakersfield) said, 'Well, I think he's guilty'?"

In a related action, Campbell

filed a complaint Thursday with the Corps Inspector General, requesting an inquiry into the conduct of the Criminal Investigation Command and the prosecution's handling of this case. In it, he claims that the prosecution withheld what he says appears to be *a suicide note written by Scott-Campbell just before she died.* [Italics added]

A Corps spokesman said the Inspector General acknowledged receipt of Campbell's complaint and has advised him to pursue it through appropriate legal channels.

The note, which Campbell said he discovered when he went to the Criminal Investigation Command's evidence room to retrieve his personal property, reads:

"Joe, I love you. You have nothing else but sleep on your mind. I have something a little more important than that on my mind. I'm a fool."

She wrote, "I love you" seven times, and then continued, "I'm so scared. I'm crazy. I think I drink too much. I think I'm an alcoholic. I know I am. I don't know what to do. I'm just like daddy I guess. I'm crazy. Just like him. I'm just so scared baby." In larger script she wrote, "I know I'm not stupid! Military is free." She drew ten lines under the word "free."

Campbell said the note shows his wife's state of mind at the time and could have aided in his defense. Hyatt, contacted late Friday, said he spent two full days at the Criminal Investigation Command office and never came across the letter.

SUMMARY

In summary, five items (of fact and inference) can be listed.

* Joseph Campbell is out of the army, honorably discharged, back in his home state, trying to pick up the pieces of his shattered life.
* The court-martial not-guilty verdict implied that Campbell definitely did not commit murder, that his wife was in the process of attempting suicide, and that the death was accidental—a rare case of an accidental death within a suicidal context. (After the

trial, a revised death certificate was issued that changed the mode of death from homicide to accident.)

• To the extent that the testimony regarding the personality of the deceased wife played a role in the court's decision, the court-martial also functioned as a psychological investigation.

• The question of the irresponsibility of the Army Criminal Investigation Command and the prosecution's handling of the case (in bringing an unwarranted charge of premeditated murder) was never resolved.

• The further question of whether or not the prosecution knew about (and advertently withheld) the wife's suicide note (which would have absolved the husband at the outset) has not been answered. However, the very presence of this vexing question about the prosecutor's behavior raises the specter of the potentiality for breakdowns in the military criminal justice system that is frightening to contemplate.

REFERENCES

Clark, D. C., and Horton-Deutsch, S. L. (1992). Assessment in absentia: the value of the psychological autopsy for studying antecedents of suicide and predicting future suicides. In *Assessment and Prediction of Suicide*, ed. R. W. Maris, et al. New York: Guilford.

Curphey, T. J. (1961). The role of the social scientist in the medicolegal certification of death from suicide. In *The Cry for Help*, ed. N. L. Farberow and E. S. Shneidman, pp. 110–117. New York: McGraw-Hill.

_____ (1967). The forensic pathologist and the multidisciplinary approach to death. In *Essays in Self-Destruction*, ed. E. S. Shneidman, pp. 463–474. New York: Science House.

Litman, R. E., Curphey, T. J., Shneidman, E. S., et al. (1963). Investigations of equivocal suicides. *Journal of the American Medical Association* 184:924–929.

Shneidman, E. S. (1969). Suicide, lethality and the psychological autopsy. In *Aspects of Depression*, ed. E. S. Shneidman and M. Ortega, pp. 225–250. Boston: Little, Brown.

———— (1973). *Deaths of Man.* New York: Quadrangle.

———— (1977). The psychological autopsy. In *Guide to the Investigation and Reporting of Drug Abuse Deaths,* ed. L. I. Gottschalk, pp. 42–56. Washington, DC: USDHEW, U.S. Government Printing Office.

Weisman, A. D. (1974). *The Realization of Death: A Guide for the Psychological Autopsy.* New York: Jason Aronson.

Acknowledgments

Grateful acknowledgment is made to the following for permission to reprint:

American Association for the Advancement of Psychotherapy for "Aphorisms of Suicide," originally published as "Aphorisms of Suicide and Some Implications for Psychotherapy," in the *American Journal of Psychotherapy*, vol. 38, pp. 319–328. Copyright © 1984. Reprinted by permission.

American Psychological Association for material from "A Psychological Approach to Suicide," in *Cataclysms, Crises and Catastrophes: Psychology in Action*, edited by G. R. VandenBos and B. K. Bryant. Copyright © 1987 by the American Psychological Association. Reprinted by permission of the publisher.

Brunner/Mazel for "Psychotherapy with Suicidal Patients," in *Specialized Techniques in Psychotherapy*, edited by T. Karasu and L. Bellak, pp. 305–313. Copyright © 1980 by T. Karasu. Reprinted with permission.

In relation to Chapter 12, "An Equivocal Death Clarified in a Court of Law," I wish to thank Attorney Dan R. Hyatt of Portland, Oregon and Jerome A. Motto, M.D., of San Francisco, California, who have permitted me to use their names. I also wish to thank the army officer who was the chief protagonist in this trial, the decedent's mother, who wrote a letter to the court in her son-in-law's behalf, and the newspaper that wrote several articles reporting this case, all of whom did not wish their names to be used. They have all permitted me to reproduce their writings verbatim (with names changed, of course). They are quoted with permission. All five of these parties have earned my abiding respect and deep gratitude.

Name Index

Subject Index

About the Author

Edwin S. Shneidman, Ph.D., is Professor of Thanatology Emeritus at the University of California at Los Angeles School of Medicine. In the 1950s, he was co-founder and co-director of the Los Angeles Suicide Prevention Center and in the 1960s, Chief of the Center for the Study of Suicide Prevention at the National Institutes of Mental Health in Bethesda, MD. He has been Visiting Professor at Harvard and at the Ben Gurion University of the Negev in Beersheva, Israel; Research Associate at the Massachusetts General Hospital and the Karolinska Hospital in Stockholm; and a Fellow at the Center for Advanced Study in the Behavioral Sciences at Stanford. He was the founder, in 1968, and the first president of the American Association of Suicidology. He is the author of *Deaths of Man* (nominated for a National Book Award in Science), *Voices of Death,* and *Definition of Suicide,* and editor or co-editor of a dozen books on death and suicide. He is the recipient of the American Psychological Association Award for Distinguished Professional Contribution to Public Service.